The making of a status symbol

Manchester University Press

The making of a status symbol

A business history of Rolex

Pierre-Yves Donzé

Manchester University Press

The right of Pierre-Yves Donzé to be identified as the author of this work has been asserted in accordance with the Copyright, Designs and Patents Act 1988.

Published by Manchester University Press
Oxford Road, Manchester, M13 9PL
www.manchesteruniversitypress.co.uk

British Library Cataloguing-in-Publication Data
A catalogue record for this book is available from the British Library

ISBN 978 1 5261 8326 2 hardback
ISBN 978 1 5261 8841 0 paperback

First published 2025

The publisher has no responsibility for the persistence or accuracy of URLs for any external or third-party internet websites referred to in this book, and does not guarantee that any content on such websites is, or will remain, accurate or appropriate.

EU authorised representative for GPSR:
Easy Access System Europe, Mustamäe tee 50, 10621 Tallinn, Estonia
gpsr.requests@easproject.com

Typeset by Newgen Publishing UK

Contents

Preface and acknowledgements

The history of the Swiss and global watchmaking industry has been a focus of my attention for some fifteen years – my first book on the subject, *Les patrons horlogers de la Chaux-de-Fonds*, was published in 2007. My academic career, which has taken me between Switzerland, Japan, and the United States, and the enriching encounters I have had with numerous colleagues and various personalities from the watchmaking world have enabled me to diversify and renew my interests. I have had the opportunity to reflect on the industrial dynamics of this sector on a local, national, and global scale, the changing role of entrepreneurs, the different innovation processes, as well as the companies that make up this industry, the sources of their competitiveness, the conditions of their growth, and the context of their demise. However, there was one striking omission from my analyses: Rolex. How can we discuss the evolution of the watch industry without giving a central place to the watch brand that became the world's most important in the 1970s and has remained so to this day? Several of my readers have sent me this very constructive criticism, but I was confronted with the limits of the historian's profession: access to archives.

In the watchmaking world and economic circles more broadly, everyone has more or less ready-made answers to explain the phenomenal success enjoyed by Rolex for more than half a century. However, these answers are rarely based on first-hand sources. Imagination plays a major role. To date, there has been no academic study, based on archival sources, that sheds light on the historical development of Rolex and the process of building this brand that symbolises individual success. Rolex is not just another brand. It is a manufacturer of excellence: it produces not only watches of exceptional quality but also narratives that value the exceptionality of those who wear them. The aim of this book is therefore to dissect – some would say "deconstruct" – the manufacture of excellence in order to understand how Rolex became what it is.

Once the research objective had been set, all that remained was to decide how to go about it. The Rolex SA archives have never been opened to historians, which is understandable given the strength of the concept developed in the 1960s (exceptional watches by an exceptional man for exceptional men). The company has no interest in encouraging narratives that contradict or contextualise the concept. Thus, I had no expectation that Rolex SA would open the doors of its archives to me. In the spring of 2021, however, I informed its CEO, Jean-Frédéric Dufour, of my intention to write this book so that my approach would be completely transparent. My knowledge of the watchmaking archives, accumulated over years of research, gave me the expertise to base this book on rich and varied documentation.

This research was made possible by the support of many institutions and individuals, such as the Musée International d'Horlogerie (MIH) in La Chaux-de-Fonds, particularly its curator Régis Huguenin and his team, and the Federation of the Swiss Watch Industry (FH) in Bienne, particularly Philippe Pegoraro, head of its statistics and economics department, for their constant availability. Pierre Fluckiger, director of the Geneva State Archives, and Serge Maillard, editor of *Europa Star* magazine, also greatly facilitated my work by making their archives available to me, and the digitisation department of the Federal Archives in Bern made a vital contribution to my work. I also thank Marc Perrenoud, who provided me with copies of documents he had consulted as part of his own research and express my thanks to the staff of the Bern State Archives, the Rubenstein Library at Duke University in the United States, and the Michael Cudlipp Research and Study Centre in Great Britain.

Preface and acknowledgements

My research was also made possible thanks to the financial support of the Japan Society for the Promotion of Science (project no. 22K01592) and the John W. Hartman Center at Duke University, as well as the Thomas K. McCraw Fellowship, which facilitated an extremely fruitful research stay at Harvard Business School, where this manuscript was completed.

Parts of this book have been presented in a seminar at the University of Alicante and at the annual conference of the Forum for Entrepreneurial Studies in Osaka. I extend my warmest thanks to the participants in these events for their suggestions and criticisms. The preparation of this book also benefited from exchanges with Rika Fujioka, Takashi Hirano, Wataru Kikuji, and Ken Sakai, with whom I am collaborating on various projects relating to the history of design management in Japan, as well as with my colleagues and friends active in the history of the fashion and luxury goods industry, in particular José Antonio Miranda, Véronique Pouillard, Emanuela Scarpellini, and Ben Wubs. During my time at Harvard Business School, Jill Avery, Rohit Deshpande, Walter Friedman, and Ryan Raffaelli gave me a better understanding of the issues surrounding advertising and brand management in the United States.

I cannot end this preface without expressing my deep gratitude for the intellectual inspiration I owe to many people. Even if they are not directly responsible for this book, they have contributed to nourishing my thoughts, opening my horizons, and sustaining my desire to continue my research. My fellow historians and academics include Vincent Barras, Patrick Fridenson, Claude Hauser, Philippe Hebeisen, Geoffrey Jones, Matthias Kipping, Takafumi Kurosawa, Stéphanie Lachat, Thierry Theurillat, and Laurent Tissot. I am also thinking of the watch journalists who know how to (or have known how to) whet my curiosity: Jean-Philippe Arm, Stéphane Gachet, Andrea Machalova, and Valère Gogniat. I also owe my knowledge of the watchmaking world to some of the industry's leading figures, who have given me a better grasp of its complexity and, at times, a better understanding of what I was discovering in the archives. My thanks go, of course, to Walter von Känel, to whom I owe a great deal, as well as to Thomas Doebeli, Christophe Savioz, and all the "Watch Boys" in Tokyo.

This volume is the English edition of a book published in French in March 2024 by Editions Alphil, Neuchâtel, Switzerland, under the title *La fabrique de l'excellence: histoire de Rolex*. It has benefited from the criticism and sound advice of Alain Cortat, director of Editions Alphil, who reviewed an earlier version of the manuscript.

Finally, as always, a special thought for Hiroko and my daughters Yuki and Natsu, without whom I would never have the energy to carry out so many projects.

Thank you to everyone!

Harvard Business School, Cambridge, MA, October 2023

Introduction

Rolex has been the world's leading watch brand for more than fifty years. It defeated its rival Omega in the 1970s and, to this day, remains the undisputed leader of the global watch market. The advent of the quartz watch, the rise of Japanese competition, the creation of the Swatch Group, the internationalisation of production networks, the arrival of luxury conglomerates, and the opening up of China have all had a significant impact on the global watch industry over the last half-century. Through it all, Rolex's leadership has remained unchanged.

Rolex's exceptional competitiveness and longevity are fascinating – and contribute to the brand's reputation. However, the reasons for this success continue to be poorly understood. Rolex has never been the subject of a social and economic history study. How did it become the world's leading watch brand? What are the sources of its competitive advantage? What explains its ability to maintain a dominant position over the long term? This book sets out to answer these questions with the sole aim of understanding this success story on the basis of academic historical research.

The company itself does not communicate its history. Unlike its competitors, it has no museum and publishes no historical works.[1] It did not publicly celebrate the centenary of its foundation, in 2005, or that of its brand Rolex, in 2008. Rolex has no history. It is timeless. It is a myth, a belief, a quasi-religion. Its successive CEOs have been, and still are, rarely interviewed in the media, while most other watch brand CEOs,

1

from Nicolas G. Hayek to François-Henry Bennahmias, via Jean-Claude Biver, have never stopped talking about their brands – and themselves. But there is nothing to say about Rolex. The brand stands on its own. To examine the conditions of its development would be to demonstrate that Rolex is the product of a historical process – and thus to deconstruct the myth.

Essentially, the brand's storytelling is limited to a simple and powerful message: Rolex is an exceptional product (the automatic, waterproof chronometer watch, available in various collections) developed by an exceptional entrepreneur (Hans Wilsdorf) for exceptional men and women (you). Rolex's ability to produce high-precision mechanical watches on an industrial scale and distribute them worldwide explains its remarkable success. The legend associated with the brand is not only communicated by Rolex SA (Montres Rolex SA between 1920 and 2002) through its website, advertisements, and a few rare publications, but also peddled by an impressive mass of books for collectors, articles in watchmaking magazines, and countless blogs, all of which take to heart the liturgy offered by the company for many decades.

Before it is a watch, Rolex is a narrative, presenting the genius of an entrepreneur and the exceptionality of his innovations. It was in 1945 that Montres Rolex SA first offered a perfectly coherent discourse on what Rolex was and what it aspired to be. The company published a small four-volume set entitled *Vade Mecum*, which means "little guide" or "reference work" in Latin.[2] It enlisted the services of two prominent figures in the Swiss watchmaking world in the first part of the twentieth century: Alfred Chapuis, a professor at the Neuchâtel School of Commerce, and Eugène Jaquet, director of the Geneva Watchmaking School. They collaborated on numerous publications and were the most widely recognised historians of watchmaking at the time.[3] Both were also appointed to the Hans Wilsdorf Foundation in 1945. Each of the four volumes of the *Vade Mecum* presents a major aspect of the brand's legend. The first volume is presented as an autobiography of Rolex founder Hans Wilsdorf. Following a classic narrative procedure in the hagiography of great entrepreneurs, this text presents an extraordinary self-made man. Orphaned at the age of twelve, Wilsdorf accumulated experience selling watches on the English market and had the brilliant idea of creating a waterproof, self-winding wristwatch, the Oyster Perpetual. The following three volumes present the different historical contexts of this innovation (the history of chronometry, the history of the waterproof watch, and the history of the self-winding watch) in order to highlight Wilsdorf's instinctive genius. This official history is the only one widely published by the company to date.[4] The message of this publication is, therefore, relatively simple: an exceptional man succeeds in developing an exceptional watch. It is on this discursive basis that Rolex has essentially developed to the present day. Although rarely cited, this *Vade Mecum* is the main, if not the only, source for many authors, journalists, and bloggers, who use it without the slightest critical perspective despite the errors and fanciful figures it contains (see p. 16).

Another historical text should also be mentioned: *Centenaire de la fabrique, 1878–1978*. Published in 1978 by the Manufacture des Montres Rolex SA in Bienne to mark the centenary of the Aegler factory (which supplied watch movements to Wilsdorf and then to Montres Rolex SA in Geneva), this limited-edition leaflet offers the classic success story of a company whose origins go back to a craftsman who started from nothing and went on to become one of the world's leading watch manufacturers thanks to the industrial talent of the Aegler family and their encounter with Hans Wilsdorf.[5] The narrative complements and reinforces the *Vade Mecum*.

The literature on Rolex is now monumental. In July 2023, Helveticat, the catalogue of the Swiss National Library, listed no fewer than 171 titles containing the keyword "Rolex" in the "printed books" category.[6] However, apart from the works published by the Group's two companies (Montres Rolex SA and Manufacture des Montres Rolex SA), this literature dates after 1990. Over the past three decades, dozens of books on Rolex have been published by independent authors, generally close to collectors' circles. The rise of wristwatch auctions has done much to stimulate interest in Rolex watches. In fact, one of the first independent books on these products was a bilingual Italian–English work published in 1992 by Osvaldo Patrizzi, the owner of the Geneva-based auction house Antiquorum, which also held an auction in Milan in the same year, with a special section devoted to Rolex. Patrizzi includes in his book the estimated value of the various models, making it an indispensable tool for collectors.[7] The book was a great success (reprinted in 1993, 1998, and 2001) and led many other authors to follow Patrizzi's example, giving rise to a vast literature in multiple languages. These numerous works share a common characteristic: they focus on the products, take the form of an annotated catalogue of watches, and offer a minimal historical account, the sources of which are generally not cited but essentially reproduce the *Vade Mecum*. The countless websites devoted to Rolex are similar in nature.

Academic publications in management and history are virtually non-existent due to the difficulty of accessing original sources that would allow a dispassionate analysis of the company's development. The company does not publish any figures – it is one of the few luxury goods companies not to be listed on the stock exchange[8] – and does not give academic researchers access to its archives. According to the Scopus database, which lists academic publications, no article has been published on Rolex's management.[9] Similarly, none of the three major international business history journals (*Business History, Business History Review*, and *Enterprise & Society*) includes a study on Rolex. The only academic analyses available are two case studies published in 2006 and 2021 by Harvard Business School. Entitled *Hans Wilsdorf and Rolex*, the first essentially repeats the firm's general discourse: Rolex's success is based on a visionary entrepreneur and an exceptional product.[10] As for the second, whose title is simply *Rolex SA*, it describes, on the basis of journalistic sources, the extraordinary growth in demand for Rolex watches since the mid-2010s.[11] Finally, among the few works that use first-hand sources is Brendan Cunningham's recent book, which draws on the archives of the J. Walter Thompson advertising agency, a long-standing partner of Rolex. However, the analysis is disappointing in that it is purely anecdotal and fails to highlight Rolex's competitive advantage on the basis of the sources used.[12]

4

Introduction

Thus, the literature on Rolex, whether written by collectors, enthusiasts or academics, is, for the most part, post-1990 – except for a few titles published by the company itself in the aftermath of the Second World War. It was, therefore, produced at a time when Rolex was already firmly established as the undisputed world market leader. The founding myth of Wilsdorf and the Oyster is never questioned and rarely placed in its historical context. The authors do not discuss the foundations of the brand's competitiveness and dominant status because doing so does not seem necessary. The exceptionality of a man and a product appears sufficient. What reinforces this perspective – and I will discuss this in detail in the following pages – is the long-term management of the brand and the company. Unlike its competitors, Rolex made no significant changes to its products, communications, and business organisation between the 1950s and the present. The apparent absence of change gives the illusion of continuity, making it unnecessary to question the process that has made Rolex the best incarnation of Swiss and world watchmaking.

Therefore, my aim in this book is to answer a few seemingly simple research questions: How did Rolex become the world's leading watch brand? Why did it adopt a luxury strategy so early on? How has it been able to maintain this competitive advantage over time? To answer these questions, I adopt an approach based on both historical research and social science. The work of the historian is based on exploiting primary sources (archives) and putting into context the facts brought to light in old documents. As the Rolex company archives are not accessible, I have used a multitude of documents produced by actors who have had dealings with the company, such as the Swiss federal government and the canton of Geneva, the commercial registers, the trade unions, the watchmaking organisations (*Chambre suisse d'horlogerie*), and other private companies (the advertising agency J. Walter Thompson and the sports agent Mark H. McCormack). I have also used the Swiss and international press. These sources, presented in detail at the end of this volume, form the documentary basis of the analysis carried out in this work.

As for the social sciences, they gave me the opportunity to build a theoretical model to make sense of the facts brought to light by the work of the historian. I was inspired by research into design management because this discipline offers tools that help explain the competitiveness of firms over the types of products developed and launched on the market. Rolex's growth and success are based precisely on products with a strong identity and remarkable longevity. Furthermore, as a historian, I introduced a dynamic perspective into the design-management models in order to understand how this perspective has evolved.

Evolutionary models developed by management researchers have shown that, from a company's point of view, the function of design has changed over time, moving from an activity limited to giving form to a manufactured good (*styling*) to the development of products in cooperation with marketing and engineering (*product design*), and to a development strategy for the company itself (*corporate design*).[13] However, for this research, I limit the scope of design management to product development in the broadest sense, my aim being to discuss the relationship between design and the ability of companies to compete in the global marketplace from a dynamic perspective. The shift from *tangible design* activities (a process focused on the physical form and characteristics of the product) to the development of products that embody the value of the brand and the company (what I call *intangible design*) is a major change in design management.[14] It enables companies to move away from a strategy focused on reducing production costs, thereby making the company more competitive, and adopt one aimed at adding more value to products.

The groundbreaking work by several European and American historians since the 1990s has helped demonstrate the value of thinking about the competitiveness of firms based on design-management strategies. While traditional historiography has focused on individual designers, design schools and iconic products,[15] a new focus of interest is the design function of companies. Hans-Ulrich Niemitz, John K. Brown, and Regina L. Blaszczyk were among the first to study how Western companies gradually integrated design knowledge and organised departments to take charge of this activity.[16] However, Blaszczyk went beyond this approach, which considered design a *styling* activity, to focus on the case of colour management in the automotive and household appliance industries. Such a focus demonstrated that design has evolved from an outsourced activity to a central department working with marketing, production development, and production planning.[17] A growing number of historians have addressed the process of internalising organisational design capabilities and their position within the company.[18]

Research carried out at Copenhagen Business School (CBS), now the world leader in business history approached from a cultural and narrative approach, offers a different perspective, arguing that design is not limited to the tangible aspects of products (size, shape, material, and colour) but includes an intangible dimension comprising the narratives associated with the products. For example, Per H. Hansen has shown that the success of Danish design in the twentieth century was as much the result of the actions of Danish furniture manufacturers, who internalised design capabilities, as of the collaboration between a network of players who worked to promote "Danish design" throughout the world.[19] As Hansen demonstrates, it's not the veracity of the narrative that counts but how these narratives are created and used and their social and economic effects.[20] If we return to watchmaking, it is possible to consider *Swiss Made* as a narrative expressing Swiss manufacturing excellence.[21] This approach has given rise to a dynamic community of researchers, mainly active in the Nordic countries, over the past decade.[22] Although this work focuses only partly on companies or industries, and some of it takes the example of nations, it perfectly underlines the narrative and symbolic dimension of design.

Drawing on this diverse body of work by management researchers and historians, I have devised an analytical model that incorporates the aspects of this literature that seem, to me, to be the most important: the gradual internalisation of design functions within the company and the transition from the tangible to the intangible. The point is to understand how these two processes operate in parallel. The French haute couture industry provides an excellent illustration of the issues involved in this dual transformation. For example, the Christian Dior company has evolved its design management from the development of material goods in the 1950s–1980s (dresses and accessories), largely based on product development by foreign companies with licensing contracts (outsourcing of design), to the formation of a global brand expressing artistic creativity in fashion, thanks to cooperation with numerous players – including star designers, a global network of mono-brand boutiques, Hollywood stars, and the mass media since the 1990s. This move towards an intangible design concept is taking place against a backdrop of verticalisation of activities and strong centralisation of control by the Paris head office (internalisation of design).[23]

The conceptual model used in this book is shown in Figure 0.1. The two main focuses are the status of organisational design capabilities within the company (vertical axis) and the nature of design activity (horizontal axis). Most companies engaged in design management focus on a tangible activity (the development of products such as a car, a radio, a garment, or a watch). This activity is carried out either by designers from outside the company (freelance designers or specialist firms), designers working in the product development department (A), or autonomous design departments (B). The transition from A to B is the first change to be studied, with the aim of understanding why and how companies have decided to internalise or outsource design, what position design occupies in the company's organisation if it is internalised, and what the implications of these changes are in terms of competitiveness. The second central question consists of analysing the company's capacity to move on to intangible design (from C to D). Intangible design includes brand and corporate identity. This evolution must be discussed in relation to the organisational resources (A or B) mobilised to carry out this operation.

I use this conceptual framework in this book to give meaning to the history of Rolex and explain the sources of its competitiveness, as it offers an original and relevant way of understanding the nature of iconic products. The manufacture of excellence is based not only on the ability to produce high-quality objects (the tangible dimension of design) but also, and above all, on the ability to embed these products in a narrative that sells dreams (the intangible dimension of design). This book is,

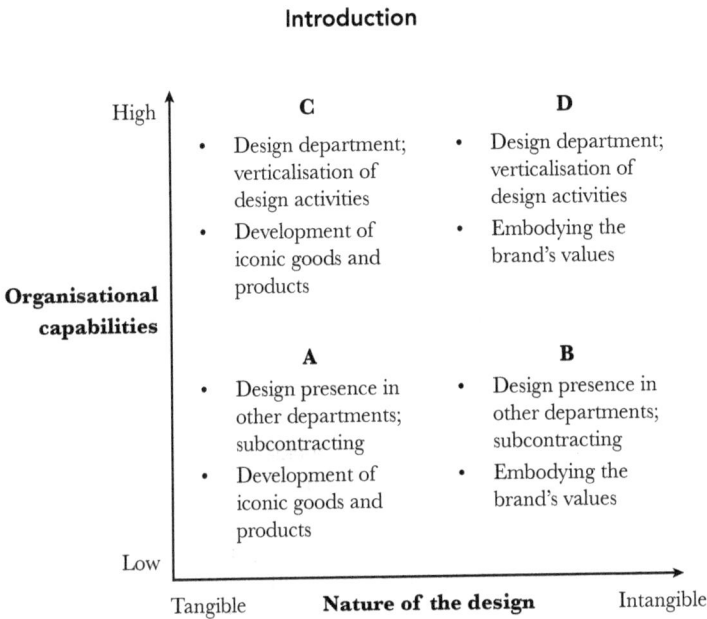

Figure 0.1 Conceptual framework for design management
Source: Author.

therefore, not a history of design at Rolex in the traditional sense. It is a historical study of the company and the brand placed in a social, cultural, and economic context that changes over time and in their competitive relationships with other companies and brands. It shows how Rolex evolved from a brand of Swiss mechanical watches to an expression of individual success.

Notes

1   In 1994, Paul Stuber, a director at Montres Rolex SA, had this to say about the museums and historical works of watchmaking rivals: "Manufacturers compete on age and give themselves an image of craftsmanship that is no longer more than fiction […]. There's no match between the book and reality. We're also trying to anchor the image of an ultra-modern tradition" (*Le Nouveau Quotidien*, 23 December 1994).
2   Montres Rolex, *Vade Mecum*, 4 volumes.
3   Donzé, *L'invention du luxe*, p. 115.

4 It should be noted that the historical texts by Chapuis and Jaquet are also collected in a book entitled *Rolex Jubilé 1905–1920–1945.*

5 *Centenaire de la fabrique, 1878–1978.*

6 www.helveticat.ch (accessed 25 July 2023).

7 Patrizzi, *Orologi da polso Rolex.*

8 Donzé, *Selling Europe to the World,* Chapter 2.

9 www.scopus.com (accessed 2 May 2022).

10 Jones and Atzberger, *Hans Wilsdorf and Rolex,* 2006. Its first author is a professor of business history at HBS.

11 Chung, *Rolex SA.* The author was then an associate professor of marketing at HBS.

12 Cunningham, *Selling the Crown.* The book's main conclusion is that Rolex benefited from the marketing know-how of former British secret agents, employed by J. Walter Thompson after 1945, for its global expansion. The work is poorly referenced and seriously lacking in historical analysis.

13 I have drawn in particular on the works of Jevnaker, "Building up Organizational Capabilities in Design"; Kretzschmar, *The Economic Effects of Design*; Cross, *Design Thinking*; Acklin and Fust, "Towards a Dynamic Mode of Design Management and Beyond".

14 Cooper, Junginger, and Lockwood, "Design Thinking and Design Management".

15 Booker, *A History of Engineering Drawing*; Meikle, *Twentieth Century Limited*; Heskett, *Industrial Design.*

16 Niemitz, *Dampfturbinenkonstruktion bei der Brown Boveri AG & Cie*; Brown, *The Baldwin Locomotive Works*; Blaszczyk, *Imagining Consumers.*

17 Blaszczyk, *The Color Revolution.*

18 Giertz-Mårtenson, "H&M"; Maielli, "Path-dependent Product Development"; Merlo and Perugini, "Making Italian Fashion Global".

19 Hansen, *Danish Modern Furniture 1930–2016.*

20 Hansen, "Business History".

21 Donzé, "National Labels and the Competitiveness of European Industries".

22 Jansen, "Designer Nations"; Melchior, "From Design Nations to Fashion Nations?"; Dahlén, "Copy or Copyright Fashion?"; Kristoffersson, *Design by IKEA*; Angell and Mordhorst, "National Reputation Management and the Competition State"; Skou and Munch, "New Nordic and Scandinavian Retro"; Pouillard and Kuldova, "Interrogating Intellectual Property Rights"; Mordhorst, "The Creation of a Regional Brand".

23 Donzé, *Selling Europe to the World,* Chapter 3.

Part I

The Swiss technical excellence (1900–1945)

At the beginning of the twentieth century, Switzerland exercised total domination over the world watch market. In 1914, it alone accounted for around 40 per cent of world production.[1] The Swiss watchmaking industry had risen to the challenge of industrialisation and transformed its production structures, without losing its ability to develop watches to suit "all countries, all requirements, all tastes and all pockets", as the Société des fabricants d'horlogerie de La Chaux-de-Fonds put it in 1912.[2]

Although the manufacturers of movement blanks and certain movement parts underwent a process of industrial concentration at the end of the nineteenth century, the diversity of products remained extremely strong and ensured Switzerland's leadership position in all markets.

The Swiss watchmaking industry was still organised on the basis of numerous small and medium-sized companies and independent workshops, alongside a few large manufacturers. In 1901, there were 627 watch factories employing a total of 23,883 workers (an average of 38.1 per factory). They included more than a hundred assemblers of finished watches, known as *établisseurs*, and a large number of component manufacturers. In addition, around 20,000 workers were employed at home.[3] The large manufacturers, which produce their own watches and most of their components, were rare. They accounted for only a small proportion of employment and production, even though their watches were the most renowned for their high precision. In 1905, the Compagnie des Montres Longines employed 853 workers, while the Omega, Tavannes Watch, and Zenith factories employed 724, 609, and 574 workers, respectively.[4] Alongside these large companies, there were also smaller manufacturers that had not adopted the mass production system, despite the use of machines, and that concentrated on specialised production of luxury products (such as jewellery watches) and grand complications. This was mainly the case for the two Geneva firms, Patek, Philippe & Cie and Vacheron & Constantin, which exercised unchallenged domination over the chronometry competitions held by the Geneva Observatory between the end of the nineteenth century and the 1950s.[5] However, these companies remained very small until the Second World War. Patek, Philippe & Cie, for example, produced just 2,000 watches in 1920, compared with more than 125,000 for Longines that year.[6] As for Vacheron & Constantin, it limited most of its sales to its boutique in downtown Geneva before the crisis of the 1930s[7]. Finally, some manufacturers, such as Audemars Piguet and Le Coultre & Cie, specialised in the production of high-quality movements and complications, which they supplied to a large clientele. They were therefore minority players with a low profile in the watch market.

Despite this great variety, the various watchmaking companies needed to distinguish themselves on the world market. The search for promising niches has led some manufacturers to develop innovative products, such as chronograph watches, world time watches and jewellery watches. This is particularly true of the Geneva-based manufacturers mentioned above. Others focus on fancy shapes and sizes. Finally, most of these companies, following the pioneering example of the major manufacturers, adopted brand development strategies. Since the adoption of the first federal law on trademarks in 1879, watchmakers have made massive use of this instrument. Giving their watches a name was a way of making their products more distinctive on the market. However, a trademark alone was not enough to stand out from the competition. It had to have a distinctive physical form and embody a strong concept. At the beginning of the twentieth century, Swiss watchmakers found it difficult to implement original design strategies. Competitiveness depended on the precision of the watch. As a result, most manufacturers concentrated on producing quality movements and developing communication activities that high-lighted their precision. On the other hand, they attached little importance to the aesthetic dimension of their brands. High-precision movements were exported as such to their main markets and boxed by local partners, thus adapting the style of the watch to the tastes of local customers. The Longines, Omega, IWC, Tissot, and Zenith brands symbolised the excellence of Swiss watchmaking but had no particular visual identity.[8]

This is the context in which Rolex was born. Hans Wilsdorf was an ambitious young watchmaking merchant. He gained experience of the market and observed his many competitors before realising the need to distinguish himself. A watch brand should not be limited to embodying high precision, but should take shape in original products. Rolex's beginnings and its first phase of expansion, up to the end of the Second World War, are explored in this first part.

Notes

1 Donzé, *The Business of Time*, p. 66.
2 Bubloz, *La Chaux-de-Fonds*, p. 12.
3 Koller, *"De la lime à la machine"*, pp. 182–183.
4 Donzé, *History of the Swiss Watch Industry*, p. 33.
5 Donzé, *Histoire sociale et économique de la chronométrie*.
6 Donzé, *History of the Swiss watch industry*, p. 138 and Donzé, *Longines*, p. 257.
7 Donzé, *L'invention du luxe*, p. 119.
8 Donzé, *"The Transformation of Global Luxury Brands"*.

1

Hans Wilsdorf's early career

In 1903, aged about twenty-two, Hans Wilsdorf moved to London to sell Swiss watches. At the time, Great Britain was the second most important market for Swiss watchmakers, after Germany.[1] It was also the main gateway to the distant markets of its colonies, particularly India, and the countries of the Far East. The British capital attracted representatives of many foreign watch manufacturers, particularly Swiss. In 1900, at least five companies from La Chaux-de-Fonds had a subsidiary in London (Petitpierre & Co, Picard & Frère, Rassmussen, Webb & Cie, Stauffer fils & Cie, and Weill & Cie).[2] In 1874, the American Watch Company of Waltham in the United States, then the largest watch company in the world, opened an office in London.[3] Finally, dozens of independent traders represented a wide range of brands. Wilsdorf was one of them.

Born in 1881 into a wealthy merchant family in a Bavarian village and orphaned in 1893, Hans Wilsdorf left his native region after school to work for a pearl merchant in Geneva. Among other things, he was in charge of exports.[4] Around 1900, he changed employer and town, joining a watch exporter in La Chaux-de-Fonds, Cuno Korten.[5] Korten, also from Germany, officially registered his company in 1899 and several watch brands until 1905.[6] His presence in this city is attested until 1908, when his company name was cancelled following his departure from La Chaux-de-Fonds.[7] He acted as an intermediary between manufacturers based in the city and foreign traders, English in particular, as attested by the advertisement that appeared in *La Fédération horlogère suisse* in 1904 (see Figure 1.1). In his *Vade Mecum* published in 1945, Hans Wilsdorf describes Korten as one of Switzerland's leading watch exporters, with a turnover of over one million francs and an extensive international network.[8] Clearly, this figure is exaggerated, considering that the Longines factory had a turnover of 2.7 million francs in 1900 when it employed more than 600 workers and was one of the largest watchmaking factories in Switzerland.[9] Korten was just one of dozens of small traders in La Chaux-de-Fonds at the time and did not belong to the city's watchmaking elite. For the young Wilsdorf, the important thing was not so much to have worked for an influential exporter but to have acquired a practical knowledge of the watchmaking trade and to understand the potential offered by the English market.

M. Bechmann
II 2552 C   de la maison   749
Baer, Bechmann & Co, L^td
de Londres
sera en Suisse à partir du 1er Août.
Offres à Monsieur Cuno Korten, Léopold Robert 49, La Chaux-de-Fonds.

Figure 1.1 Advertisement published in *La Fédération horlogère suisse*, 31 July 1904
Note: Cuno Korten, watch merchant in La Chaux-de-Fonds and employer of Hans Wilsdorf, announces the presence in town of one of his British clients.

In 1903, Wilsdorf left Korten and crossed the English Channel. He settled in London and worked as a representative for an unknown Swiss watch manufacturer.[10] Two years later, at the age of 24, he joined forces with an English partner, Alfred Davis, and founded the general partnership Wilsdorf & Davis. Davis later married Wilsdorf's younger sister and became his brother-in-law.[11] The business model of this trading company remained similar to Wilsdorf's up to that point: it acted as an intermediary between Swiss manufacturers and markets linked to Great Britain. In the mid-1900s, Wilsdorf was actively looking for companies to represent in the British Empire and Asia. He published several advertisements in the journal *La Fédération horlogère suisse* in 1906 and 1907 (see Figure 1.3) and made trips to La Chaux-de-Fonds to meet his business contacts, staying at the Hôtel de la Fleur de Lys, where many salesmen linked to the watchmaking business used to stay.[12] Finally, around 1907, Wilsdorf & Davis opened an office in La Chaux-de-Fonds. The *Davoine* directory for 1908 mentions an address in the town.[13]

Initially, Wilsdorf & Davis were pure intermediaries who did not own any brands. Their watches bore their customers' names on the dial, following the example of the jewellers Asprey and Goldsmiths.[14] However, the two partners soon realised the importance of having their own brands. In 1907, they registered the trademarks Lusitania, Mauretania, and The Eastern Watch in Switzerland, followed by Rolex in 1908 (see Figure 1.4), and three others between 1909 and 1912.[15]

It was during these years that business relations began with the Aegler factory in Bienne, which supplied the movements used in the watches marketed by Wilsdorf & Davis. However, until at least 1911, Wilsdorf & Davis purchased from several manufacturers. Until that date, they continued to publish advertisements in *La Fédération horlogère suisse*.

An important step was taken in 1912 with the strengthening of ties between Wilsdorf and Aegler, the development of the Rolex brand, and concentration on the British market. The branch in La Chaux-de-Fonds was closed that year, and a new one was opened in Bienne in January 1913. At the same time, the two partners concentrated increasingly on the Rolex brand, although it was not the only one used. Wilsdorf & Davis

Figure 1.2 Hans Wilsdorf

Note: Born in 1881 into a family of wealthy German merchants, Hans Wilsdorf completed a commercial apprenticeship and settled in La Chaux-de-Fonds in 1900.

Source: Rolex SA.

Soumettez

NOUVEAUTÉS

H 1467 C   ·pour   453

l'Angleterre et ses colonies la Chine et le Japon

à la maison

Wilsdorf & Davis

Horlogerie en gros

83, Hatton Garden

London E. C.

Figure 1.3 Advertisement published in *La Fédération horlogère suisse*, 19 April 1906

Note: Wilsdorf & Davis acted as an intermediary between watch manufacturers in La Chaux-de-Fonds and retailers in the British Empire. Its head office was in London, but it sourced its watches from Switzerland.

protected this trademark in Great Britain (1912) and Aegler SA also registered it in Switzerland (1913) and the United States (1914).[16] Finally, the two companies changed their names. The Bienne-based company was renamed Les Fils de Jean Aegler, Fabrique de montres Rebberg, Final et Rolex (1912; it became Aegler SA, Fabrique de montres Rolex in 1915), while Wilsdorf & Davis became The Rolex Watch Company Ltd.[17] Finally,

19

Eintragungen. — Enregistrements.

N° 24001. — 2 juillet 1908, 8 h.
Wilsdorf & Davis, fabricants,
Chaux-de-Fonds (Suisse).

Montres, parties de montres et étuis.

ROLEX

Figure 1.4 First registration of the Rolex brand
Note: *The Rolex brand was registered in Switzerland by the local office of a foreign company: the London firm of Wilsdorf & Davis.*
Source: Feuille officielle suisse du commerce (FOSC), *1908*.

Figure 1.5 Map of Switzerland
Source: Author.

the company's roots in Great Britain were strengthened. In 1914, Hans Wilsdorf, who had obtained British nationality in 1911,[18] registered a whole series of trademarks linked to the British Empire: King George Lever, Princess Royal Wristlet, Prince of Wales Lever, Crown Jewels Lever, Queen Alexandra Wristlet, and The Sailor King Wristlet.[19]

Transfer of the registered office to Switzerland

The outbreak of the First World War had a considerable impact on Rolex's business. However, it was not so much the fighting or the conflict itself that had a negative influence on business but the political decisions taken to underwrite the war effort. In 1915, Great Britain introduced a 33.3 per cent custom duty on luxury goods, including watches,[20] based on the notion that national wealth should not be wasted on unnecessary consumption. According to Wilsdorf, this decision led him to transfer his head office to Switzerland,[21] thus avoiding paying import duties on watches re-exported from London. Above all, however, a new British tax policy was adopted, targeting companies, in particular, with the aim of helping to finance the war. In the same year, the British authorities passed the War Profits Act, which applied to profits made in the UK as well as those made abroad by British companies.[22] In this context, it was no longer in Wilsdorf's interest to make London the centre of his international business activities.

In the autumn of 1915, he decided to leave Great Britain and continue his business from Bienne. The arrival of "a whole host of young Englishwomen"[23] in Bienne was noticed and criticised for the risk of technology transfer it entailed. Since the 1890s, the export of watchmaking components and the opening of assembly workshops abroad – a process known as *chablonnage* – had been booming, contributing to the development of a competing industry in Germany, the United States, and Japan.[24] The Bienne-based newspaper *L'Express* claimed that these young Englishwomen were there "no doubt to learn a bit about watchmaking and then use their knowledge in their own country".[25] However, the reality was different. *The Fédération horlogère* explained shortly afterwards that Wilsdorf had "rented larger premises and brought over several of his employees from London to carry out his shipments from Bienne to the English colonies or other parts of our globe. This measure was no doubt taken to avoid the new duties, delays, etc. created by the current situation".[26] Commercial activities were repatriated to Bienne. Wilsdorf's business partner, Alfred Davis, also moved to Switzerland at this time, staying at the Hôtel des Alpes in Montreux until the early 1920s.[27] However, Wilsdorf remained at the head of the firm.

The following year, in 1916, a new limited company, Wilsdorf & Davis Export SA, was founded in Bienne with 6,000 francs capital.[28] Managed by Emile Béha, Wilsdorf's trusted man in Switzerland, the company's mission was to export watches for the Bienne branch of Wilsdorf & Davis. It, therefore, took over the activities transferred from London. After the war, in 1919, Hans Wilsdorf, whose personal residence was now in Geneva, wound up the Swiss subsidiary of Wilsdorf & Davis and the export company. He set up a new marketing and sales company in Bienne as a simple partnership: Hans Wilsdorf.[29] There was continuity in terms of management, however, as Béha took over the helm.

In addition, the link with movement manufacturer Aegler was strengthened. In 1919, Hermann Aegler, son of the founder and head of the family firm, would have received a 15 per cent stake in Wilsdorf's British company, The Rolex Watch Company. It was also at this time that the Aegler factory would have become the exclusive supplier of movements to Rolex. As for Davis, he would have gradually withdrawn from the business between 1920 and 1924.[30] There is however no primary sources to confirm these assertions.

Finally, in 1920, Wilsdorf founded Montres Rolex SA in Geneva, with capital of 100,000 francs. The Board of Directors comprised three people: Hermann Aegler (chairman), Hans Wilsdorf (executive director), and Emile Béha.[31] The tax increases following the end of the war led Wilsdorf to wind up the London company, under unknown circumstances, and to transfer all its activities – sales and marketing, as well as movement casing and decoration – to Geneva.

The beginnings of the Aegler factory

The watch manufacturer who gradually became Wilsdorf's sole supplier during the 1910s was one of the many entrepreneurs who helped make the town of Bienne one of Switzerland's leading watch production centres during the last two decades of the nineteenth century. The town's population grew from 16,579 in 1880 to 32,136 in 1910[32] and saw the establishment of numerous companies that adopted modern watchmaking production technologies. In 1913, Bienne had a total of ninety-four watch manufacturers,[33] including Brandt & Frère, Omega Watch SA – Switzerland's largest watch manufacturer. Founded by their father in La Chaux-de-Fonds in 1848, the company was moved to Bienne in 1880 by brothers Louis Paul and Charles César Brandt. They adopted mass-production methods and launched the Omega movement in 1894. The reluctance of watchmaking workers in La Chaux-de-Fonds to change production methods meant that the company had to move to a more favourable environment.[34] By the end of the First World War, Bienne was one of the main cities in which watchmaking factories, several machine-tool manufacturers, and hundreds of skilled workers were concentrated. It was an ideal environment for innovation in terms of products and manufacturing processes.

Jean Aegler was one of these many manufacturers. Little is known about his training and early career.[35] Born in 1850 in the village of Krattigen at the foot of the Bernese Alps, he learnt the watchmaking trade and settled in Bienne under unknown circumstances. In 1878, aged less than thirty, he and his wife founded a factory, which was legally registered in 1883.[36] He quickly became one of the city's largest manufacturers and established himself as one of the leaders of the employers' movement in Bienne. In 1886, he was one of the speakers at a meeting attended by around 300 people.[37] He was also one of the founders of the Syndicat des fabricants d'horlogerie, a trade association of Swiss watch manufacturers, in 1888.[38] Together with a group of Bienne-based manufacturers, he also took part in the Universal Exhibition in Paris in 1889.[39] Following his death in 1891, his wife Maria continued the company as a simple partnership under the name Vve Jean Aegler. In 1902, she appointed her son, Hermann, as authorised representative to run the business. Four years later, in 1906, the two brothers Hermann and Hans Aegler took over the family firm under the name Les Fils de Jean Aegler, Fabrique Rebberg. It was transformed into a limited company with a capital of 600,000 francs in 1913. The structure of the capital and the composition of the board of directors are not known, but it was the two brothers who managed the company.[40] Hans Aegler died in 1918 and was not replaced. From then on, Hermann Aegler managed the family business alone until his death in 1944.

Despite the lack of archives to analyse the company's growth in detail, some clues suggest the adoption of industrial methods and strong business development during the period 1880–1910. First of all, the Aeglers showed great dynamism in terms of product development. Jean worked on improving the pendant winding system, for which he obtained a patent in 1889, which he also used in his communication (see Figure 1.6). But it was above all for its contribution to the development of the wristwatch that the company became known in the 1890s. The ladies' wristwatch was a collective innovation developed largely by Bienne-based manufacturers, notably Louis Müller and Omega. According to Sylvie Béguelin, the Aegler factory was one of the first companies capable of making wristwatches with lever escapements. Manufactured since 1896, these are more precise than the cylinder escapements that equipped the first wristwatches because they are easier to miniaturise.[41] Clearly, this was a strategy aimed at establishing a foothold in a new market with quality products, as wristwatches were then perceived as timepieces with little precision.[42] At the beginning of the twentieth century, the wristwatch with lever escapement became the quality standard in the watchmaking industry.

However, despite Aegler's contribution to the development of the wristwatch, it is important to avoid adopting a teleological interpretation of innovation at this company. Not only did it continue to produce pocket watches until the 1910s, but it also developed research activities in this field. Of the seven patents filed by the company between 1900 and 1910, four relate to pocket-watch cases and dials. The most recent was a patent for dials with radium indexes, filed in 1915. This was obviously in response to a request from Wilsdorf, who also filed a patent in Great Britain in 1917 for improved radium luminous indicators. As for wristwatches, they were the subject of three patents registered between 1915 and 1917, two of which concerned the water resistance of the case, which

Fabrique d'horlogerie

JEAN AEGLER

au Rebberg

B I E N N E (SUISSE)

Spécialité de remontoirs au pendant

qualité soignée et garantie

Nouveau système de mise à l'heure
le plus perfectionné qui existe.

Brevet pris en Suisse sous Nº 243.

Figure 1.6 Advertisement published in *La Fédération horlogère suisse*,
11 May 1889

Note: The Aegler factory emphasised its capacity for innovation in its advertising. Here, it mentions the development of a time-setting system that is "the most advanced in existence" and protected by the new patent legislation.

became one of the main subjects of research during the interwar period (see Chapter 2).[43] The Aegler brothers carried out various research projects in parallel, illustrating the uncertainty of the market at the beginning of the twentieth century. The wristwatch was certainly an innovative product, but pocket watches were still widely consumed. Indeed, in 1913, the Aegler company emphasised the variety of its products in an advertisement aimed at watchmaking merchants (see Figure 1.7).

The company then adopted industrial production methods. An advertisement published in 1905 announced that the Aegler factory produced its watches using "modern mechanical processes" and operated according to the "interchangeable system" (see Figure 1.8). At the beginning of the twentieth century, the technical direction of the company was handed over to a young technician, Charles Billeter, who had graduated from the Neuchâtel Watchmaking School.[44] He developed numerous machine

Aegler S.A. Bienne (Suisse)

2230 (Maison fondée en 1878) H 1463 U

Fabrique de montres de dames : Rebberg, Final, Rolex

7 lig., 9 lig., 10 lig., 11 lig., 12 lig., 13 lig.

Montres de poche, bracelets, boutons, pendantifs, en tous métaux.

Bureau de vente à La Chaux-de-Fonds : Rue Daniel Jean Richard 43.

Figure 1.7 Advertisement published in *La Fédération horlogère suisse*, 18 October 1913

Note: On the eve of the First World War, Aegler SA was a generalist watch manufacturer. It produced pocket watches as well as wristwatches, worked in all available metals, and made watches in fanciful shapes.

tools for the manufacture of watch components and established himself as an independent consulting engineer in Neuchâtel in the mid-1920s, founding his own mechanical engineering company there in 1930.[45] The Aeglers, therefore, recruited a qualified technician who enabled them to modernise their industrial equipment.

The violent social conflict that shook Bienne in 1916 highlighted the strong position held by the mechanical workers at the Aegler factory, which had already been a hotbed of union activity in the city since the outbreak of war.[46] With the cost of living rising sharply because of the war, the company's workers demanded their first pay rise in 1914, but the owners refused. The union's lack of influence in the company prevented effective negotiation, with the union representative regretting that he "could not reject what the workers had freely accepted".[47] Wage demands continued in 1915 and became insistent in 1916, with the workers arguing that "machine manufacturers are enjoying a period of the greatest prosperity and that it is right, in these conditions, that mechanical workers who are offered very high wages outside the country should make their work worth what it is actually worth".[48] The Aegler brothers were forced to make a few concessions to the watch fitters and assemblers but refused to deal with the machinists.[49] The conflict spread to all the city's factories, and led to a gathering of the watchmaking employers of the whole canton of Bern within a new trade association, the Association cantonale bernoise des fabricants d'horlogerie (ACBFH), which was created for the occasion and of which Aegler SA was a founding member. The ACBFH signed an initial agreement with the Fédération des ouvriers sur métaux et horlogers (FOMH), the largest workers' union in the watch industry.[50] In the end, a pay rise was granted, putting an end to the conflict.[51] Over and above the industrial action itself, this episode highlighted the leadership of mechanics in the workshops of the Aegler factory, a phenomenon that reflected the advances in industrial production at this firm.

The Aeglers not only aimed for mass production but also for the development of quality watches. They submitted their first watch with the Bienne Watch Control Office in 1910, an institution set up in 1878 within the town's watchmaking school to help improve the precision of watches.[52] The watches submitted were subjected to a series of technical tests and were awarded operating reports (*bulletins de marche*) with or without mention if they met the minimum standards defined by the

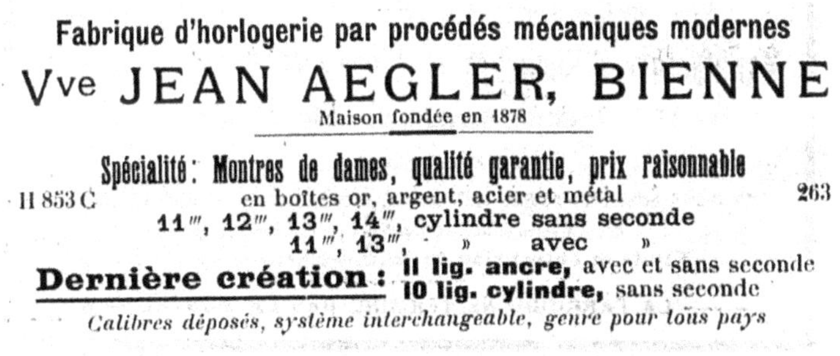

Figure 1.8 Advertisement published in *La Fédération horlogère suisse*, 2 February 1905

Note: *The wide variety of products was not the only characteristic of Aegler. It also used modern production methods, which gave the company a positive image.*

Office. These tests enabled manufacturers to assess the quality of their work and improve the manufacture of their watches. In addition, in 1913, Aegler deposited watches with the chronometric services of the Observatories at Kew (Great Britain) and Neuchâtel (Switzerland). These establishments certified the accuracy of the watches based on stricter tests than those of the Swiss Watch Control Offices. They awarded the title of "chronometer" to watches that passed the tests.[53] Watch manufacturers used the bulletins issued by these institutions for advertising purposes, presenting them as official recognition of the excellence of their products. This is what the Aegler factory did in 1914 when it showcased its chronometric successes in an advertisement published in *La Fédération horlogère suisse* (see Figure 1.9).

CHRONOMÈTRES DE DAMES
Montres 9 et 11 lignes Bracelets

Mars 1910 :
Date où le Bureau d'observation de Bienne a délivré à une montre Rolex 11 lignes le premier bulletin de marche.

Janvier 1913 :
Date où le Bureau d'observation de Bienne a délivré à une montre Rolex 9 lignes le premier bulletin de marche. — Première montre grandeur 9 lignes avec bulletin de marche.

Février 1913 :
Date où l'Observatoire de Kew a délivré la première fois à une montre 9 lignes un bulletin pour réglage chronométrique. — C'est à la Rolex qu'appartient ce record.

Mars 1913 :
Date où l'Observatoire de Kew a délivré pour la première fois à une montre 11 lig. un bulletin avec la mention très-satisfaisant et il s'agit de nouveau de la Rolex.

Décembre 1913 : 3190
Date où l'Observatoire de Neuchâtel a délivré à une montre 11 lig., à notre avis, le premier bulletin de réglage chronométrique, avec résultat, créant un nouveau record pour la **Rolex.** (Ecart moyen pour la marche diurne 0,26 secondes.)

Aegler s. A., Bienne (Suisse)

Manufacture de Montres de dames : Rolex, Rebberg et Final, de 7 à 13 lig.

☞ Bureau de Vente à **La Chaux-de-Fonds**, Daniel JeanRichard, 43 ☜

Figure 1.9 Advertisement published in *La Fédération horlogère suisse*, 24 February 1914

Note: At the beginning of the twentieth century, the successes achieved by watch control offices and observatory chronometry competitions became a selling point. They were presented as recognition by scientific institutions of the high quality of the watches produced.

The adoption of a strategy to develop a strong brand also accompanied this communication based on excellence. The 1914 advertisement repeatedly emphasised that it was Rolex-branded watches that had achieved the results presented as exceptional at Kew and Neuchâtel. Although the Aegler manufacturers understood the importance of branding for some time, they had not yet succeeded in building a single, strong brand. The "Jean Aegler" brand had been registered with various logos on several occasions between 1885 and 1910. The Aegler brothers also registered the trademarks Précision (1890), Final (1909), Marukoni (1913), The Bee (1913), and Rolex (1913).[54]

The watch manufacturer that became Wilsdorf's partner in the early twentieth century was, therefore, an innovative company, investing in both the development of new products (ladies' wristwatches, chronometer watches) and the modernisation of its production facilities. In 1912, the Aegler brothers added the Rolex brand to their company name, which became Les Fils de Jean Aegler, Fabrique de montres Rebberg, Final et Rolex. Transformed into a public limited company the following year, the company took on a new name in 1915 that more strongly expressed its proximity to its new partner: Aegler SA, Fabrique de montres Rolex.[55] The name change followed a rapprochement between the two partners. Wilsdorf is said to have placed an order for £125,000 of movements in 1912 (worth approximately 3.1 million francs in 1912 and more than 30 million francs in 2020) to ensure its long-term supply.[56]

However, the tie-up with Wilsdorf did not result in an exclusive relationship. At the same time, Hermann Aegler did business with other partners active in other markets. In particular, he sought to strengthen his position in the German market, the main outlet for Swiss watches at the beginning of the twentieth century. He was close to the Alliance Horlogère, a trading company that brought together Swiss watch manufacturers and German traders, whose aim was to provide a network of retailers and jewellers in Germany. It was founded in 1911 and Hermann Aegler joined its board of directors in 1914. He sat alongside Paul W. Brack, owner of the Lavina factory in Villeret (a village close to Bienne), Henri Bornhauser, a merchant in Bienne, and two watchmaking merchants based in Berlin and Bremen, respectively. However, the company ran into difficulties during the First World War and was wound up in 1917.[57] Nonetheless, Hermann Aegler continued to do business with the German partners until the early 1930s (see Chapter 3).

Conclusive remarks

The years 1900–1920 saw the emergence and growth of a new watch brand, Rolex, based on collaboration between a merchant and a manufacturer. This business model was not in itself original. Since the eighteenth century, it had been followed by the watch industry, enabling Swiss watches to dominate the world market.[58] Like dozens of other traders at the beginning of the twentieth century, Hans Wilsdorf established business relationships with distributors and retailers in a particular market – London and the British Empire – where he sold Swiss-made watches. He soon began sourcing from a single manufacturer, the Aegler factory in Bienne, one of whose main characteristics was that it aimed to mass-produce quality watches.

Rolex watches were, therefore, co-developed by two companies. The identity of the brand in its early years was essentially intangible but intrinsically linked to the technical characteristics of the product: Rolex stood for precision in the measurement of time. Here too, there was nothing original about the positioning. Wilsdorf's company was a small, newly created enterprise that adopted a follower's strategy. It imitated the major Swiss watch manufacturers such as Longines, Omega, and Zenith. The visual and material identity of the first Rolex watches was underdeveloped, as precision was the basis of the brand's reputation and competitiveness on the world market. It was during the interwar years that Rolex adopted an original approach that enabled it to stand out from its competitors.

Notes

1 Scheurer, *Les crises de l'industrie horlogère dans le canton de Neuchâtel*, pp. 148–149.

2 Davoine directory, 1900.

3 Donzé, *The Business of Time*, p. 12.

4 Montres Rolex, *Vade Mecum*, vol. 1, pp. 7–8. To my knowledge, there are no other sources to confirm this information. All the literature on Rolex is based on this original account.

5 Ibid.

6 *Feuille officielle suisse du commerce (FOSC)*, 1899–1905.

7 Davoine directory, various years, and *FOSC*, 1908, p. 408.

8 Montres Rolex, *Vade Mecum*, vol. 1, p. 8. In a speech given in 1958, Wilsdorf is said to have articulated the figure of 80,000 francs in sales. Quoted in Brunner, *The Watch Book*, p. 16.

9 Donzé, *Longines*, appendices.

10 Montres Rolex, *Vade Mecum*, vol. 1, p. 9.

11 According to Brozek, *The Rolex Report*, p. 23.

12 *La Fédération horlogère suisse*, 21 January 1906.

13 Davoine directory, 1908, p. 198.

14 According to Brozek, *The Rolex Report*, p. 24.

15 *FOSC*, 1907–1912.

16 Intellectual Property Office database, London, https://trademarks.ipo.gov.uk (accessed 20 January 2023); *FOSC*, 1913, p. 1835; and United States Patent and Trademark Office database, Trademark Electronic Search System (TESS), https://tmsearch.uspto.gov (accessed 3 October 2023).

17 Brozek, *The Rolex Report*, p. 28; *FOSC*, 1912–1915.

18 House of Commons Parliamentary Papers, Aliens (Naturalization), 24 April 1912.

19 *FOSC*, 1915.

20 *La Fédération horlogère suisse*, 13 November 1915.

21 Montres Rolex, *Vade Mecum*, vol. 1, p. 18.

22 Billings and Oats, "Innovation and Pragmatism in Tax Design".

23 Quoted in *La Fédération horlogère suisse*, 13 November 1915.

24 Donzé, *The Business of Time*, Chapter 3.

25 Quoted in *La Fédération horlogère suisse*, 13 November 1915.

26 *La Fédération horlogère suisse*, 20 November 1915.

27 According to Izuishi, *Rorekkusu no himitsu*, p. 61. Several editions of the *Journal et Liste des Etrangers de Montreux* confirm this assertion (e.g., 23 August 1913 and 16 December 1922).

28   *FOSC*, 1916, p. 1355.
29   *FOSC*, 1919, p. 1473.
30   According to Brozek, *The Rolex Report*, pp. 28–29. He does not cite his source, and the *Vade Mecum* makes no mention of this acquisition.
31   *FOSC*, 1920, p. 307.
32   Anne-Marie Dubler and Tobias Kästli, "Bienne (commune)", in: *Dictionnaire historique de la Suisse (DHS)*, https://hls-dhs-dss.ch/fr/articles/000222/2018-01-23/ (accessed 15 April 2021).
33   Davoine directory, 1913.
34   Donzé, *Les patrons horlogers*, p. 85.
35   Christoph Zürcher, "Aegler, Jean", in *Dictionnaire historique de la Suisse (DHS)*, https://hls-dhs-dss.ch/fr/articles/029786/2001-03-09/ (accessed 15 April 2021).
36   *FOSC*, 1883, p. 414.
37   *Le Jura*, 29 October 1886.
38   *La Fédération horlogère suisse*, 13 March 1889.
39   *Le Jura*, 26 April 1889.
40   *FOSC*, 1913, p. 1753.
41   Béguelin, "Naissance et développement de la montre-bracelet".
42   Izuishi, *Rorekkusu no himitsu*, p. 46.
43   Espacenet database, https://worldwide.espacenet.com/ (accessed 15 April 2021).
44   *Cinquantenaire de l'Ecole de mécanique et d'horlogerie de Neuchâtel*, p. 41.
45   *FOSC*, 7 January 1930.
46   According to the minutes of local union meetings. AEB, V Unia 578–585 Uhrenarbeiter/Horloger, Protokollbuch Vorstand, 1900–1956.
47   AEB, V Unia 580, 4 July 1914.
48   Article from the trade union newspaper *Le Métallurgiste* quoted in *La Fédération horlogère suisse*, 19 April 1916.
49   *La Fédération horlogère suisse*, 23 September 1916.
50   Donzé, *Histoire d'un syndicat patronal horloger*.
51   *La Lutte syndicale*, 28 October 1916.
52   Donzé, *Histoire sociale et économique de la chronométrie*, p. 52.
53   Ibid., pp. 40–47.
54   *FOSC*, 1885–1913.
55   *FOSC*, 1912–1915.
56   Izuishi, *Rorekkusu no himitsu*, pp. 51–52. No source is mentioned.
57   *FOSC*, 1911–1917.
58   Donzé, *The Business of Time*; Veyrassat, "Sortir des montagnes horlogères".

2

Development of the Oyster (1920–1945)

The interwar period was a decisive moment in the history of Rolex. It was during this period that Hans Wilsdorf and Hermann Aegler developed the product that made Rolex such a worldwide success: the waterproof watch with automatic movement. This two-stage story – the patenting of a water-resistant case in 1926 and the development of an automatic movement in 1931 – is well known and an integral part of the brand's legend. It represents the main event of this founding period and is widely discussed in collectors' books and blogs. To understand how Rolex became the world's leading watch brand it is necessary to explain the context in which this innovation took place, its place among the other products sold by Rolex during the interwar period, and the conditions under which it was commercially exploited.

The waterproof, dustproof watch developed in response to a need. In the first decades of the twentieth century, the watch became an object worn on the wrist and was therefore subject to a range of new environmental constraints. The consumption and social use of watches underwent profound changes as the product transitioned from pocket watches to wristwatches. The latter represented only 24.6 per cent of the volume of Swiss watch exports in 1920, but the proportion had become 50 per cent by 1930 and by 1945 had risen to 92.7 per cent.[1] To function properly while worn on the wrist, watches had to be resistant not only to water and dust but also magnetism and shocks.

In this context, the watchmaking industry launched a series of research projects to improve the quality of watches (artificial stones, new alloys insensitive to magnetism and heat, shock absorbers, etc.). This was also the reason for the creation in 1921 of the first joint research centre, the Laboratoire de Recherches Horlogères (LRH).[2] LRH's initial work focused on balance springs because of their essential influence on watch movement. The physicist Charles-Edouard Guillaume developed a new material (elinvar), which enabled the design of non-magnetic balance springs, produced since 1919 by the Société des fabriques de spiraux réunies.[3] This material was subsequently improved to produce new types of balance springs, in particular the Nivarox balance spring (non-magnetic, invariable, and stainless), created by Reinhardt Straumann, an engineer at Thommen SA in Waldenburg, and produced by the company of the same name since 1933.[4] The LRH, for its part, had been conducting research into the influence of magnetism on watches since the 1920s, publishing its main findings in 1933 in the annual bulletin of the Swiss Chronometry Society.[5] Finally, industrialists used this work to develop non-magnetic components. The use of non-magnetic balance springs (notably Nivarox) became the norm during this period. It should also be noted that some companies used this innovation for advertising purposes. Shock-absorbing components were developed in the 1930s by Le Porte-Echappement Universel SA (Portescap). It was not until the 1950s, however, that watch manufacturers began incorporating Incabloc shock absorbers into their movements.[6]

Thus, the boom in research into the water resistance of watch cases took place in the context of improving the resistance of timepieces to external stresses. In an article published in 2010, David Boettcher highlighted the fact that the water and dust resistance of pocket watches had been a subject of study in Europe and the United States since the end of the nineteenth century.[7] One of the first to file patents in the United States on this subject was Ezra C. Fitch, an inventor and investor who became president of the American Watch Company in Waltham in 1883.[8] Fitch invented the idea of the screw-down crown, which Rolex later adopted with its Oyster. Around ten years later, Swiss industrialists based in the

Bienne region launched similar research and obtained several patents for hermetic cases, the licences for which were then sold to watch manufacturers such as the firm Edouard Heuer & Cie, giving rise to a veritable "market in watchmaking patents", as Nicolas Chachereau showed.[9] Therefore, the development of a water-resistant watch was not a new idea when Wilsdorf launched the Oyster on the market (see Figure 2.1). It emerged from an innovative environment that had been active for several decades.

The development of a water-resistant watch case was the focus of attention of several manufacturers during the 1920s. Wilsdorf, who realised the potential of such a product early on, launched research activities and bought out the patents of subcontractors and competitors. The aim was to limit the Oyster's rivals.

However, although the development of the water-resistant, self-winding wristwatch was presented by Montres Rolex SA after 1945 as the fruit of Wilsdorf's genius, a detailed analysis of the patents filed by Wilsdorf and Aegler reveals the wide variety of research subjects during the interwar period. The two entrepreneurs experimented and dabbled, developing various watch models, including pocket watches, in parallel with their work on the water resistance of the case. Their research and development (R&D) activities illustrate this diversity of interests.

The R&D activities of Wilsdorf and Aegler

Putting the R&D carried out by Wilsdorf and Aegler into perspective helps us to go beyond the traditional discourse on the two-stage design of the water-resistant watch (the winder and the case) and understand the conditions under which this innovation was achieved. A systematic analysis of the patents filed by the two men provides an excellent insight into these conditions. Some economists and historians of technology have rightly argued that patents only imperfectly express the level of innovation of companies, in the sense that some manufacturers prefer secrecy and do not appear to be innovative through the use of patents as a

Figure 2.1 First Rolex Oyster, 1926
Source: Rolex SA.

source.[10] However, this does not apply to the Swiss watchmaking industry, which is characterised by a high level of technical knowledge and strong competition between hundreds of independent manufacturers. To avoid copying, watchmakers generally patented their innovations. Indeed, they have been among the main proponents of legal protection for inventions.[11] They have also made extensive use of this institutional framework.

A long-term quantitative analysis of the patents filed by the Aegler family, Hans Wilsdorf, and the Rolex companies in Bienne and Geneva reveals three main periods of intense R&D activity: the interwar period, the 1950s, and the period since 1990 (see Figure 2.2). Between 1920 and 1945, Aegler and Wilsdorf filed eighty-two patents, mainly in Switzerland but also in the UK and Germany.[12] What did these innovations represent during this period?

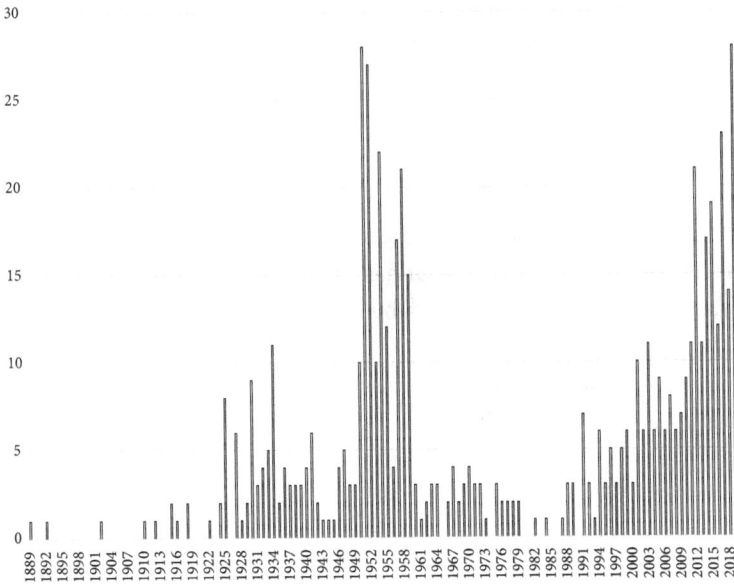

Figure 2.2 Patents filed by Rolex, 1889–2019

Note: This graph includes patents registered by the Aegler family and company by Hans Wilsdorf and by the Rolex companies in Bienne and Geneva. Patents are listed by the earliest publication date.

Source: Espacenet database, https://worldwide.espacenet.com/ (accessed 15 April 2021).

The main area of their research concerned the water resistance of watches, with a focus on crown-winding mechanisms (seventeen patents) and wristwatch cases (ten patents). But the two partners also developed two devices for screwing knurled backs onto the bodies of hermetically sealed watch cases (1931) and for checking the water resistance of cases (1936). As for the automatic movement, it was the subject of seven patents during these years. Therefore, the water-resistant automatic watch, which symbolised the first stage of the Rolex success story, according to the brand's legend, was the focus of particular attention between 1920 and 1945. However, its design accounted for just over 40 per cent of all patents registered during this period.

Two other major areas were the focus of intense R&D activity. The first is the watch's regulating components (balance wheel, escapement, gear train, etc.), for which fifteen patents were obtained. This focus demonstrates the determination to develop a high-precision movement and improve the components that had a direct impact on precision. These research activities are therefore linked to the desire to establish Rolex as one of the leading watch brands in observatory precision competitions. The research supported Rolex's marketing objectives.

Research also resulted in the development of new products to meet changing customer tastes. Rolex patented thirteen watch models, ranging from a watch with jumping hour hand to a watch in a case and a system for attaching a pocket watch to a buttonhole (see Figure 2.4). Regarding this last innovation, the patent, published in 1925, explains that "golfers, mountaineers and other sports enthusiasts who, during exercise, climbing, etc., do not generally wear jackets or waistcoats, will conveniently carry such a watch in the trouser pocket, where it is safe from shock, moisture and accidental snagging".[13] The wristwatch was not the only object of research. A patent for a pocket watch case was filed in 1925 – but attention to this type of product subsequently disappeared. Watch movements were also often improved and developed to offer new functions to consumers (nine patents). For example, in 1924, Rolex obtained a patent for a shaped watch movement with a second hand: "To satisfy public taste,

Hans Wilsdorf

Brevet N° **120851**
1 feuille

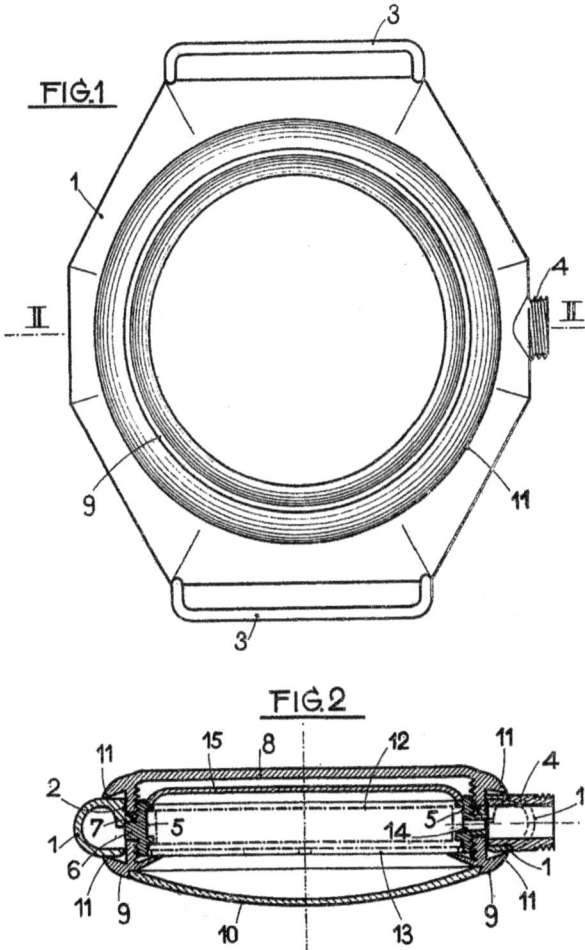

Figure 2.3 Patent no. 120851 for a water-resistant Oyster watch case, published in 1927

Note: The water-resistant case was the subject of much research between the wars. Between them, Aegler and Wilsdorf registered a total of ten patents in this field, including this one for the first Oyster watches (see Figure 2.1).

Source: Espacenet, https://worldwide.espacenet.com/ (accessed 15 April 2021).

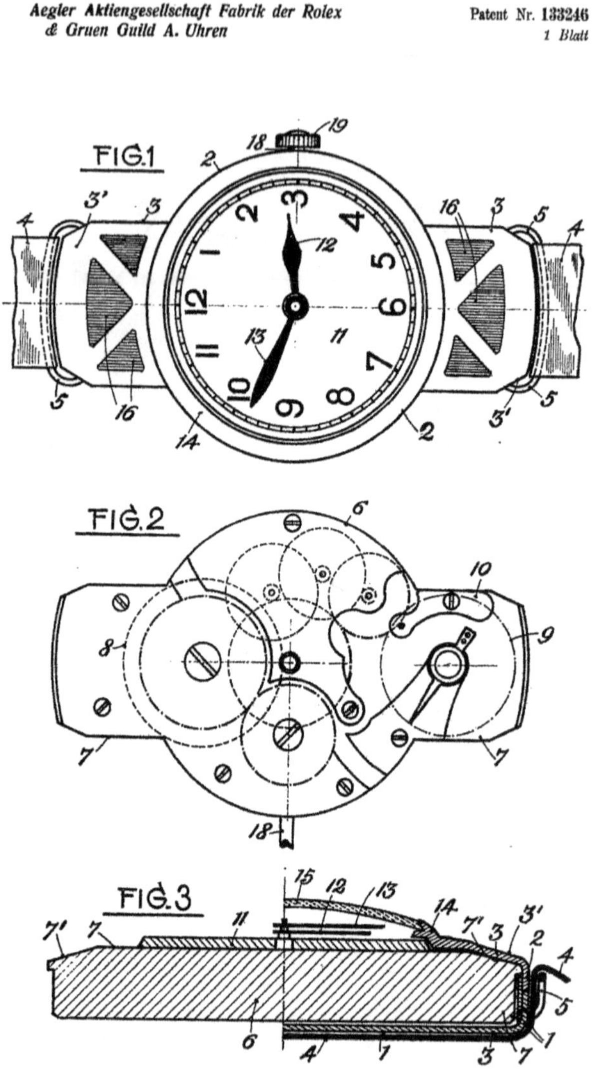

Aegler Aktiengesellschaft Fabrik der Rolex
& Gruen Guild A. Uhren

Patent Nr. 133246
1 Blatt

Figure 2.4 Patent no. 133246 for a watch model, published in 1929

Note: Alongside their work on the water resistance of cases and automatic movements, Aegler and Wilsdorf worked on the development of several types of new watch models. This wide range of interests illustrates their determination to create a new product that would meet with consumer approval.

Source: Espacenet, https://worldwide.espacenet.com/ (accessed 15 April 2021).

small-shaped watch movements should be provided, like full-size movements, with a second hand placed in the usual position on the dials."[14]

These few examples reveal a great deal of attention to products as they are consumed. On the other hand, patents are too limited a source to have a precise idea of the development of Rolex's interest in the aesthetics of watches. Patents are often not obtained for the development of new watch styles or cases, as technical innovation is often absent from these new products. A single patent was obtained for a bracelet in 1925 and another for a dial in 1941.

However, since 1888, Swiss companies have also been able to register designs and models to protect the style of the objects they develop.[15] Watchmakers made extensive use of this instrument, including to protect calibres, movements, or specific watch parts that were not technically innovative enough to qualify for a patent but whose stylistic originality allowed them to be legally protected. The Manufacture des Montres Rolex SA in Bienne registered numerous watch movements and calibres in the 1920s and 1930s. Regarding components, it obtained design protection for seventeen dials in 1925–1928 and twelve watch cases in 1928. However, by the end of the 1920s, these activities were being carried out mainly in Geneva. Between 1927 and 1937, Hans Wilsdorf personally registered five wristwatch models, five dials, six watch cases, and one wristwatch bezel. Subsequently, the company Montres Rolex SA, which had already protected two cases in 1928, took charge of all model registrations. Between 1938 and 1945, it applied for protection for eighteen watch case designs, some of which included the bracelet, four types of hands, and a watch-case bezel (see Figure 2.5).[16] This intense model protection activity illustrates the desire to internalise the creation of the style of Rolex watches launched on the market at the end of the 1920s. Although Rolex depended on external suppliers for producing dials and parts, Rolex itself determined the aesthetic characteristics. The tangible dimension of design was therefore internalised. What is more, this resurgence of activity in the field of watch styling is the perfect expression of a product development strategy that remains versatile. Attention was not focused on the Oyster model.

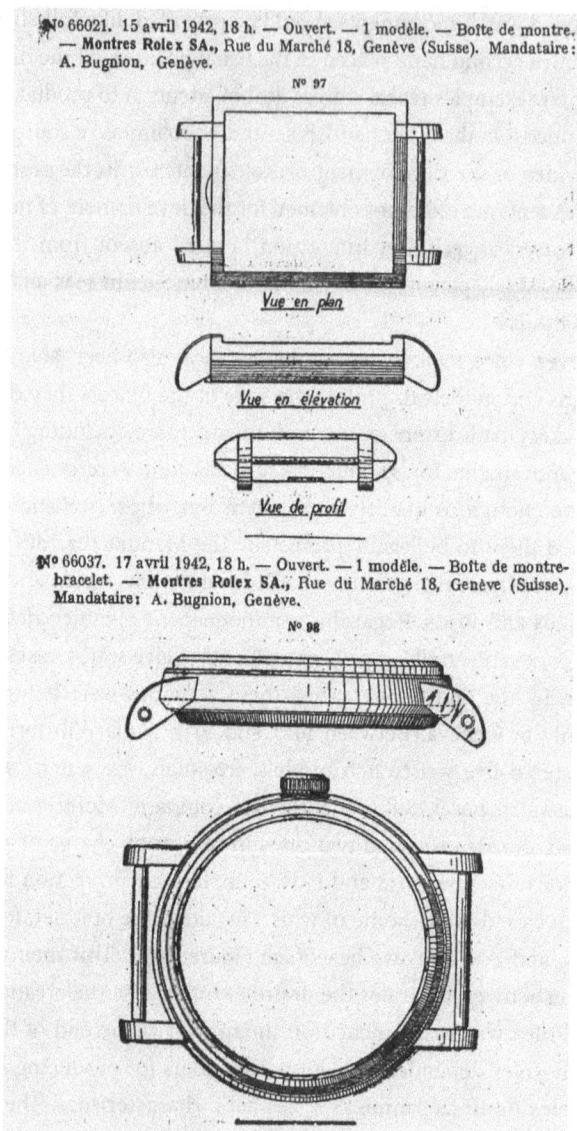

N° 66021. 15 avril 1942, 18 h. — Ouvert. — 1 modèle. — Boîte de montre. — **Montres Rolex SA.**, Rue du Marché 18, Genève (Suisse). Mandataire : A. Bugnion, Genève.

N° 97

Vue en plan

Vue en élévation

Vue de profil

N° 66037. 17 avril 1942, 18 h. — Ouvert. — 1 modèle. — Boîte de montre-bracelet. — **Montres Rolex SA.**, Rue du Marché 18, Genève (Suisse). Mandataire : A. Bugnion, Genève.

N° 98

Figure 2.5 Watch-case model registered by Montres Rolex, 1942

Note: The stylistic diversity of Rolex watches before the 1950s can also be seen in the many different types of watch-case shapes used. Square cases were very popular in the 1930s and 1940s.

Source: Feuille officielle suisse du commerce, 18 May 1942.

This brief analysis of the patents and designs filed by Rolex during the interwar period highlights three main areas of interest for Wilsdorf and Aegler: the water-resistant automatic watch, high-precision movements, and the launch of products in line with consumer tastes.[17] However, this intense patenting activity does not mean that the two partners developed their innovations solely in-house. They acquired patents developed by others on the market, with the aim of incorporating inventions into their own work.

Boettcher's study of the development of the water-resistant winding crown by Rolex is a good illustration of this strategy of internalisation.[18] In 1925, Paul Perregaux and Georges Perret, from La Chaux-de-Fonds, filed a patent application for a winding watch that solved "the problem of the watertightness of the joints separating the crown respectively the winding stem from the watch case".[19] These two inventors were not precisely identified, but their absence from watchmakers' directories suggests that they were not independent entrepreneurs but rather employees of companies in the city. Moreover, the patent application mentions an address at which no factory was established (Rue du Succès 3), which suggests that the patent was granted in a personal capacity. Finally, neither Perregaux nor Perret is mentioned in the list of people who obtained at least ten watchmaking patents between 1888 and 1945.[20] They were not, therefore, watchmakers specialising in R&D. The water-resistant remontoir was an innovation they developed in isolation under unknown conditions. On 19 July 1926, they transferred ownership of this patent to the company C.R. Spillmann & Cie SA of La Chaux-de-Fonds, which transferred it to Hans Wilsdorf five days later.[21] At the time, Spillmann was one of the city's leading watch-case manufacturers.[22] According to an analysis of the hallmarks on several Oyster watch cases between 1926 and 1937, this company was a supplier to Rolex.[23] Therefore, the hypothesis that Perregaux and Perret were employees of Spillmann working on the design of a water-resistant case is highly plausible. Wilsdorf would have acquired this patent to control its use by his case maker – and reserve it for himself. The innovation was subsequently improved by Aegler and Wilsdorf, leading to the two men filing various patents.

Moreover, in some cases, the purpose of acquiring a patent was to prevent the exploitation of an innovation that might compete with the Rolex waterproof watch. This happened in 1927 when Wilsdorf bought a patent for a winding waterproof watch from Philippe Weiss of La Chaux-de-Fonds.[24] Weiss' family owned a small watch factory, the White Star.[25] The possibility of competition led Wilsdorf to take control of this patent. Two years later, in 1929, he also bought out the patent for a winder registered the previous year by one of Le Locle's largest case manufacturers, Huguenin Frères.[26] This strategy of buying out competing patents continued over the following decade. In February 1934, Rolex explained that it jointly held "patent No. 120558 for dust cover crowns with the firm J. Boninchi et ses fils, in Geneva".[27]

Limiting competition by buying out patents was accompanied by public threats to potential counterfeiters. From 1929, Hans Wilsdorf and Montres Rolex SA regularly published advertisements in La Fédération horlogère suisse, the leading watch industry newspaper, announcing their intention to take legal action against any imitation of the hermetic winding watch. Some were even signed by the company's lawyer, Albert Rais, future president of the Swiss Watchmaking Chamber (Chambre suisse d'horlogerie, CSH) (see Figure 2.6).[28] Similar announcements continued to be made regularly throughout the Second World War. Sometimes they were followed by action. In 1937, the Federal Court ruled in favour of Hans Wilsdorf, who had lodged a complaint against Schmitz Frères & Co. of Grenchen.[29] The following year, the latter assigned its patent to Wilsdorf.[30]

Hans Wilsdorf thus made extensive use of the system of legal protection of innovation to ensure that he would dominate the production and sale of water-resistant watches as far as possible. It should be noted, however, that the automatic movement did not give rise to a strategy of acquiring patents, although threats to potential counterfeiters were published in 1944.[31] Such a commitment expresses the strategic choice to have a single product – the high-precision water-resistant automatic watch – to embody the Rolex brand. Technical innovations were accompanied by a marketing strategy aimed at communicating the excellence and originality of the product.

MISE EN GARDE

Monsieur Hans Wilsdorf, Rolex Watch Co., à Genève, propriétaire du brevet No. 120.558, constatant que des fabricants cherchent à imiter la couronne de remontoir faisant l'objet de ce brevet, informe les tiers qu'il est décidé à poursuivre toute contre-façon de manière rigoureuse. La couronne brevetée est reproduite ci-contre.

963   **Par mandat:**

Albert Rais, avocat.

Figure 2.6 Advertisement published in *La Fédération horlogère suisse*, 27 July 1930

Note: *Wilsdorf retained the services of Albert Rais, a prominent lawyer in the Swiss watchmaking community. At the time, he was a radical deputy for the canton of Neuchâtel on the National Council (Swiss federal parliament) and became president of the Swiss Watchmaking Chamber in 1935.*

Commercial exploitation of an innovation

Despite the foundation of Montres Rolex SA in Geneva in 1920, the brand's marketing activities were not centralised until the early 1930s. Initially, the Aegler factory in Bienne registered its own brands, notably Rebberg in 1903. Although it supplied certain manufacturers with movements, this company was independent at the time and sold its own watches. It needed to protect its brands and has done so on several occasions since the mid-1880s. However, the development of business with Wilsdorf gradually led it to abandon its marketing activities and concentrate on production. Only four trademarks were registered between 1910 and 1940.

The Geneva-based company, Montres Rolex SA, was responsible for decoration, final assembly, and marketing. The company grew rapidly, with its capital rising from 100,000 francs when it was founded in 1920 to 500,000 francs in 1927 and 1.4 million francs in 1945.[32] Sales trends during these years are not known and have not been estimated. However, the level of capitalisation shows that Rolex was one of the country's leading watch manufacturers between the wars. By way of comparison, the capital of the Société suisse pour l'industrie horlogère SA (SSIH), formed from the merger of the Omega and Tissot manufactures, amounted to 5.3 million francs when it was founded in 1930.[33] This had risen to 7.4 million francs by 1947.[34] It was then the largest watchmaking group in the country. As for the Compagnie des Montres Longines, its capital stood at 2.4 million in 1914,[35] and Patek, Philippe & Cie in Geneva saw its capital fall from 1.6 million to 800,000 francs in 1934.[36] The latter had great difficulty coping with the crisis of the 1930s because of its dependence on the American upper class and the lack of rationalisation in its production system.[37] Montres Rolex SA was a medium-sized company in the interwar period, but this was because it did not produce its own movements, which had an impact on the level of investment in means of production and therefore on its balance sheet.[38]

However, the increase in capital was not the only source of financing for Montres Rolex SA. The company reinvested its profits massively in developing the business, including conducting expensive advertising campaigns.[39] Self-financing seems to be the company's main source of capital. In 1951, in an appeal to the Swiss Federal Supreme Court against the tax authorities regarding tax on war profits, Maurice Merket, the lawyer for Montres Rolex SA, stated that "since its creation in 1905, Montres Rolex SA has never distributed anything by way of dividend or cash payment, except in 1946 and the following financial years, and this was for the sole purpose of providing income for the [Wilsdorf] Foundation".[40] Bank loans were an additional source of funds. Montres Rolex SA's bank debt amounted to 3.1 million francs on 31 December 1950.[41] By way of comparison, the Swiss watch industry was characterised by a generous distribution of profits to shareholders in the form of dividends. In 1939, these amounted to an average of 8.2 per cent of capital, compared with an average of 6.1 per cent for Swiss industrial companies in general. This trend continued and accelerated until at least the mid-1950s.[42] Exchanges between Merket and the Federal Administration also provide information on the average net return, an index used by the federal government to determine the amount of tax on war profits. It corresponds to net profit after depreciation and amortisation in relation to invested capital (share capital and reserves).[43] For Montres Rolex SA, the return was 27.93 per cent in 1937–1939 and fell to 20.45 per cent in 1939–1947 due to increased capital and slower profit growth.[44] Sources are too sparse to compare with other watch manufacturers of the time, but these proportions are high by today's standards, illustrating the excellent financial health of Montres Rolex SA.[45]

We know little about this company's activities. In the absence of sources, it is difficult to know exactly where watches were made. But it can be said that in 1922, Montres Rolex SA imported certain cases directly from its English customers, into which it placed its movements manufactured in Bienne and then re-exported the finished watches to Great Britain.[46] These customers were the case manufacturers Dennison Watch Case Co. in Birmingham and Willis & Sons in Melbourne.[47] It thus continued a business model built up in the early twentieth century, which was undoubtedly based on exporting bare movements and assembling them with English cases on British territory. After the First World War, however, this type of relationship became anecdotal. The volume of transactions was extremely low (a few dozen units). Montres Rolex SA continued to import foreign cases during the 1920s, however, prompting the Swiss Watchmaking Chamber (CSH) to take action against the hallmark, suggesting that the cases were made in Geneva.[48] A few years after developing its famous Oyster, Montres Rolex SA replied to the Swiss customs authorities that "it is not the case that is the main part of a watch, but the movement".[49] The Geneva manufacturer asked for more time to adapt, arguing that "you can't stop using cases that are already made from one day to the next".[50] In a letter to the Geneva Chamber of Commerce, Montres Rolex SA explained that "we no longer buy silver cases abroad", except for certain special models, including the one in question.[51] It used Swiss cases for gold and silver, although it continued to import gold-plated cases.[52] After 1929, the Swiss Federal Archives no longer held any documents relating to Rolex's imports of cases, which suggests that the company was now sourcing its supplies exclusively from Switzerland. In 1930, Wilsdorf invested in a case factory in Geneva (see below, p. 50).

The watches were cased and shipped in Geneva. Montres Rolex SA was located in the city centre, at Rue du Marché 18, but had sufficient space for these activities. In 1937, the *Journal de Genève* mentioned the existence of "vast workshops" on the fifth floor of the building.[53] The company was managed by Emile Béha until his death in 1926, when it was taken over by Antoinette and Marguerite Gagnebin. The Board of Directors was limited to just three members: Hermann Aegler, who was chairman until 1935, Hans Wilsdorf, and Emile Béha, who also ran Wilsdorf's business in Bienne (see Table 2.1).

The company's growth led to a reorganisation in the second half of the 1930s, which was characterised by a strengthening of operational management. Aegler's departure as chairman in 1935 was no doubt due to the difficulties he was experiencing at his Bienne factory (see Chapter 3). He did not express any fundamental disagreement with Wilsdorf. In fact, six years later, Wilsdorf again gave Aegler the post of chairman. The strengthening of the management took the form of making the two secretaries, Marguerite and Antoinette Gagnebin, authorised representatives in 1935. In 1938, they were also appointed to the Board of Directors, although they left the following year in favour of the first administrator from outside the firm: the Geneva business lawyer Fernand Lilla.[54] He played a minor role in Rolex's management and acted as a lawyer to defend the company in dealings with other companies and the authorities. Finally, in 1944, Wilsdorf took over as executive director and appointed two other directors to work alongside him: Werner Ryser and René-Paul Jeanneret.[55] Jeanneret was to play a decisive role in developing the marketing strategy after the Second World War (see Chapter 5). In 1944, two other new directors, Lucie-Flora Monnier and Marie Blanche Joséphine Meinen, were also appointed. Finally, in 1945, Emil Borer, chairman and executive director of the Aegler factory in Bienne, was entrusted with the presidency of Rolex Watches on the death of his father-in-law, Hermann

Aegler. He did not, however, hold the company's signature. His appointment was intended to strengthen the coordination of activities between the Group's two main companies.

The change in governance between 1935 and 1944 led to an expanded management team that responded to the need to manage a larger number of businesses. First, the growth in sales necessitated a growing commitment to production activities linked to the assembly of watches. Movements were delivered from Bienne and assembled in cases produced in Geneva. In 1938, a burglary at Montres Rolex SA by its main case supplier, in association with a bandit from Lyon, led to the publication in the local press of information about the relationship between Rolex and its subcontractor. For the historian, this is an essential source for understanding how the manufacturer internalised its assembly. The *Journal de Genève's* investigation reveals that the watch-case manufacturer Robert Meylan, who employed around twenty workers in 1939, "had received a great deal of help from the Rolex management as soon as he set up [the] workshop".[56] He appeared in 1930 as a case fitter at watch business

Table 2.1   Board of Directors of Montres Rolex SA, 1920–1945

Period	Name	Function	Career
1920–1960	Hans Wilsdorf	Member, chairman (1935–1941)	Executive director and owner of Rolex Geneva
1920–1944	Hermann Aegler	Member, chairman (1920–1935 and 1941–1945)	Executive director and owner of Rolex Bienne
1920–1926	Emile Béha	Member	Executive director of Hans Wilsdorf in Bienne
1938–1939	Antoinette Gagnebin	Member	Authorised representative
1938–1939	Marguerite Gagnebin	Member	Authorised representative
1939–1972	Fernand Lilla	Secretary	Lawyer in Geneva
1945–1968	Emil Borer	Chairman (1945–1961)	Executive director and owner of Rolex Bienne

Source: FOSC, 1920–1945.

directories. In addition, between 1932 and 1933, he registered three patents, two of which related to hermetic watch cases, illustrating the proximity of his interests to Rolex.[57] After Meylan's conviction, his factory was taken over by a new company, Genex SA, founded in 1940 with capital of 50,000 francs. It was co-managed by the brothers Jean and Noël Gay, who were also members of the board of the company, alongside Hans Wilsdorf.[58] This was Rolex's first vertical integration of watch production. The Gay brothers also ran a watch-strap factory established in Geneva in the early part of the nineteenth century. Clearly, they were suppliers to Rolex. The final assembly of Rolex watches has been carried out in Geneva workshops since the late 1920s, using components produced by companies in the city.

Second, the management of ancillary companies, whose registered offices were in the offices of Montres Rolex SA, represents another type of extension of activities. This was essentially the case of a small company with capital of 7,500 francs, founded in 1928 under the name Montres Huître SA (Oyster Watch Ltd.), whose purpose was to manufacture and sell waterproof watches. Its directors were the same as those of Montres Rolex SA. The Board of Directors in 1928 was made up of Hans Wilsdorf and Marguerite and Cécile-Antoinette Gagnebin. Its capital increased to 100,000 francs in 1942, and it remained in business until being wound up in 1969.[59] The purpose of this company is not identified, but it was probably created for tax reasons. It did not own any watch brands – all those in the group were owned by Montres Rolex – and probably acted as an intermediary between the Rolex factory and certain markets. The other companies managed by the directors of Montres Rolex SA were the property companies managing Hans Wilsdorf's personal fortune (La Perle du Lac SA and Escale SA, founded in 1924 and 1939, respectively).[60]

Third, advertising and communication became major activities for the Geneva company with the launch of the Oyster waterproof watch. In collaboration with the Aegler manufacturer, Wilsdorf worked to establish Rolex as a brand expressing the excellence of Swiss watchmaking. This marketing strategy is analysed in Chapter 5.

Conclusion

The Oyster waterproof watch was, above all, a technical innovation. It was not, however, a breakthrough or disruptive innovation that would enable Rolex to adopt a new marketing strategy and stand out from its competitors. The innovation was incremental; it reinforced Rolex's positioning as a manufacturer of high-quality watches. The design of the Oyster initially remained essentially intangible but was linked to the technical nature of the product. This watch expressed precision and quality – a first step towards a stronger stylistic identity with the verticalisation of case development. However, the variation of the first models meant that visual identification was not immediate. Moreover, it should not be forgotten that the Oyster was just one model among many until the Second World War. The Rolex brand was also used to sell watches with technical and aesthetic characteristics quite distinct from the Oyster. This is the case, for example, with the Rolex Prince, launched in 1928 as a fashion item for men (see Chapter 4, p. 87).

Rolex was not alone in the hermetically sealed watch segment. On the one hand, case manufacturers' research into mastering this technology dates back to the 1880s and 1890s if patent applications are to be believed. The major watch manufacturers also launched diving watch models a few years after the creation of the Oyster. In 1932, Omega launched its Marine watch, equipped with a waterproof case patented two years earlier. Its technical characteristics were widely promoted in advertising to reinforce the brand's image of excellence. This product led to a new diver's watch in 1957 called the Seamaster.[61] Later, Blancpain designed its Fifty Fathoms (1952) and Longines a collection of diving watches (1959).[62] All these companies used military divers, explorers, and sportsmen and women to showcase their watches and emphasise their durability and extremely high quality.[63] In addition, post-war watch manufacturers benefited from the research carried out by certain watch-case manufacturers to develop water-resistant cases. Piquerez SA and Ruedin SA in Bassecourt, for example, mastered this technology and, from the 1950s, began supplying the entire Swiss watch industry.[64]

Rolex's second major innovation of the interwar period, the self-winding movement, was also the subject of great rivalry between many companies. While the idea for the technical principle of this innovation dates back to the eighteenth century, the first wristwatches equipped with this technology appeared after the First World War – the automatic watch of British watchmaker John Harwood, developed in 1923, being one of the first.[65] In Switzerland, Hans Wilsdorf was the first to register and exploit a patent, in 1931. He was followed a few years later by Omega (1943), Longines (1945), and Eterna (1948). As with the hermetically sealed case, the automatic movement is presented as an illustration of technical excellence.

Faced with the growth of these companies, traditional luxury watch manufacturers struggled to expand and remained concentrated on their niche markets. Patek, Philippe & Cie, saved from bankruptcy by the Stern family in the early 1930s, found a balance between continuing to manufacture a large number of complicated watch models, which expressed the excellence of its expertise, and a limited rationalisation of its production system, illustrated by the launch of the Calatrava watch in 1932.[66] As for its rival, Vacheron & Constantin SA, it faced insurmountable managerial and financial difficulties and was taken over by the Jaeger Le Coultre group in 1938.[67] Here too, the aim was to better control production costs by rationalising the number of movements supplied by Le Coultre & Cie. In 1931, Le Coultre & Cie decided to diversify strategically into the finished watch market in collaboration with its French partner Jaeger, a Parisian watch merchant with an international distribution network, who placed orders with Le Coultre for watches.[68] It was in this context that the Reverso model was developed.[69] However, Le Coultre & Cie remained first and foremost a diversified industrial company, which, in addition to producing watch movements, also produced clocks, counters, and various instruments. Although watch sales were growing rapidly – 2.5 million francs for just over 54,000 pieces in 1947[70] – this company did not focus its communication on the excellence and high precision of its products. In fact, none of these traditional manufacturers represented head-on competition for Rolex, Omega, and the other industrial manufacturers because they were positioned in different market segments.

Rolex's intensive R&D did not aim to create a wide variety of highly complicated watches. Rather, its objective was to establish itself as a dominant brand within the Swiss and global watchmaking industry. Although it was a small company in the early 1920s, it adopted a follower strategy rather than radical innovation. It ensured its growth by adopting the business model of the country's leading watch manufacturers. However, alongside the product innovation explored in this chapter, it is worth analysing the first steps towards mass production, which enabled the company to establish itself as a large enterprise (Chapter 4), and the way in which Rolex communicated to its customers (Chapter 5).

Notes

1   *Statistiques historiques de la Suisse*, p. 627.
2   Perret et al., *Microtechniques et mutations horlogères*, Chapters 1 and 2.
3   Pasquier, La *"Recherche et Développement" en horlogerie*.
4   Boillat, *Les véritables maîtres du Temps*, p. 417.
5   Laboratoire de recherches horlogères, "L'influence du champ magnétique".
6   Pasquier, La *"Recherche et Développement" en horlogerie*, p. 185.
7   Boettcher, "The Rolex Screw Down Crown".
8   Moore, *Timing a Century*.
9   Chachereau, *Les débuts du système suisse des brevets d'invention*, p. 294.
10 This is particularly true of German manufacturers of electrical equipment, such as Siemens, who preferred secrecy over patents. However, their American competitors, such as General Electric, made massive use of patent protection for innovation. Donzé and Nishimura, "Patent Management and the Globalization of Firms". For a critique of patent filing statistics as an expression of innovation, see, for example, Mazzucato, *The Entrepreneurial State*.
11 Chachereau, *Les débuts du système suisse des brevets d'invention*.
12 I only mention here the countries of first deposit.
13 Espacenet, patent no. CH 109335, https://worldwide.espacenet.com/ (accessed 15 April 2021).
14 Espacenet, patent no. CH 106817, https://worldwide.espacenet.com/ (accessed 15 April 2021).

15 Chachereau, *Les débuts du système suisse des brevets d'invention*, pp. 296–298.

16 *FOSC*, 1920–1945.

17 Remaining patents comprise the non-watertight crown winding mechanism (two patents), casing devices (two patents), a watch component (one patent), and a watch display stand (one patent).

18 Boettcher, "The Rolex Screw Down Crown", p. 682.

19 Espacenet, patent no. CH 114948, espacenet, 30 October 1925, https://worldwide.espacenet.com/ (accessed 30 June 2023).

20 Musée international d'horlogerie (MIH), Robert Berthoud, Répertoire des brevets horlogers, 1954.

21 *La Fédération horlogère suisse*, 1 September 1926.

22 Donzé, *Les patrons horlogers*, p. 147.

23 Analysis by David Boettcher on his blog, www.vintagewatchstraps.com/blogoystercase.php (accessed 20 January 2023).

24 Boettcher, "The Rolex Screw Down Crown", p. 687.

25 Davoine directory, 1927, p. 344.

26 *FOSC*, 1930, p. 161.

27 *La Fédération horlogère suisse*, 14 February 1934.

28 Isabelle Jeannin-Jaquet, "Rais, Albert", in *Dictionnaire historique de la Suisse (DHS)*, version of 2 August 2010, https://hls-dhs-dss.ch/fr/articles/006050/2010-08-02/ (accessed 30 April 2021).

29 *Gazette de Lausanne*, 28 October 1937 and decision of the Federal Court, BGE 63 II 277, https://entscheide.weblaw.ch/dumppdf.php?link=BGE-63-II-277 (accessed 30 April 2021).

30 *FOSC*, 1938, p. 65.

31 *La Fédération horlogère suisse*, 23 March 1944.

32 *FOSC*, 1920–1945.

33 Richon, *Omega Saga*, p. 29.

34 *FOSC*, 11 August 1947.

35 Donzé, *Longines*, p. 89.

36 *FOSC*, 15 August 1934.

37 Foulkes, *Patek Philippe*.

38 In 1943, the share capital of Manufacture de Montres Rolex SA in Bienne increased from 500,000 francs to one million francs. Taken together, the balance sheets of the Rolex companies in Bienne and Geneva represented around half that of the SSIH at the end of the war.

39 In 1925, Hans Wilsdorf decided to invest heavily in advertising in the British press. Montres Rolex, *Vade Mecum*, vol. 1, p. 16.

40 Swiss Federal Archives (SFA), 6300B#19692223#273, Appeal to the Swiss Federal Court, 19 January 1951. Rolex's lawyer complained of "excessive taxation" and "a rigour that cannot be explained and which will inevitably lead to the abolition or transfer abroad of certain parts of the administrative apparatus". However, the appeal was rejected.

41 Ibid.

42 Rieben, Urech, and Iffland, *L'horlogerie et l'Europe*, p. 193.

43 SFA, 6300B#19692223#273, Response to administrative law appeal, 9 February 1951.

44 SFA, 6300B#19692223#273, Appeal to the Swiss Federal Court, 19 January 1951.

45 The rate of return calculated by the Confederation is close to the current return on equity (ROE). Between 1983 and 2022, Swatch Group had an ROE of more than 20 per cent on only four occasions (1991, 1992, 1993 and 2013). For the years 2010 to 2019, its average ROE was 11.8 per cent. Swatch Group, Annual Reports, 1983–2022.

46 That year, Montres Rolex SA applied for an exemption from import duties for cases from Great Britain and reshipped complete watches to that country. SFA, 6351-C.01#10001041#601, letter from the Geneva Office of Swiss Customs to the Directorate General of Customs, 23 March 1922. Authorisation was obtained for twenty-four cases.

47 SFA, 6351-C.01#10001041#601, letter from the Geneva Office of Swiss Customs to the Directorate General of Customs, 24 August 1922.

48 SFA, 6351E#10001043#8042, letter from the Swiss Chamber of Watchmaking to the Directorate General of Customs, 15 March 1929.

49 SFA, 6351E#10001043#8042, letter from Montres Rolex SA to the Directorate General of Customs, 25 March 1929.

50 Ibid.

51 SFA, 6351E#10001043#8042, letter from Montres Rolex SA to the Geneva Chamber of Commerce, 7 May 1929.

52 SFA, 6351E#10001043#8042, letter from the Geneva Chamber of Commerce to the Swiss Watchmaking Chamber, 10 May 1929.

53 *Journal de Genève*, 26 July 1938.

54 *Journal de Genève*, 8 February 1972.

55 *FOSC*, 1945, p. 1274.

56 *Journal de Genève*, 17 February 1939.

57 Espacenet database, https://worldwide.espacenet.com/patent/ (accessed 6 May 2021).

58 *FOSC*, 1940, p. 348.

59 *FOSC*, 1928–1969.

60 *FOSC*, 1924, p. 541, and 1939, p. 1943.
61 Richon, *Omega Saga*, pp. 134–135.
62 Lachat, *Le Temps Longines*, p. 131.
63 *The Millennium Watch Book*.
64 Kleisl, *Le patronat de la boîte de montre dans la vallée de Delémont*.
65 Jewkes, Sawers, and Stillerman, "Self-Winding Wrist-Watch".
66 Foulkes, *Patek Philippe*.
67 Jequier, *De la forge à la manufacture horlogère*, pp. 504–506.
68 Ibid., pp. 472–474.
69 At the time, this watch was just one model among many. Following its relaunch in the 1980s, Jaeger-LeCoultre made it an iconic product illustrating the brand's creative genius. *Europa Star*, Europe Edition, 1983, no. 139, p. 34.
70 Jequier, *De la forge à la manufacture horlogère*, p. 541.

3

The mass production of chronometers (1920–1945)

The business model devised by Wilsdorf and Aegler was not limited to the development of a water-resistant automatic watch. The challenge was to mass-produce – and sell – high-quality watches, whatever their design or technical characteristics. The industrialisation of quality watches was not unique to Rolex. The major watch manufacturers of the early twentieth century – International Watch Company (IWC), Longines, Omega, and Zenith – all adopted mechanised production of quality products. They were not only the largest Swiss watchmaking companies but also the first prize winners in the Neuchâtel Observatory competitions.[1] In this context, Rolex's originality lies not in its desire to establish itself as one of these manufacturers but in doing so with a reduced number of models. The Japanese company Seiko was among the rare examples of other watch companies that followed the same path as Rolex.[2]

The company Aegler SA, Fabrique de Montres Rolex, in Bienne, was responsible for the development and manufacture of movements. After Hans Aegler's death in 1918, his brother Hermann took over sole operational management of the company until his own death in 1944. Hermann Aegler adopted an ambitious development policy. By 1920, the company's capital had increased from 600,000 to 1.5 million francs. The following year, a reduced Board of Directors was appointed, with Hans Wilsdorf as chairman and Hermann Aegler and Emile Béha as members. Within the firm, Aegler was assisted by a technical manager, his nephew Emil Borer.[3] Born in 1898 and trained as a watchmaking technician, Borer was appointed authorised representative in 1926, succeeding Charles Billeter as the company's technical director.[4] He became executive director of the company on the death of his uncle in 1944. Borer implemented the mass production of movements in the workshops and directed the company's research and development activities. In fact, he is mentioned as the inventor of some thirty patents filed by Rolex, but none published before the Second World War – the company then being mentioned as the inventor of patented innovations.[5] The literature generally identifies Emil Borer as the technician who developed the automatic Rolex Perpetual watch with Wilsdorf in 1931. However, there are no original documents available to substantiate this claim. Hermann Aegler was assisted by a certain Eduard Baumgartner, who was also appointed an authorised representative in 1926. He was probably in charge of the administrative management of the factory and remained in this position until 1955.[6]

During the 1920s, the Aegler company followed the classic pattern of developing many calibres to equip pocket watches and wristwatches of different shapes and sizes. The advertisements produced during this period are an excellent illustration of this phenomenon (see Figure 3.1). They highlight the need to offer a wide variety of products.

Publications by Rolex watch collectors and enthusiasts provide another source for examining product development, as they offer a detailed record of the various models introduced to the market. The problem is that these publications generally focus on movements used by the Rolex brand and do not discuss the possible existence of movements developed for other clients with whom Aegler worked in the 1930s and into the 1940s. According to the movement census published by John Brozek in 2002, Aegler SA produced a total of twenty-five different movements between 1932 and 1945.[7] Most were based on similar calibres and should therefore be considered as new variations of an existing model rather than fundamentally different movements. Of these twenty-five movements, seven are self-winding. In 1939, Aegler SA also developed two chronograph movements based on calibres designed by Valjoux SA, which at the time was the main independent manufacturer of chronograph movements – before it was taken over by Ebauches SA in 1944.[8]

Figure 3.1 Rolex advertisement, 1927

Note: One year after the launch of the Oyster, Rolex advertisements continued to showcase the wide variety of watches that bore this brand name. It was their precision that was the focus of the company's communication – and the competitiveness of its brands.

Two years earlier, in 1937, Rolex had launched its first chronographs on the market, made with a movement produced by this supplier.[9] This was a fashionable product, the production of which most manufacturing companies subcontracted to small independent companies.[10]

By comparison, during the same period, Omega launched a total of 139 new calibres while continuing to use movements developed before 1932.[11] Its competitor Longines was also characterised by the wide diversity of its product portfolio, with technical director Alfred Pfister explaining as early as 1915 that "all types in various sizes and thicknesses, simple and complicated, come out of the Longines workshops; they can satisfy all public tastes".[12] As for Patek, Philippe & Cie, although positioned in a distinct segment (semi-artisanal production of complicated watches), the excessive variety of its products, and therefore the impossibility of rationalisation, led to insurmountable financial difficulties during the first part of the 1930s.[13] Compared with the major luxury watch manufacturers in Geneva, the variety of movements Aegler produced was limited, which made it easier to set up a mass-production system. At Longines, the rationalisation of calibres, characterised by the adoption of greater interchangeability between them, was introduced in the 1920s to improve production costs.[14] Similarly, the takeover of Patek, Philippe & Cie by the Stern family in the mid-1930s was followed by an in-depth reorganisation of the company and a rationalisation of product development, illustrated by the launch of the Calatrava.[15] As for Hattori & Cie, which launched the Seiko brand in 1924, it created only a total of twenty-five models of watches between 1895 and 1939.[16] Moreover, most of them were improved versions of former movements. As the goal of this firm was to mass-produce high-quality watches, standardising their movement was a major step. This demonstrates that Rolex and Seiko had similar strategic goals during the interwar years.

At the same time as setting up a mass-production system, Emil Borer worked to internalise the know-how linked to the watch's regulating organs. The manufacture of chronometer watches required direct control over the development and production of the parts that influenced the watch's precision. In 1932, Manufacture des Montres Rolex SA bought a small workshop specialising in assortments and moved its equipment and workers to its own factory.[17] Three years later, in 1935, it began manufacturing balance wheels, a move that met with strong opposition from Fabriques des Balanciers Réunies SA, which had held a monopoly on the production of this component since it was founded in 1932. In 1940, after lengthy negotiations with the Federal Department of Economic Affairs, Manufacture des Montres Rolex obtained authorisation to produce in-house balance wheels "for your own calibres and your own needs".[18]

However, the absence of archival documents enabling even a rough estimate to be made of changes in production volumes makes it difficult to assess the conditions under which production technologies were developed at Aegler. In addition, no patents were filed for these technologies before 1945, which makes analysis difficult. However, two types of sources show that the Aegler factory entered a phase of mechanised mass production during the interwar period: the annual statistics of the Bienne Watch Control Office and press articles relating to industrial disputes at the company.

Collaboration with the Bienne Watch Control Office

The Aegler company registered its first watch with the Bienne Watch Control Office (WCO) in 1910 (see p. 27). This institution had been founded in 1878 within the town's watchmaking school, with the aim of providing manufacturers with information about the quality of their watches, which were subjected to a series of technical tests. In fact, the bulletins issued after these tests were soon used as guarantees of precision in advertising.[19]

Until 1925, the WCO concentrated on the analysis of pocket watches, a product that was of secondary importance to the Aegler company. As a result, Aegler only registered a very small number of movements. In 1924, for example, it submitted just eight movements, compared with a total of fifty-three for Omega, which dominated submissions to the WCO in Bienne (49.5 per cent of the total number of bulletins issued in 1924). In 1925, Aegler submitted six pocket watches in Bienne (compared to

100 for Omega), as well as one watch in each of the Le Locle and Saint-Imier WCOs.[20] The aim was undoubtedly to assess the quality of the work offered by these various organisations. The WCO in Bienne was preparing to accept wristwatches, and Aegler was determined to benefit from the services of this institution.

The deposit of watches in a WCO can serve two distinct purposes. First, a manufacturer can use the control tests to improve the quality of its watches and its production system – which is the primary objective of these WCOs. WCO tests provide precise technical information that can be used to assess the construction of a new movement, the use of new components, or the use of a particular type of machine tool. Second, companies work with WCOs as part of their communication policy. The bulletins issued by the WCOs are used in advertising as an expression of the quality of the watches, in the same way as the documents issued by the chronometric services of the observatories. In fact, there was no consensus on the definition of "chronometer" until the end of the Second World War, and companies played on this ambiguity to present their watches that had been issued with WCO as chronometers.[21]

The Aegler company made massive use of the WCO in Bienne after it opened to wristwatches. The number of deposits rose from 423 in 1926–1927 to a peak of more than 3,300 in 1930 (see Figure 3.2). Subsequently, the economic crisis and the difficulties encountered by the company (see pp. 65–66) led to a fall in the number of deposits, to less than 200 per year in 1936–1937. However, despite these sharp fluctuations, there was a considerable increase in the number of watches receiving bulletins "with honours" (*avec mention* in French). Their proportion rose from just 10.8 per cent of submissions in 1926–1927 to an average of 63.1 per cent in 1932–1937 – the peak of 84 per cent in 1935 was an exception caused in part by the low number of submissions. Between 1927 and 1932, Emil Borer, who was the firm's technical director at the time, worked to improve the construction of his movements and the conditions for their mass production. Stability was achieved by the mid-1930s.

A major change occurred in 1938, with a return to growth in filings, which was accompanied by a sharp fall in the rate of bulletins with

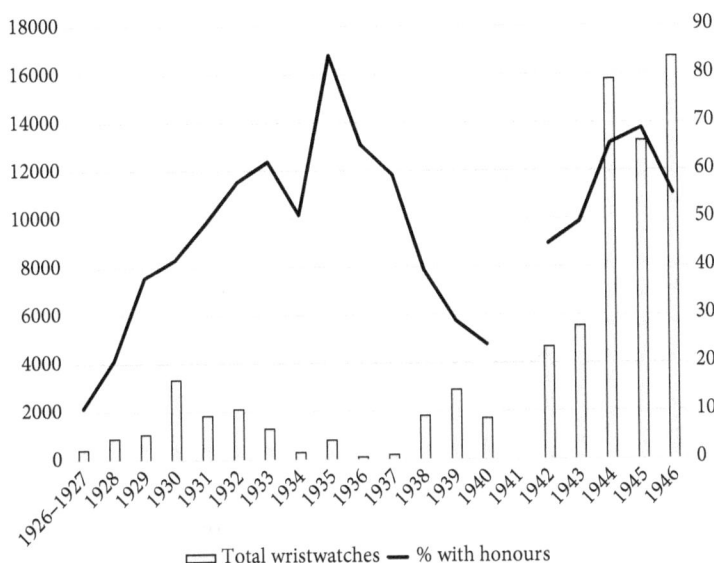

Figure 3.2 Bulletins obtained by Aegler SA at the WCO in Bienne, 1926–1946
Note: Figures for 1941 are not included in this publication.
Source: La Fédération horlogère suisse, *various issues.*

honours. By 1940, it had dropped to 23.9 per cent. However, this decrease did not indicate a decline in the quality of Rolex watches – it reflected the launch of new models, particularly the first automatic chronometer movement, launched in 1936. The automatic rotor watch was patented in 1932 and has been produced since 1933.[22] This chronometer accounted for 73 per cent of registrations in 1938–1940.[23] With mass production of this chronometer in development phase, Aegler used the services of the WCO in Bienne to identify how it could be improved. Furthermore, according to an advertisement that appeared in a British magazine in 1938, Rolex claimed to be able to issue chronometry certificates for all its watches.[24] The statistics from the Bienne office show strong growth in the early 1940s, suggesting systematic registration. After 1942, the reports no longer gave details of the various models analysed, but the growth in the number of registrations, which reached more than 16,000 movements in

1946, and the improvement in the rate of bulletins with honours, which returned to the level of the mid-1930s, demonstrate that the Aegler company had managed to achieve a stability that allowed the mass production of automatic chronometer watch movements during the Second World War. It was on this industrial base that Rolex's extraordinary growth after 1945 was founded.

It should also be noted that the strategy implemented during the interwar period was unique. Before 1940, Omega registered only a handful of wristwatch models at the WCO in Bienne. Their numbers rose to several hundred during the war but remained far behind Rolex, which dominated the Bienne office (90.5 per cent of the total number of bulletins issued in 1942–1946).

Relations with the labour movement

Trade union sources are the second type of document that shed light on the transformation of production methods at Aegler between the wars. The industrial dispute of 1916 had already revealed the strong position held by mechanics within the company, a sign of the advance of mechanisation in the firm's workshops (see Chapter 1).

Six years later, there was another industrial action at Manufacture des Montres Rolex SA over "inadequate wages".[25] The main watchmaking union, the Fédération des Ouvriers sur Métaux et Horlogers (FOMH), exercised strict control over its members to guarantee its ability to exert pressure on the employers. It informed workers wishing to join Aegler as case fitters – which meant that not all watches were cased in Geneva – that they should contact its secretariat to find out what wage conditions they would have to accept.[26] The FOMH wanted to present a united front to the employers and demand an improvement in working conditions. The conflict was short-lived – it left no trace in the minutes of the union's meetings, which detail wide-ranging social disputes.[27] It was resolved following the intervention of the Association Cantonale Bernoise des Fabricants d'Horlogerie (ACBFH), "in return for a small concession".[28] However, the main information on this industrial action was provided by the trade association journal *La Fédération horlogère suisse*, which explained in September 1922 that "it was not a question of a wage cut, but of new rates for a new calibre, with *a new working method*".[29] This mention, which is not followed by any details, shows that the technical direction of the Aegler company was concentrating not only on developing new movements but also on transforming the way work was organised in the workshops. The aim was undoubtedly to speed up the mechanisation and standardisation of the manufacturing process in order to increase production volumes while cutting costs. There were no industrial disputes between 1923 and 1930.[30]

Finally, new tensions arose during the Great Depression of the 1930s. Workers sought to defend their wages against a backdrop of declining business due to the economic crisis. However, the issue of work organisation was not linked to these demands. In January 1930, the Bienne-based management of Rolex attempted to cut wages by up to 35 per cent in certain activities. A consultation meeting with the workers was organised at the Bienne Chamber of Commerce.[31] However, positions remained polarised. In February, the management stated that it would be necessary to dismiss staff "because the refusal of the workers to accept a reduction meant that the company could no longer compete".[32] To avoid this eventuality, the workers agreed to a 10–20 per cent average reduction in their rates, but management rejected the proposal. The dispute remained unresolved in April 1930. It is not possible to ascertain from the available sources how the crisis was resolved, but union mobilisation remained strong at the Aegler factory in the autumn of 1930.[33] Tensions were still high in 1931 when, on 1 May, the Aegler, Bulova Watch and La Champagne factories saw the intervention of the FOMH and a work stoppage in their workshops. The investigation carried out by the ACBFH revealed that at the Aegler factory, "posts set up by the union from 7 a.m. prevented workers and even some visitors from approaching the factory entrance".[34]

However, the economic crisis was particularly severe. The volume of Swiss watch and movement exports fell from a peak of 20.8 million pieces in 1929 to 8.2 million pieces in 1932. It was not until 1937 that the 1929 level was again reached.[35] Under these conditions, employers were often unable to respond to workers' legitimate demands and were forced to lay off some of them. In November 1934, the FOMH's newspaper, *La Lutte syndicale*, wrote an article describing the ravages of the crisis in Bienne's factories: "We feel an unspeakable sadness as we contemplate the many empty Rolex workshops. Here and there, a watchmaker still works behind his board, and that's all."[36] This crisis is the main one to date suffered by Rolex.

The social conflicts linked to the transformation of the mode of production, as revealed by trade union sources, were limited to the period between 1916 and 1922, undoubtedly the years that saw the most profound organisational changes. It should also be noted that these years were marked by a sharp rise in prices, particularly during the First World War, with employees the main victims, and a short but violent conversion crisis in 1921–1922.[37] This difficult context exacerbated tensions arising from changes within the workshops.

After 1922, the organisation of work in the factory was no longer an issue. The mechanisation of production and the new hierarchy between the technical director, the visitors (workshop managers) and the workers were now accepted. The easing of social tensions was also due to the paternalism of the Aegler family. The details of these activities are not known, but in 1925, on the death of Maria Aegler, widow of the company's founder, the socialist newspaper *La Sentinelle* paid tribute to her, pointing out that "the deceased was discreetly and extensively involved in local charities".[38] This practice was continued by subsequent generations of the company's directors. In 1939, for example, Rolex was cited as one of the companies that paid part of its wages to mobilised workers, with thanks from the FOMH.[39]

Moreover, Hermann Aegler was one of the main promoters of corporatism in the Swiss watchmaking industry between the wars. He supported the idea of creating a professional community, bringing together workers and employers bound by a collective agreement.[40] Such a position could only contribute to social peace in his workshops. It was also his desire to defend the competitiveness of Swiss watchmaking companies and jobs in Switzerland that led him to strongly criticise the actions of the federal government and employers' organisations in 1932 and 1933.[41] He called for strong and decisive action to get out of the crisis: banning the export of watch components, including the machine-tools used to produce these parts, and cooperating with the workers' unions.[42] He was one of the leaders of the Comité d'action de la Restauration horlogère, a movement of a corporatist nature, bringing together "the smallest worker to the head of the largest company"[43] and aiming to maintain industry and employment in Switzerland.[44]

Aegler also intervened with the federal authorities to denounce a rumour – unfounded – that Tavannes Watch, one of the largest watch manufacturers at the time, was considering relocating its activities to Japan.[45] This position won him the support of the Socialist Party. In January 1934, the newspaper *La Sentinelle* denounced this transfer of production, adding: "For those who have not read it, we strongly recommend the report by Mr H. Aegler, of the Manufacture Rolex, in Bienne, which deals with this question with a competence that no one will dispute."[46] He was one of those who called for energetic intervention by the federal authorities to put an end to technology transfer through the export of watch components, which would be done in 1934.[47]

Aegler's various markets

Despite cooperating with Wilsdorf on the development of a water-resistant watch with an automatic movement and the presence of the latter as chairman of the Board of Directors, the Aegler company continued to work with other customers during the interwar period, mainly in the United States and Germany. This undoubtedly explains Wilsdorf's difficulties in penetrating these two major Swiss watchmaking markets. It should not be forgotten that Wilsdorf's business remained modest until the end of the 1920s. He ran a small company specialising in the British market, which did not have the financial and human resources to expand on a global scale. Cooperation was necessary. In June 1914, Aegler SA applied for protection of the Rolex brand in the United States.[48] In 1928, the year before the Wall Street crash, Germany and the United

States accounted for 42.6 million francs (14.2 per cent of the total) and 30.2 million francs (10 per cent), respectively, of watch and movement exports.[49] They were, therefore, the two most important markets for Swiss watchmaking.

In the United States, Aegler joined forces with The Gruen Watch Company, a watch manufacturer based in Cincinnati.[50] Its origins lie in the activities of Dietrich Gruen, a German watchmaker who had trained in the Black Forest and immigrated to the United States in 1866, where he founded his own company in the early 1870s under the name Columbus Watch. The company went bankrupt in 1893 and was taken over by its creditors. In 1894, Gruen set up a new company with his son Frederick, a young graduate of the Glashütte School of Watchmaking, in Germany. During the 1890s and 1900s, they invested in a movement factory in Germany, as well as a watch factory and two case factories in the United States. The business model was typical of the new trans-national watch companies born out of the export of components.[51] However, by the early 1900s, business relations with the German movement supplier had broken down. Consequently, in 1903, the Gruen family decided to open their own movement factory in Madretsch, on the outskirts of Bienne, in Switzerland. The Gruen Watch Manufacturing Company was a Swiss enterprise founded at this time. It probably took over the assets of Alfred Aeby's factory, which had been registered in 1883 and struck off in 1903.[52] Aeby was indeed appointed director of the Gruen company in Switzerland. Gruen applied for several patents, trademarks, and designs in the 1900s, 1910s, and 1920s. In 1906, it also acquired the right to use a patent relating to a combined winding and time-setting mechanism using the crown stem, registered in 1904 by Fritz Köhli, a watchmaker based in Bienne.[53] Köhli had been one of the leading manufacturers researching the water resistance of watch cases since the mid-1890s.[54] Finally, in 1923, Gruen bought the right to use a patent for a winding and time-setting mechanism registered by Aegler in 1921.[55]

Gruen Watch's ambitions in Switzerland were not just technical. American entrepreneurs invested heavily. The company's capital, which stood at 60,000 francs in 1903, increased to 350,000 francs in 1914 with the takeover of the United Watch Company (a small watch factory founded in Madretsch in 1910 by an accountant, Eduard Gasser)[56] and then to 1.5 million in 1919 and 2.5 million in 1921.[57] In 1925, the Cincinnati-based brothers Frederick and Georg Gruen each acquired a 10,000-franc limited partnership in Marc Favre & Co, Manufacture de Montres Siva, in Bienne.[58] By the 1920s, Gruen had become one of the most important watch manufacturers in Switzerland in terms of capitalisation, patents, and brands.

Gruen produced its own standard-quality movements in-house but sourced high-quality movements from Aegler. Reports from Bienne WCO show that Gruen only registered a limited number of timepieces under its own name (a total of 598 wristwatches in 1926–1935), most of which (58.7 per cent) did not receive a mention.[59] The close relationship between Aegler and Gruen was further strengthened in the mid-1920s when the Gruen brothers acquired a stake in the Aegler company – for an unknown amount. In 1927, they were appointed to its Board of Directors.[60] The company also changed its name in 1925, becoming Aegler SA, Fabrique de Montres Rolex et Gruen Guild. The cooperation between Aegler and Gruen was probably the reason why Rolex did not enter the American market until 1937. Some Gruen watches sold in the United States during this period had movements identical to those of Rolex watches, since they came from the same supplier.[61]

As for expansion in the German market, this had been based since the 1910s on cooperation with the Alliance Horlogère sales network (see above, p. 29). This company was dissolved in 1926, probably for reasons linked to the difficulties of the German economy after the First World War.[62] Aegler then joined forces with another cooperative present on the German market, Alpina, which comprised a group of watch retailers spread throughout Germany. They each had an exclusive representation in their hometown and sourced quality watches from Swiss manufacturers.[63] In 1929, Hermann Aegler became a member of the Board of Directors of the Bienne-based company associated with this cooperative, called Alpina Gruen Guilde Uhrenaktiengesellschaft. He worked alongside the Gruen brothers and several watch manufacturers from Bienne and Geneva.[64]

It was the economic difficulties resulting from the crisis of the 1930s that put an end to these partnerships in the German and American markets. In 1931, Hermann Aegler withdrew from the Alpina Board of Directors.[65] As for the Gruen brothers, they were severely affected by the Great Depression. Their company had been accumulating deficits since 1932 and was radically restructured in 1935, with the departure of Frederick Gruen from operational management.[66] That year, the capital of the Bienne subsidiary was reduced to one million francs,[67] and the Gruen brothers withdrew their capital from the Aegler factory and left its board of directors. In 1936, the company was renamed Manufacture des Montres Rolex, Aegler SA.[68] The following year, the Gruens also divested Marc Favre, Alpina, and even their own Bienne subsidiary. Gruen Watch Manufacturing was bought by new investors led by Betty Fiechter, who four years earlier had taken over the management of Rayville SA, the successors to Blancpain, in Villeret.[69]

Conclusion

Aegler organised the mass production of high-precision watches in the interwar period, using the services of the Watch Control Office in Bienne to ensure the quality of its production system. In addition, the industrialisation of production was accompanied by the adoption of a paternalistic policy that enabled the social integration of workers. The Aegler family's social and industrial initiatives were supported by the socialist newspaper *La Sentinelle*.

In 1940, the Manufacture des Montres Rolex SA employed a total of 338 workers, ten of whom worked from home.[70] At the same time, Longines employed 720 workers, a figure similar to that of Omega two years earlier.[71] Of course, the Rolex figures only include the Bienne factory, to which we would have to add those of the Geneva company to obtain an accurate comparison. However, it is reasonable to estimate that Rolex remained behind the two largest Swiss watch manufacturers in terms of size. It was also far behind the Japanese company that manufactured Seiko watches. By 1940, it had become the world's largest producer of watches and employed more than 4,000 workers.[72] However, Manufacture des Montres Rolex SA was larger than a company like IWC, which employed 186 people in 1944.[73] Aegler can therefore be described as a medium-sized watch manufacturer.

Moreover, until the early 1930s, Aegler did not work exclusively for Wilsdorf. It had customers in other markets, notably the United States and Germany, where it developed its own business with well-established companies. However, it was severely affected by the crisis of the 1930s, as evidenced by the fall in its watch deposits at the Bienne WCO and articles in the trade union press. Relations with its German and American partners also broke down. The conditions under which the company survived are not known, but the company undoubtedly owed a great deal to its relationship with Hans Wilsdorf and the development of the automatic watch. The crisis of the 1930s proved to be a major turning point, turning the destiny of Aegler into that of the Rolex brand.

Notes

1   Donzé, *Histoire sociale et économique de la chronométrie*, pp. 79–93.
2   Donzé, "The Hybrid Production System".
3   *Journal suisse d'horlogerie*, 1967, p. 554.
4   *FOSC*, 1926, p. 2222.
5   Espacenet database, https://worldwide.espacenet.com/patent/ (accessed 6 May 2021).
6   *FOSC*, 1926, p. 2222, and 27 December 1955.
7   Brozek, *The Rolex Report*, pp. 172–185. He does not explain why his census does not include movements developed before 1932.
8   Boillat, *Les véritables maîtres du Temps*, p. 427.
9   Brozek, *The Rolex Report*, p. 35.
10 Valjoux SA was bought out in 1944 by Ebauches SA. Gilbert Marion, "Reymond, John", in *Historical Dictionary of Switzerland (DHS)*, version of 11 May 2012, https://hls-dhs-dss.ch/fr/articles/030814/2012-05-11/ (accessed 14 May 2021).

11 Richon, *Omega Saga*, pp. 179–189.

12 Longines Archives, *Annual Report of the Technical Director*, March 1915.

13 In 1926, *Journal de Genève* praised the superiority of this business model over industrial manufacturing. *Journal de Genève*, 25 March 1926.

14 Donzé, *Longines*, pp. 97–99.

15 Foulkes, *Patek Philippe*, Chapter 8.

16 Donzé, "The Hybrid Production System", p. 366.

17 SFA, 7004#19727#8, letter from the Federal Office for Industry, Trade and Labour to Manufacture des Montres Rolex-Aegler SA, 8 December 1938. This move was made without prior authorisation and Rolex was reprimanded.

18 SFA, 7004#19727#8, letter from the Federal Office for Industry, Trade and Labour to Manufacture des Montres Rolex-Aegler SA, 4 December 1939 and 23 February 1940.

19 Donzé, *Histoire sociale et économique de la chronométrie*, pp. 113–127.

20 *La Fédération horlogère suisse*, 26 June 1926. Depots were again set up at the WCOs in Saint-Imier, Le Locle, and La Chaux-de-Fonds in 1928.

21 Donzé, *Histoire sociale et économique de la chronométrie*, pp. 113–127.

22 Brozek, *The Rolex Report*, p. 48.

23 The reports from the WCO in Bienne published in *La Fédération horlogère suisse* give details by movement size. For the years 1938–1940, they mention a round model with a diameter of 26.4 mm, which corresponds to the automatic chronometer launched in 1936, according to Brozek, *The Rolex Report*, p. 175.

24 MIH, Chambre suisse d'horlogerie (CSH), letter from the CSH to Rolex Watch, 23 July 1938.

25 *Le Droit du Peuple, Organe officiel du Parti socialiste suisse, des Partis ouvrier-socialiste vaudois et ouvrier-socialiste lausannois*, 18 August 1922.

26 *La Lutte syndicale*, 26 August 1922.

27 State Archives, Berne (AEB), V Unia 578–585 Uhrenarbeiter/Horloger, Protokollbuch Vorstand, 1900–1956.

28 *La Fédération horlogère suisse*, 16 September 1922.

29 Ibid. Emphasis added.

30 According to the minutes of the local branch of the FOMH. AEB, V Unia 578–585 Uhrenarbeiter/Horloger, Protokollbuch Vorstand, 1900–1956.

31 *La Lutte syndicale*, 25 January 1930.

32 *La Lutte syndicale*, 8 March 1930.

33 *Journal du Jura*, 5 November 1931.

34 Association Patronale de l'Horlogerie et de la Microtechnique (APHM), ACBFH, Box 1727, *Enquête sur les événements du 1er mai 1931*.

35 Annual Swiss Foreign Trade Statistics, 1929–1937.

36 *La Lutte syndicale*, 24 November 1934.

37 Donzé, *History of the Swiss Watch Industry*, p. 75.

38 *La Sentinelle*, 12 December 1925.

39 *La Lutte syndicale*, 17 June 1939.

40 The process is described in detail in Boillat, *Les véritables maîtres du temps*, pp. 441–446.

41 SFA, E 7004/1967/12/195, Hermann Aegler, *Rapport sur la situation horlogère*, Bienne, 1933. I would like to thank Marc Perrenoud for providing me with a copy of this report.

42 *La Sentinelle*, 6 December 1933.

43 SFA, E 7004/1967/12/195, Aegler, *Rapport sur la situation horlogère*.

44 Boillat, *Les véritables maîtres du temps*, p. 442.

45 SFA, E 7004 Uhreninndustrie 1967/12, Band 39, letter from Rolex Watch Co Ltd to the Federal Department of Economic Affairs, 2 December 1932, and letter from Rolex Watch Co Ltd to the Federal Office for Industry, Trade and Labour, 24 December 1932.

46 *La Sentinelle*, 18 January 1934.

47 Boillat, *Les véritables maîtres du temps*.

48 United States Patent and Trademark Office, Trademark Electronic Search System (TESS), https://tmsearch.uspto.gov (accessed 3 October 2023). It is not known when this trademark was transferred to Rolex Watch USA, a subsidiary of Montres Rolex SA, Geneva.

49 Official Swiss foreign trade statistics, quoted in *La Fédération horlogère suisse*, 2 February 1929.

50 Dietrich, *A Brief History of the Gruen Watch Company*, and the German Historical Institute website, www.immigrantentrepreneurship.org/entries/dietrich-gruen/ (accessed 30 June 2023).

51 Donzé, *The Business of Time*, Chapter 4.

52 *FOSC*, 1883–1903.

53 *FOSC*, 1906, p. 1423.

54 Chachereau, *Les débuts du système suisse des brevets d'invention*, pp. 292–293.

55 *FOSC*, 1923, p. 1013.

56 *FOSC*, 1910, p. 2102.

57 *FOSC*, 1920, p. 1342, and 1921, p. 970.

58 *FOSC*, 1925, p. 958.

59 Reports from Bienne WCO, quoted in *La Fédération horlogère suisse*.

60 *FOSC*, 1927, p. 89.

61 Brozek, *The Rolex Report*, pp. 29 and 35.

62 *FOSC*, 1932, p. 2006.

63 *Deutsche Uhrmacher-Zeitung*, 1925, vol. 3, pp. 46–47.

64 *FOSC*, 1929, p. 1698.

65 *FOSC*, 1931, p. 2586.

66 www.immigrantentrepreneurship.org/entries/dietrich-gruen/#_ednref70 (accessed 30 June 2023).

67 *FOSC*, 1935, p. 922.

68 *FOSC*, 1936, p. 2047.

69 Emma Châtelain, "Blancpain SA", *Dictionnaire du Jura*, https://diju.ch/f/noti ces/detail/6135Als (accessed 28 May 2021).

70 SFA, 7004#19727#8, letter from the Federal Office for Industry, Trade and Labour to Manufacture des Montres Rolex-Aegler SA, 23 February 1940.

71 Donzé, *Longines*, p. 257; Richon, *Omega Saga*, p. 30.

72 Hirano, *Seikosha shiwa*, appendices, p. 22.

73 Seyffer, *Die Unternehmensgeschichte von IWC Schaffhausen*, p. 615.

4

Communication and marketing positioning (1920–1945)

What communication strategy did Rolex adopt in the first part of the twentieth century? How did Wilsdorf position his brand in the watch market, and what messages did his advertisements send consumers? The answers to these questions are essential to understanding the origins of the brand's success.

Wilsdorf and Aegler designed and mass-produced several high-precision watches, including the Oyster model, a technically innovative product that ran alongside more traditional watches. The marketing of these various watches was accompanied by communication aimed at conveying the values attached to the Rolex brand. This chapter analyses the brand's marketing strategy up to the Second World War. One of the objectives is to identify the place occupied by the Oyster.

At the end of the nineteenth century, watchmaking companies adopted new communication practices based on the use of brands and advertising.[1] In the context of industrialisation, the increasing distance between the manufacturer of standardised goods and its customers, through a complex network of distributors and retailers, made the use of brands necessary. Brands provide instantaneous information to consumers and make it easier to identify the nature of products.[2] In Switzerland, the first federal law on the protection of trademarks was passed in 1880,[3] and watchmakers made massive use of this new legal instrument. The number of new trademarks registered rose from sixty-two in 1881 to 230 in 1900 and 346 in 1920.[4] In addition, the use of trademarks was accompanied by various actions aimed at building the identity of the brand and distinguishing it from its competitors. Modern advertising arose from the use of brands for communication purposes. Until the 1960s, advertising was intended to be informative: it explained to consumers the specific features and quality of the products embodied by the brand.[5] Through a range of media, from shop windows to press advertisements and posters, watch manufacturers promoted their brands and products.

Until the advent of the quartz watch in the 1970s, the reputation of a timepiece depended on its precision. Precision was, therefore, at the heart of brand communication strategies.[6] A Longines, Omega, or Zenith watch is considered a top-of-the-range product first and foremost because of its precision. Companies communicated intensely on this notion and the values attached to it, such as astrology, sporting achievement, and speed. Technical innovation was also strongly present, in the sense that it reinforced the precision and durability of the watches. Alongside precision and performance, some companies associated their brands with elegance, beauty, and glamour. Watches were also fashion accessories, and brands insisted on the aesthetics of their products – even if iconic products with a strong aesthetic identity were still extremely rare. This was particularly true of ladies' watches. Finally, ordinary quality watch brands did not insist on precision but on the affordability of their products. The makers of Roskopf watches fall into this category.

Establishing itself as a brand of excellence

What about Rolex? Since Wilsdorf's ambition was to mass-produce high-precision watches, it was logical for him to adopt a marketing strategy aimed at establishing his brand among those that claimed Swiss and world watchmaking excellence. Since the beginning of the twentieth century, the top-of-the-range watch market has been occupied by a dozen or so manufacturers. Rolex was a newcomer that had to make its mark in a market dominated by brands with a largely similar message. Wilsdorf was not particularly innovative in the advertising field. He did not question current practices in top-of-the-range watchmaking but used them to Rolex's advantage. He adopted a follower's strategy. The main action was to take part in chronometric competitions organised by observatories. Since the 1870s, watchmakers had been using annual rankings and accuracy records in advertisements to promote their watches.[7] This use became widespread in the interwar years to the extent that a handful of major manufacturers monopolised the top ranks of the Geneva and Neuchâtel competitions. For Rolex, it was, therefore, imperative to take part in these contests. The objective was not to participate but to win. From the mid-1920s, Manufacture des Montres Rolex SA regularly took part in the world's four main chronometry competitions, organised by the observatories at Kew (Great Britain), Besançon (France), Geneva, and Neuchâtel.[8] At Kew in 1927, Rolex lagged far behind Zenith, Longines, Omega, and Nardin,[9] so it decided to invest in high-precision timing. Up to then it had used the services of independent timers; now, it hired one of them and set up an in-house chronometry department. A similar practice was observed at the same time among the Geneva manufacturers.[10] The fierce competition between watch manufacturers led them to invest heavily in timing. Jean Matile, an independent timer from the town of Bienne, headed the department at Manufacture de Montres Rolex SA from 1926–1927[11] until his death in 1961.[12]

The main purpose of in-house expertise in timing was to develop watches specially designed to win chronometric competitions. Before 1941, the Neuchâtel Observatory was not the preferred venue for Rolex competitions because it did not have a specific category for small calibres (wristwatches), which put manufacturers that had abandoned pocket watches at a disadvantage.[13] According to an advertisement published by Rolex in 1946, it used the chronometric services of the Kew Observatory in Great Britain, where it registered wristwatches, and much more exceptionally in Geneva, Neuchâtel, and Besançon. Since 1942, Rolex has played an active role in the Neuchâtel concours – the most important in Switzerland. In 1932, Rolex claimed to be the only manufacturer to have obtained first-class bulletins for small wrist chronometers at the four observatories in Besançon, Geneva, Kew, and Neuchâtel.[14] The following

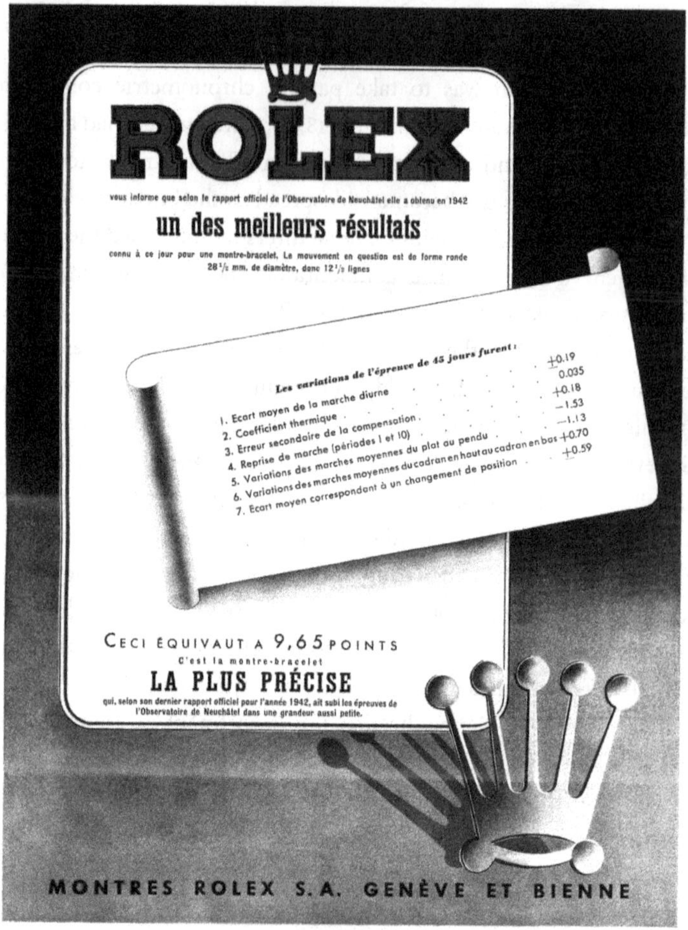

Figure 4.1 Advertisement published in *La Fédération horlogère suisse*, 2 September 1943

Note: Participation in observatory chronometry competitions was the preferred way for Swiss watch manufacturers to establish the reputation of their brands on the world market. It was the high precision of the watches that gave the brands a competitive edge. Rolex also adopted the same marketing strategy followed by its competitors since the end of the nineteenth century.

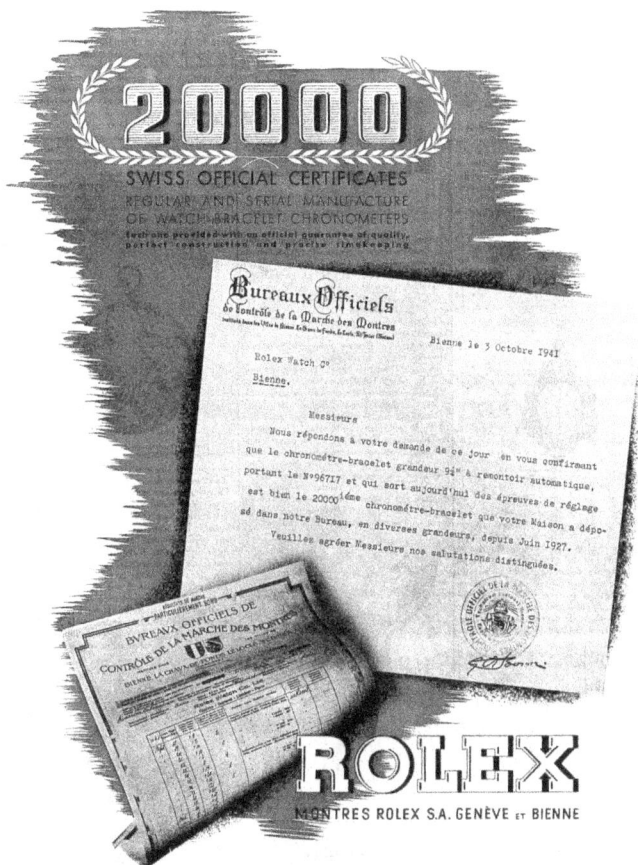

Figure 4.2 Advertisement published in *La Fédération horlogère suisse*, 13 August 1942

Note: The official watch control offices did not issue official chronometry certificates in the strict sense of the term until 1952, but they did attest to the proper functioning of watches, which they sometimes referred to as "chronometers". Companies, particularly Omega and Rolex, played on this confusion in their communications.

year, Omega beat the precision record – with a large chronometer – at Kew and claimed the world record for chronometry, as this was the only establishment open to all manufacturers worldwide.[15] This advertising rivalry underlined the fierce competition between watch manufacturers to present themselves as high-precision brands.

In the 1930s and 1940s, Rolex succeeded in gaining recognition as one of the great names in chronometry, alongside older manufacturers. Like its rivals, Rolex communicated the results obtained in these tests extensively, which legitimised its ability to embody Swiss watchmaking excellence (see Figures 4.1 and 4.2).

The use of sporting exploits

On 24 November 1927, Rolex published a full-page advertisement in the *Daily Mail*, Britain's leading conservative newspaper. It featured a wide variety of models accompanied by messages celebrating their technical excellence and beauty (see Figure 4.3). This type of advertisement was nothing new – it was exactly what watch manufacturers had been doing since the end of the nineteenth century. However, the November 1927 advertisement was innovative in the way it presented the new Rolex Oyster as "the wonder watch that defies the elements" to the general public: "Being hermetically sealed the Rolex Oyster is proof against changes of climate, dust, water, damp, heat, moisture, cold, sand or grease." The Swiss manufacturer refers to the feat of a young British woman the previous month, Mercedes Gleitze, who swam the English Channel wearing a Rolex Oyster.

As is so often the case, the operation was staged. Mercedes Gleitze was no stranger to London. Since the beginning of the 1920s, she had received notable sporting accolades, such as beating the record for the longest swim in the Thames in 1923.[16] She was also the first woman to swim the English Channel, achieving this feat in early October 1927 after several unsuccessful attempts in previous years. However, challenged by a competitor, she was forced to attempt a new crossing a few weeks later – which was unfortunately aborted due to poor weather conditions. It was at this point that Hans Wilsdorf stepped in, realising the media potential

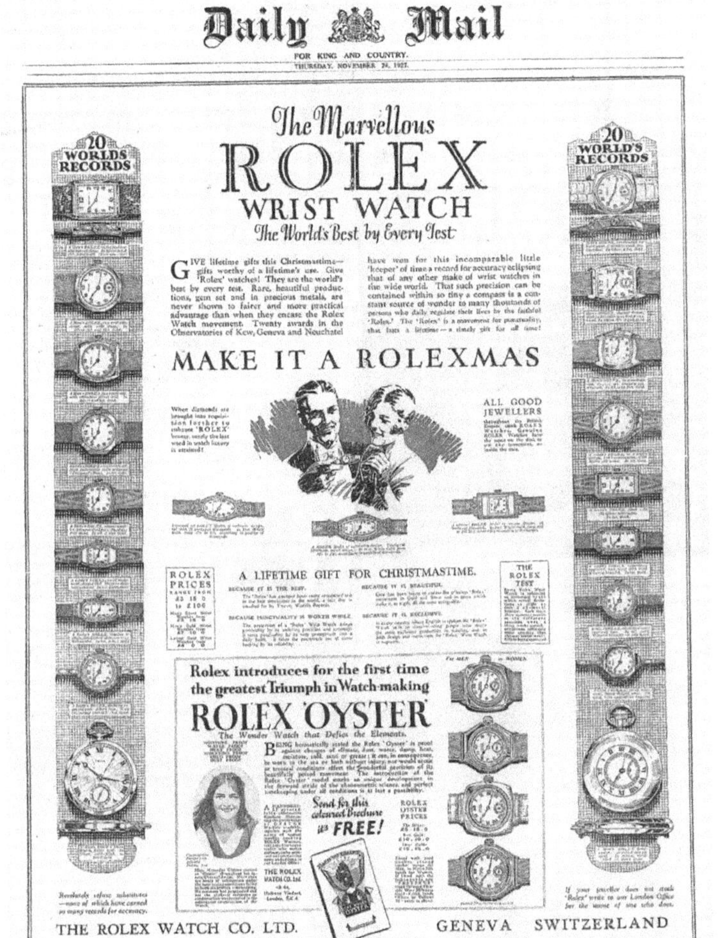

Figure 4.3 Advertisement published in the *Daily Mail*, 24 November 1927

of the swimmer's prowess. Mercedes Gleitze's numerous failures between 1922 and the summer of 1927 were widely reported in the press, which had not encouraged potential sponsors to get involved. It was only after her success that Wilsdorf approached the champion. Although Gleitze only

Figure 4.4 Contemporary version of the 1927 advertisement, reworked by the Rolex communications department

Note: The full-page Daily Mail article mentioning swimmer Mercedes Gleitze's achievement is an excellent expression of the fact that Rolex's product development and communications strategy at the time was not focused on the Oyster. The Oyster was just one of a wide range of models for men and women, including wristwatches and close-up watches. It was not until several decades later, when the story told by the company – and picked up by the unanimous specialist press – had been refocused on the Oyster, that the layout of this advertisement was reworked with this in mind. This layout is generally used today in publications by the company, journalists, and bloggers.

Source: © Rolex SA.

wore a Rolex Oyster on her aborted attempt, the extreme conditions of this trial demonstrated the great resistance capabilities of the new Rolex watch. Therefore, the Swiss manufacturer decided to exploit this collaboration in the British press. The advertising page in the *Daily Mail* would have cost the sum of 42,000 francs (a value of more than 270,000 francs in 2020).[17] As for the young swimmer, she continued her sporting career, crossing the Straits of Gibraltar in 1928, but without a Rolex on her wrist.

The collaboration between Rolex and the English swimmer was not in itself original. Since the beginning of the twentieth century, the major Swiss watch manufacturers had been participating in the exploits of extreme athletes and adventurers to build brands that expressed high precision, top quality, and resistance to extreme environments. Prizes won in chronometry competitions were not enough to distinguish brands on the global market. Consumers needed strong, emotional messages that highlighted the high quality of the brands. In his history of the *Journal Suisse d'Horlogerie*, Sébastian Vivas states that "the reliability of chronometers was no longer legitimised by physicists working in observatories, but by heroic users".[18] For example, Longines equipped the explorers who set out to conquer the North Pole in 1899 and 1904–1905, before embarking on a fruitful collaboration with aviation pioneers in the 1920s and 1930s. In particular, the company was involved in the first non-stop, solo flight between New York and Paris by Charles Lindbergh aboard the *Spirit of St Louis* in May 1927. Longines had also been a partner of several major sporting events since the 1910s, including providing sports timekeeping for car races and ski competitions.[19] Omega, which had been producing chronographs since the 1890s, began developing large clocks for football stadiums at the end of the 1920s and worked with divers. However, it was above all its collaboration with the Olympic Games, from 1932 onwards, that established the brand's legitimacy. It has been used extensively in Omega's communications ever since.[20]

The collaboration with Mercedes Gleitze was part of a general trend to promote watch brands through participation in exploits that appeal to a wide audience. Their choice expressed a desire to build a specific brand identity. For Rolex, all the attention was focused on the waterproof Oyster

Figure 4.5 Rolex advertisement, 1936

Note: Putting Rolex Oyster watches in extreme situations allowed the company to communicate facts about their great resistance. This type of advertising, which made Rolex out to be indestructible, continued regularly until the end of the twentieth century.

watch. This was not just a chronometer or a high-precision watch but a timepiece that could withstand the most extreme conditions. With the advent of the wristwatch, water resistance became an important quality element, subject to harsher conditions than a pocket watch. Wilsdorf understood the need to communicate on this point and to distinguish its chronometers from those of its competitors. In the 1930s, advertisements featuring Rolex Oyster watches in aquariums were published in newspapers and other media around the world. The manufacturer also installed them in the windows of some of its boutiques worldwide (see Figure 4.5).[21]

Building a brand portfolio

Hans Wilsdorf was a salesman with a highly developed sense of the market. He decided to establish Rolex as a brand of Swiss watchmaking excellence, notably through the Oyster model. However, he did not focus all his attention on this one model. At the same time, he resorted to various sub-brands to fill the lower or special segments of the market. Indeed, there was a significant increase in brand registrations after the First World War, under the decisive action of Hans Wilsdorf (see Figure 4.6).

Wilsdorf & Davis registered its first three trademarks in Switzerland in 1907, before registering Rolex the following year. After the dissolution of this firm, it was the simple firm of Wilsdorf that took charge of registering numerous trademarks: it recorded fourteen in the 1910s and forty-seven in the 1920s, including some emblematic of Rolex's technical development, such as the Oyster (1926) and Huître (1927) trademarks.[22] It was also at this time that the crown symbol was registered as a logo (1925). The company ceased trading in the early 1930s and was officially wound up in 1933.[23] Trademark registration was continued by Hans Wilsdorf in his personal capacity. From 1931, he had been registering trademarks for his group, with an address at the Hôtel des Bergues in Geneva and then at his personal home – nineteen trademarks in all during the 1930s. After 1940, these trademarks were transferred to Montres Rolex SA, which also began registering them in its own name in 1939. The reasons for this transfer are not known. They were no doubt aimed at Wilsdorf's personal

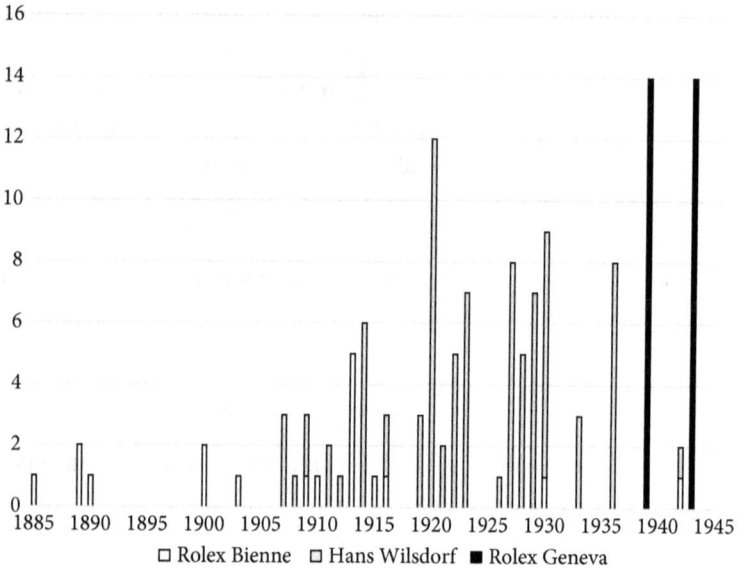

Figure 4.6 Trademark registrations by Rolex, 1885–1943
Note: These figures include trademark registrations in Switzerland. They do not include renewals, cancellations, or transfers.
Source: MIH, Archives de l'horlogerie, various locations and publishers, 1880–1943.

enrichment and the development of brand management skills within the Montres Rolex company.

These figures on trademark registrations perfectly illustrate the importance Hans Wilsdorf attached to marketing. He did not limit himself to developing a technically innovative product but incorporated it into a brand strategy designed to ensure its renown. For example, while the Rolex group registered seventy-one patents between 1920 and 1940, the total number of trademarks for the same period was eighty-one. It is of course impossible to put a precise figure on the real value of a patent or trademark, but this comparison shows that the efforts of Aegler and Wilsdorf were not limited to technical innovation.

Of the many sub-brands registered, only a few were used to develop products that complemented the main Rolex and Oyster brands. The challenge was first and foremost to offer a second brand in a lower segment to maintain a coherent positioning for the main brand and to prevent the emergence of new competitors who would have become dominant at a lower range. The merger of Omega and Tissot into the Société Suisse pour l'Industrie Horlogère SA (SSIH) in 1930 resulted in the two brands being positioned separately, with Omega at the top end of the market and Tissot in a lower segment.[24] As for Longines, it had tried unsuccessfully to launch a sub-brand for simple, inexpensive products in the 1880s and 1890s. Its importers on the American market repeatedly asked it to launch such a product after the Second World War.[25] The idea of maintaining a main brand in the expensive but high-quality watch segment, and protecting it with a simpler, more accessible complementary brand, was therefore widespread in the Swiss watchmaking industry in the first part of the twentieth century, although it was relatively little used due to the small size of most companies. It should also be remembered that this is by no means unique to watchmaking. In many industrial sectors, product and brand segmentation was introduced during the interwar period, following the innovative example of General Motors in the US car industry.[26]

Wilsdorf adopted a similar strategy, designed to better identify its main products. The idea, however, was not to create a second brand, positioned in a lower segment, but rather various sub-brands for particular watches. Nor was the link with Rolex broken or hidden. On the contrary, the name of the sub-brand generally appeared to be associated with the main "Rolex" name. During the interwar period, the main brands were Marconi, Prince, and Tudor. The first of these, Marconi, was registered in 1911. It was used from the 1920s to the 1940s for models in a lower range than the Oyster, generally equipped with calibres produced by ébauches factories independent of Rolex, such as the Fabrique d'ébauches de Fontainemelon.[27] It appears in advertisements aimed at the Japanese market. The second brand, Prince, was one of the first successful models. It was originally a rectangular timepiece with an art deco dial, launched in 1928 and representing the brand's top-of-the-range line.[28] Popular in the 1930s, it gradually disappeared when the Oyster Perpetual became the incarnation of Rolex. Production ended in the 1940s.[29] Finally, the

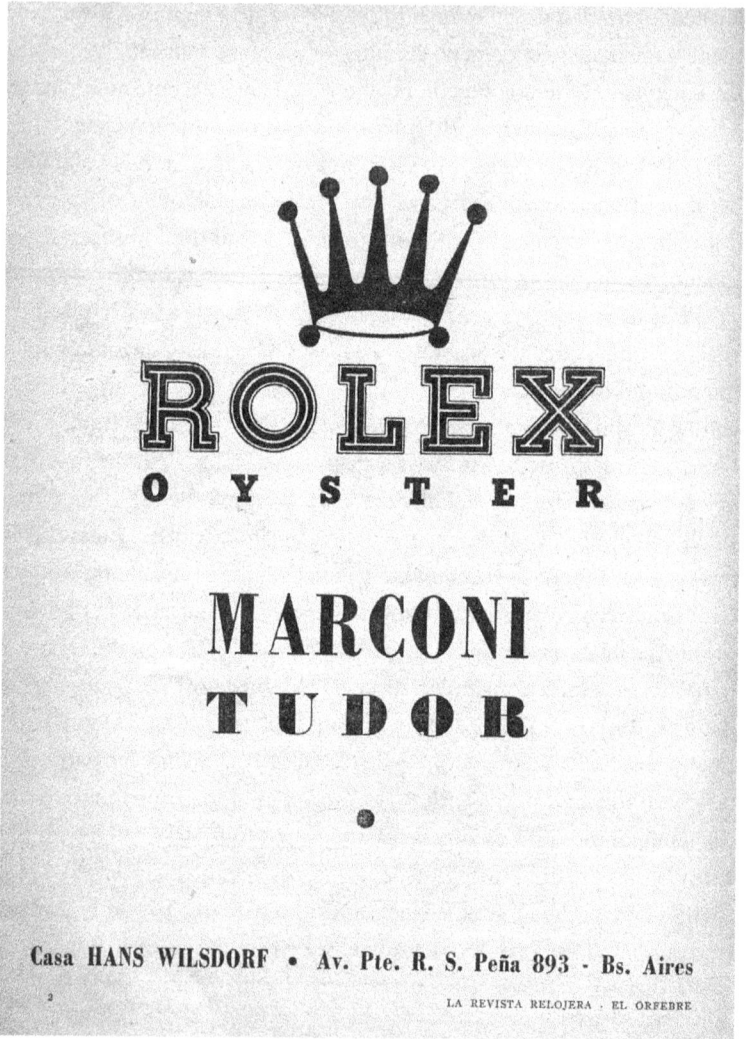

Figure 4.7 Rolex advertisement, 1946

Note: Although Rolex Oyster established itself as the company's main brand after the Second World War, it was still accompanied by other brands positioned in a lower price segment. The watches were generally sold side by side by retailers until the 1950s.

Source: La Revista Relojera, 1946, no. 48, p. 6. © Europa Star Archives.

Tudor brand was acquired by Hans Wilsdorf in 1936 and registered two years later by Montres Rolex SA.[30] It had been registered in 1926 by a small watchmaking company in Colombier, in the canton of Neuchâtel, the Veuve de Philippe Hüther.[31] The company had been founded in 1917 by Philippe Hüther and continued by his wife after he died in 1926.[32] It was therefore at the time of the change of management that the Tudor brand was registered. Its name suggests that it was a brand for Great Britain and its empire. According to some watch journalists, Wilsdorf collaborated with Hüther to penetrate the Australian market before 1936, but there are no original documents to confirm this.[33] The Davoine directory for 1928 states that Veuve Philippe Hüther specialised in "anchor and cylinder watches for all countries".[34] This was a small workshop whose activities are not known.

The commercial expansion of Rolex

When he moved to Geneva in 1920, Hans Wilsdorf explained to the local police that "my business is solely that of Swiss watchmaking, from which I export several million francs annually to the English colonies and Great Britain".[35] The British Empire remained Rolex's main market until the early 1930s. Despite its presence in other markets, commercial diversification remained limited. Hermann Aegler's agreements with the Gruen brothers and with German traders meant that Rolex was absent from two of Switzerland's main watchmaking markets: the United States and Germany.

In 1924, Wilsdorf signed an agreement with the Lucerne watch retailer Bucherer, marking the start of the Swiss market's development in the second half of the 1920s.[36] While the nature of the contract is not known, it was an important partnership that enabled Rolex to benefit from a distribution network reaching wealthy foreign customers during their stay in Switzerland as Bucherer had representatives in the main luxury resorts.

The company's origins lie in a hardware shop opened in Lucerne in 1888 as a subsidiary of a Basel trading company.[37] Managed by Carl Bucherer, this subsidiary became independent in 1892 and specialised in the sale of toys, taking the name Grand Bazar Suisse two years later.[38] In 1897, Bucherer opened a single company in his own name, still in Lucerne, specialising in jewellery and luxury goods.[39] A small goldsmith's workshop was also opened in 1900.[40] Bucherer tried unsuccessfully to expand into the German market, opening a boutique in Berlin between 1915 and 1925, before concentrating on the Swiss market. He added the sale of watches to his company name in 1926, then successively opened jewellery stores in top tourist destinations like Interlaken (1927), Lugano (1928), the Hotel Rigi in Lucerne (1930), and Saint-Moritz (1931).[41] After the First World War, tourism experienced a new boom, marked by an increase in overnight stays from less than 12,000 in 1918 to a peak of more than 22,000 a year in 1928–1930.[42] Bucherer and Rolex took advantage of this expansion in tourist demand, which was based essentially on high-income travellers, to develop their business in the Swiss market. However, the economic crisis of the 1930s and then the Second World War put a temporary halt to this strong growth.

Outside Switzerland, Hans Wilsdorf also used independent agents, with British business networks supporting this expansion into Asia. In Japan, Charles Burton Bernard, a long-established English merchant, was Rolex's agent in the early 1920s.[43] After he ceased trading around 1930, the agency was taken over by F.W. Schulz of Kobe and then by the Swiss trading company Liebermann & Waelchli.[44] In Shanghai, Wilsdorf used the services of the sales subsidiary of the British silverware manufacturer Alexander Clark Co., at least since 1929.[45] Rolex placed advertisements in English-language newspapers published in Asian countries, such as the *Japan Times* and the *China Weekly Review*, demonstrating that it was targeting the foreign community established in these countries, the British in particular. Moreover, the advertisements highlighted the results obtained at the Kew Observatory.

Apart from these details relating to the Swiss and Asian markets, it is not possible to identify and discuss Rolex's commercial expansion during the 1920s from the available sources. What is certain, however, is that the crisis of the 1930s represented a turning point in the diversification of outlets. The devaluation of the sterling in 1931 came as a shock. To limit its losses in Swiss francs, Wilsdorf had to sharply increase its prices in pounds, which led to serious commercial difficulties in the British Empire, on which Montres Rolex SA depended.[46]

Market diversification, therefore, became urgent. In 1931, the Société française des Montres Rolex was founded in Paris to exploit the French market.[47] Sales to Italy had also been recorded since 1929, but remained modest (709 watches on average per year from 1929 to 1934).[48] Interest was also shown in Latin America, where sales representatives were sent.[49] Walter Luthy, who was to become one of the main managers of Rolex's export department after the war, spent long and fruitful periods there.[50] Montres Rolex SA also exploited the Swiss diplomatic network. In 1934, for example, it asked the CSH for a report on the Malaysian market prepared by the Swiss consulate in Singapore.[51]

However, market diversification was made extremely difficult by the new political and institutional context. After 1931, Switzerland's trade with many countries was conducted under bilateral clearing agreements, which introduced controls on foreign trade to avoid currency swaps. In each country, importers paid for their purchases in local currency to the central bank, which then allocated these amounts to exporters. Balancing trade in this way avoided the need to send money back and therefore avoided exchange controls. In Switzerland, these amounts were managed by the National Bank, and since 1934 by the Swiss Clearing Office. They adopted quotas by industry and by company, based on the number of exports in previous years.[52] In the watch industry, the allocation per company was supervised by the Swiss Watchmaking Chamber (CSH). This complex system, which remained in force until the end of the 1950s, mainly regulated trade with European countries, while the United States maintained free trade and the movement of capital. An important feature of this system is that it made it difficult to diversify outlets quickly: companies were allocated maximum quotas by country according to their exports in previous years. In the case of the watchmaking industry, the CSH only had small amounts available each year outside the quotas, which it could allocate to certain exceptional cases.

The clearing agreements delayed Rolex's expansion into certain countries, leading to numerous complaints from Geneva-based Montres Rolex SA to the CSH and the federal authorities. Moreover, in some countries, specific protectionist measures were taken to limit imports. In 1935, for example, Fascist Italy decided to make imports of gold watches subject to a licence, while silver watches remained subject to the quota decided under the clearing agreement.[53] Similarly, the British market remained difficult to access, as Montres Rolex SA explained in 1944: "The English markets are completely closed to us; the maximum prices imposed on importers in mainland and in the British colonies rule out any possibility of supplying Rolex watches, which are very expensive."[54] The bureaucratic control of foreign trade left its mark on the archives, enabling the historian to identify the countries to which Rolex exported after 1931. Applications for export permits, dependent on the quotas allocated to Rolex, were submitted to the CSH for the following countries: Egypt (first mentioned in 1936), Canada (1936), France (1940), Croatia (1941), Jamaica (1941), Poland (1941), Bulgaria (1942), Denmark (1942), Venezuela (1942), Hungary (1942), Portugal (1942), Iceland (1942), Iraq (1943), and Sweden (1943), as well as for the whole of Latin America in 1943.[55] Export volumes are not known, but these references illustrate Rolex's determination to expand, despite the war, throughout Europe, the Middle East, and the entire American continent.

However, the United States was the focus of the strategy to diversify outlets. Until 1930, Gruen Watch sold the movements manufactured by Aegler on the American market. During their collaboration, this firm is said to have supplied Aegler with between 1,000 and 1,200 "precision movements" per week.[56] As we have seen, it was Aegler that registered the Rolex brand in the United States in 1914 (see Chapter 3, p. 67). In 1931, however, Gruen's difficulties meant that Manufacture des Montres Rolex SA had to find a new solution and try to expand into this market with the help of its partner in Geneva. The challenge was described as: "the enormous task of introducing to the American market a brand that was totally unknown there".[57] At first, everything seemed to indicate that Rolex was only exporting movements to the

United States – there is evidence of a similar practice in Canada in 1943 and in France in 1944.[58] This was the way most Swiss watch manufacturers exported to the United States at the time – in order to avoid the heavy customs duties on finished watches and to offer watches in a style that suited the tastes of American consumers.[59] This was the business model followed by Gruen Watch. In 1935, Montres Rolex SA requested information from the CSH on the regulation of the watch-case industry in the United States in order to respond correctly to the demands of its partner on the other side of the Atlantic.[60] In addition, since 1936, foreign watch manufacturers had been obliged to declare to the American authorities the names of their importers in that country and to indicate this on their movements. Rolex did business with the following partners: Oppenstein Bros., Kansas City (1936), Louis Friedlander, Seattle (1936), Zell Bros., Portland (1936), Paul Breguette Watch, Washington, DC (1937), Shreve, Treat and Eacret, San Francisco (1937), Stokes Jeweler, Beverly Hills (1937), and J.P. Bouret, Puerto Rico (1938).[61] These companies imported movements, cased them, and sold Rolex-branded watches through their retail networks. Some of them negotiated exclusive contracts, like H.I. Stokes of Beverly Hills, which in 1937 obtained representation for the whole of the western United States, including California. H.I. Stokes developed the Rolex brand there "by means of considerable and costly advertising".[62] These various collaborations enabled Rolex to enter the United States.

However, Wilsdorf wanted to take control of Rolex in this important market. In 1940, he sent his commercial director, Luthy, with the aim of creating a subsidiary in New York. An office was opened in 1941 under the name Rolex Watch Corporation.[63] It took charge of importing Rolex watches into the United States and distributing them throughout the country, gradually breaking the exclusive contracts signed during the 1930s.[64]

However, the Swiss National Bank's (SNB) decision in June 1941 to restrict the dollar led to major difficulties[65] not limited to the American market. They extended to the whole of Latin America, where Rolex carried out its transactions in US dollars.[66] As the dollar quotas were calculated on the basis of average export figures for the years 1937, 1938, and 1940, at a time when Rolex had little involvement on the American continent, it was only allocated small amounts.[67] Despite the intervention of the Geneva government with the federal authorities, Rolex did not benefit from an extension of its quota, especially as other manufacturers were calling for a similar measure.[68] In January 1944, when the SNB allocated Rolex a monthly sum of 40,800 francs for the purchase of US dollars, the latter complained to the CSH: "The figure that you are giving us does not even allow us to envisage making our factory work 'idle'. As far as we are concerned, the only valid solution is immediate closure and the complete redundancy of all our workers."[69] It also recalled the new strategy adopted around 1941: "We would point out that, even in the USA, we only ship complete watches, adjusted in-house and ready to be worn. We flatly refused to send a single bare movement. The Swiss precision watch industry undoubtedly benefits from the prestige enjoyed by Rolex."[70] The virulence of the reactions towards the SNB suggests that, despite the evidence of exports to a great many countries, it was indeed the United States that became Rolex's main outlet during the Second World War. In 1942, Rolex Watch Corporation took possession of a sales space on Fifth Avenue in New York, in the prestigious building at No. 580. At the same time, the Longines Wittnauer Watch Company, which also distributed Vacheron & Constantin in the United States, acquired space in the same building.[71] The American subsidiary of Rolex and Longines Wittnauer worked closely together on commercial matters. Since at least 1943, the Tourneau Watches boutique on Madison Avenue has offered Rolex watches as part of a range of luxury timepieces that also includes Longines and Vacheron & Constantin.[72] Despite business difficulties and an unfavourable institutional context since 1941, Rolex managed to establish its presence in the United States during the Second World War. In January 1944, Wilsdorf explained the reasons for the success of this operation: "We have spent a fortune to achieve the result we have obtained in this country."[73]

Conclusion

The marketing strategy adopted by Wilsdorf in the interwar period aimed to establish its brand as a representative of Swiss watchmaking excellence. Participation in chronometric competitions and support for sporting exploits, widely reported in the written press, served as the basis for the company's advertising. From this perspective, communication is a direct extension of product development. It is informative in nature and aims to pass on to consumers a series of facts, such as prizes and records won in observatories or recognition of the water resistance of cases, which attest to the high quality of Rolex watches. This strategy is not in itself original. It has been pursued by the major Swiss watch manufacturers since the end of the nineteenth century. Therefore, Wilsdorf was not particularly innovative in terms of its marketing positioning. Rolex was a new entrant to the top-of-the-range watch market, but it did not adopt a disruptive strategy. It did not challenge the fundamental principle of competitiveness in this market: the technical excellence of the product.

It is also worth highlighting a second feature of Rolex's positioning in the interwar watch market. Until the early 1930s, its geographical presence was essentially limited to Great Britain, its empire, and its sphere of influence – including the Far East – as well as a few European markets, including Switzerland. The early 1930s marked a major turning point. First, the British market collapsed following the devaluation of the pound and the adoption of protectionist measures. These difficulties continued during the Second World War, especially as the British authorities suspected Hans Wilsdorf of Nazi sympathies and refused him visas to export his watches to the UK.[74] In January 1943, Wilsdorf considered separating his house in London from his business in Dublin, "a measure that would not suit the English".[75] Rolex then used the Swiss diplomatic bag to correspond with its agent in Ireland "in order to avoid British censorship".[76] Finally, in 1946, when Montres Rolex SA sought to resume relations with regions under British influence, such as South Africa, Egypt, and Palestine, it faced administrative hassles from the British authorities in granting visas and travel documents to its representative – himself a

British citizen.[77] Second, the diversification of outlets in Europe was made difficult by the clearing agreements, the protectionist measures of many countries, and the war. The period 1930–1945 was not favourable for the arrival of a new top-of-the-range watch brand in the various European markets. The case of Italy is emblematic. The quotas issued by the CSH and the restrictions on gold watch imports imposed by the Fascist government prevented Rolex from meeting the growing demand.[78] Third and finally, it was during the 1930s that Rolex made its entry into the United States. Although the beginnings were difficult, the Swiss manufacturer opened a subsidiary in New York, which soon became the heart of its expansion in this country, where it experienced significant growth during the first part of the 1940s. In 1943, Montres Rolex SA recruited staff in the Neuchâtel mountains.[79] Within two years, it had considerably increased its capital (see Chapter 2). It was precisely on the American market that Rolex became an icon of affordable luxury after the Second World War.

Notes

1   Paratte, *Marketing et publicité dans l'horlogerie*; Vivas, *L'ancre et la plume*; Huguenin and Bernasconi, *L'heure pour tous*.
2   Chandler, *Scale and Scope*; da Silva Lopes and Duguid, *Trademarks, Brands, and Competitiveness*.
3   Anne-Marie Dubler, "Marques", in *Dictionnaire historique de la Suisse (DHS)*, version of 23 August 2013, Online: https://hls-dhs-dss.ch/fr/articles/013728/2013-08-23/ (accessed 4 June 2021).
4   MIH, *Archives de l'horlogerie, 1881–1920*. Recordings began in November 1880.
5   Chessel, *La publicité*.
6   Huguenin and Bernasconi, *L'heure pour tous*.
7   Donzé, *Histoire sociale et économique de la chronométrie*, pp. 47–51.
8   *La Fédération horlogère suisse*, 1 March 1946.
9   *La Fédération horlogère suisse*, 7 March 1928.
10 Donzé, *Histoire sociale et économique de la chronométrie*, p. 45.
11 According to the results of the Neuchâtel Observatory competitions published in *La Fédération horlogère suisse*, the last time Jean Matile took part in these competitions as an independent timer was in 1926. His last entry as an independent timer in the Davoine directory was in 1927.

12 *La Sentinelle*, 12 July 1961.

13 Donzé, *Histoire sociale et économique de la chronométrie*, pp. 88–89.

14 *La Fédération horlogère suisse*, vol. 5, 1946.

15 Donzé, *Histoire sociale et économique de la chronométrie*, pp. 119 and 124.

16 Doloranda Hannah Pember, "Gleitze, Mercedes (1900–1981)", Oxford Dictionary of National Biography, www.oxforddnb.com/ (accessed 15 June 2023).

17 The sum of 42,000 francs is mentioned in a Rolex advertisement in the *Journal de Genève*, 22 March 1956.

18 Vivas, *L'ancre et la plume*, p. 101.

19 Donzé, *Longines*, pp. 128–129.

20 Richon, *Omega Saga*, Chapter 2. It should be noted that other companies, notably Longines, have taken part in the timekeeping of the Olympic Games. See Tonnerre, "Une question de prestige dans le domaine international de l'industrie horlogère".

21 Brozek, *The Rolex Report*, p. 31.

22 *FOSC*, 1926–1927.

23 *FOSC*, 1933, p. 521.

24 Richon, *Omega Saga*, pp. 28–29; Fallet, *Tissot, 150 ans d'histoire*.

25 Donzé, *Longines*, pp. 56, 177, and 192.

26 Chandler, *Strategy and Structure*.

27 Izuishi, *Rorekkusu no himitsu*, p. 63.

28 Brunner, *The Watch Book*, pp. 68–73.

29 Patrizzi and Cappelletti, *Investir dans les montres Rolex*, pp. 22–25 and 316.

30 *FOSC*, 1936, p. 2750, and 1939, p. 903.

31 *FOSC*, 1926, p. 682.

32 *FOSC*, 1917, p. 1229, and 1926, p. 367.

33 See for example *Europa Star*, no. 303, 2010, p. 6.

34 Davoine directory, 1928, p. 436.

35 State Archives, Geneva (AEG), Residents' Police, letter from Hans Wilsdorf to the Residents' Police of the canton of Geneva, 23 February 1920.

36 According to the company's website, www.bucherer.com/ch/en/buchererworld/company/our-history (accessed 15 December 2024).

37 *FOSC*, 1888, p. 780. The company in question was K. Bucherer, officially registered in 1883. Renamed Métraux-Bucherer in 1905, it continued its hardware business and became one of the leading sellers of carnival masks between the wars. The company's official history emphasises its specialisation in the manufacture and sale of watches and jewellery since its foundation, in an attempt to construct a narrative that stresses the permanence of

its luxury positioning. See Bucherer, "Célébration de 125 ans d'histoire suisse du temps".

38 *FOSC*, 1892, p. 961, and *FOSC*, 1894, p. 962.

39 *FOSC*, 1897, p. 113.

40 *FOSC*, 1901, p. 9.

41 *FOSC*, 1926, p. 1946, and 1930, p. 1250. He also opened a watchmaking workshop in 1926 and marketed his own watches under the Novidar brand. *FOSC*, 1927, p. 256, and 1928, p. 884.

42 Laurent Tissot: "Tourisme", *DHS*, version of 25 February 2014, https://hls-dhs-dss.ch/fr/articles/014070/2014-02-25/ (accessed 18 June 2021).

43 *The Japan Times*, 14 January 1923. For Bernard's career, see www.meiji-portra its.de/meiji_portraits_b.html (accessed 3 July 2021).

44 *The Japan Times*, 11 February 1930; MIH, CSH, letter from CSH to Rolex Watch, 26 June 1934.

45 According to an advertisement in *The China Press*, Shanghai, 18 December 1929.

46 Montres Rolex, *Vade Mecum*, vol. 1, p. 27.

47 *Archives commerciales de la France*, 11 December 1931, p. 5651.

48 MIH, CSH, letter from the CSH to Rolex Watch, 17 October 1935. Export quotas for 1935 were allocated based on this average.

49 AEG, Secrétariat général du Département de l'Economie publique (DEP), 1986 va 9.18.58, letter from Montres Rolex to the CSH, 27 January 1944.

50 *The Eastern and Jeweller and Watchmaker*, 1953, no. 16, p. 49.

51 MIH, CSH, letter from CSH to Rolex Watch, 13 January 1934.

52 Martin Meier, "Clearing", *DHS*, version of 18 December 2003, https://hls-dhs-dss.ch/fr/articles/013779/2003-12-18/ (accessed 4 August 2023).

53 MIH, CSH, letter from CSH to Rolex Watch, 17 December 1935.

54 AEG, Secrétariat général du Département de l'Economie publique (DEP), 1986 va 9.18.58, letter from Montres Rolex to the CSH, 27 January 1944.

55 MIH, CSH, correspondence between Rolex Watch Co. and the CSH.

56 AEG, Secrétariat général du Département de l'Economie publique (DEP), 1986 va 9.18.58, letter from Montres Rolex to the CSH, 27 January 1944.

57 Ibid.

58 MIH, CSH, letter from CSH to Rolex Watch, 16 November 1943 and 16 May 1944.

59 Donzé, *The Business of Time*, Chapters 3 and 4.

60 MIH, CSH, letter from CSH to Rolex Watch, 12 February 1935.

61 MIH, CSH, letter from CSH to Rolex Watch, 15 July 1936, 30 September 1936, 19 May 1937, 13 August 1937, 26 November 1937, 10 August 1938.

62 MIH, CSH, letter from CSH to Rolex Watch, 11 June 1943.

63 MIH, CSH, letter from CSH to Rolex Watch, 17 March 1941.
64 MIH, CSH, letter from CSH to Rolex Watch, 25 September 1943.
65 Martin Meier, "Contrôle des changes", *DHS*, version of 5 November 2003, https://hls-dhs-dss.ch/fr/articles/013743/2003-11-05/ (accessed 4 August 2023).
66 AEG, Secrétariat général du Département de l'Economie publique (DEP), 1986 va 9.18.58, letter from Montres Rolex to the CSH, 27 January 1944.
67 AEG, Secrétariat général du Département de l'Economie publique (DEP), 1986 va 9.18.58, letter from the CSH to the Département du Commerce et de l'Industrie du Canton de Genève, 7 February 1944.
68 AEG, Secrétariat général du Département de l'Economie publique (DEP), 1986 va 9.18.58, correspondence between the CSH, the Département du Commerce et de l'Industrie and the Département fédéral de l'économie publique, February 1944.
69 AEG, Secrétariat général du Département de l'Economie publique (DEP), 1986 va 9.18.58, letter from Montres Rolex to the CSH, 27 January 1944.
70 Ibid.
71 *New York Times*, 21 April 1942; Donzé, *Longines*, pp. 176–178.
72 According to an advertisement in the *New York Times*, 13 June 1943.
73 AEG, Secrétariat général du Département de l'Economie publique (DEP), 1986 va 9.18.58, letter from Montres Rolex to the CSH, 27 January 1944.
74 AF, E2001E#196878#9624, letter from the Geneva Chamber of Commerce to the Federal Political Department (Foreign Affairs), 24 May 1941. In June 1941, the British authorities investigated Hans Wilsdorf, a British citizen but of German origin, whose brother was allegedly active in the German Ministry of Propaganda. They contacted the Swiss authorities (AF, E2001E#196878#9624, confidential letter to the Federal Public Prosecutor's Office, 25 June 1941). An investigation by the security police of the canton of Geneva, carried out at the request of Werner Balsiger, head of the police department of the Federal Public Prosecutor's Office, concluded: "The information gathered shows that Wilsdorf is a fervent admirer of the Hitler regime. He does not hide his satisfaction when events favourable to Germany occur. However, we have not seen or heard of any pro-Hitler propaganda or suspicious activity on his part. The above-mentioned person is not unfavourably known to our judicial services and has not been convicted and our town. From a political point of view, Wilsdorf is known to our services as a 'Nazi'. A check of his correspondence was carried out in 1940, but nothing suspicious was found at that time" (AF, E2001E#196878#9624, report by the security police of the canton of Geneva, 9 August 1941). No further action was taken on this investigation. The State Archives in Geneva (AEG) do not

hold any archival documents from the Security Police for this period (email from AEG to the author, 10 February 2023). Many watch bloggers and journalists emphasised Wilsdorf's open support for British officers held in prison camps in Germany. The sources for these assertions are never cited, and most of them relate to events after 1943. Such actions may have been taken to improve Rolex's image in Britain. In the absence of access to the company's archives, however, it is not possible to substantiate such a hypothesis.

75 AF, E2001E#196882#397, note from a telephone call to Hans Wilsdorf, 8 January 1943.

76 Ibid. Although against diplomatic practice, the Confederation agreed that certain companies could use its consular network to send private correspondence during the Second World War, as Rolex did, for example, to Ireland, Argentina, Italy, and occupied France in 1943 and 1944 (AF, E2001E#196882#397).

77 Montres Rolex SA tried unsuccessfully to get the Confederation to intervene on its behalf through the Geneva branch of Crédit Suisse. AF, E2001E#196878#4455, letter from Crédit Suisse to the Federal Political Department (Foreign Affairs), 11 April 1946.

78 In particular, Rolex sold parts to Panerai & Fils in Florence, which supplied Italian combat swimmers according to the brand's official history. MIH, CSH, letter from CSH to Rolex Watch, 22 February 1943 and Panerai website, www.panerai.com/en/about-panerai/history.html (accessed 4 August 2023).

79 A CSH report cites Montres Rolex SA as one of several Geneva watchmaking companies that recruited workers in La Chaux-de-Fonds in 1943, through advertisements in the newspaper L'Impartial. AEG, Secrétariat général du Département de l'Economie publique (DEP), 1986 va 9.18.58, report of Solvil company, 2 December 1943.

Part II

The creation of new collections (1945–1960)

At the end of the Second World War, Switzerland enjoyed a position of strengthened dominance on the world market. It accounted for more than half the world's watch production.[1] At the same time, the economic and political difficulties of the interwar period were forgotten. The world economy was entering a period of strong growth that benefited Swiss watchmaking companies. The volume of Swiss watch exports rose from 18.8 million watches and movements in 1945 to 24.2 million in 1950 and 41 million in 1960. This growth was based primarily on the American market (44 per cent of exports in 1945, 36.8 per cent in 1950, and 30 per cent in 1960), especially for low-cost products,[2] but it was the expansion on a global scale that was the main feature of the post-war period.

The expansion of the global market represented an opportunity for many watch companies. It also means much stiffer competition, especially as foreign companies such as Bulova in the United States and Seiko in Japan experienced strong growth in their respective domestic markets.[3] The need to stand out from the competition and offer products with a strong identity has led watch companies to adopt a new strategy for their top-of-the-range watches.[4] First, they abandoned the practice of exporting movements, which had become common after the First World War because it enabled them to bypass the customs barrier affecting finished products and to adapt to the tastes of local customers thanks to on-site casing. High-quality finished watches were then brought together in specific collections, bearing a particular name and generally determined by the watch's function. Omega, which in 1940 was one of the first Swiss watch manufacturers to set up a design department, entrusted to a young designer, René Bannwart, successively launched the Seamaster collection for water-resistant watches (1948), the Constellation collection for wristwatch chronometers (1952), and the Speedmaster collection for chronographs (1957).[5] Its rival Longines soon imitated this new strategy. In 1954, it decided to create the Conquest collection for its self-winding watches, with the company's sales management explaining the choice of "a pleasant-sounding name, easy to pronounce in all languages",[6] and appropriate for a product classified as a luxury watch, for which "worldwide advertising"[7] was set up, i.e., a global advertising campaign that did not vary according to market. In the years that followed, the success of the Conquest led to the design of new collections such as Silver Arrow (1955) and Flagship (1957).

It was no longer importers and distributors in the various markets who ordered the products of their choice from the manufacturers, but the latter who designed them and launched them on the market. This change in perspective was part of a drive to limit dependence on the American market and to expand outlets worldwide. Real marketing studies began to be carried out, including product design, choice of name and, ultimately, the worldwide advertising campaign.[8] The success of these iconic products led most watch companies to launch models with their own specific technical and aesthetic features from the 1960s onwards. In terms of design management, this change clearly expresses the internalisation of skills relating to tangible design (watch styling).

At Rolex, the development of product collections with a clearly identified design was not a fundamental break. As we saw in the previous chapter, the company internalised watch decoration in the second half of the 1920s and, with the design of the Oyster, had the opportunity to develop a model with very specific technical characteristics and identity. During the years 1945–1963, Rolex continued and developed this strategy, creating a number of complementary models that embodied the brand's values in various variations. However, the major change Rolex made after 1945 was the rapid concentration of its marketing strategy on these iconic products when, as we have seen in the previous chapters, the Oyster was still just one model among many on the eve of the world conflict. The series of new models created during this period forms the basis on which Rolex continues to develop today. It abandoned the great variety to concentrate on a few iconic products.

Notes

1 Donzé, *The Business of Time*, p. 88.
2 The average value of a complete watch exported to the United States in the 1950s was 24 francs, compared with 31 francs for the world as a whole. Source: Federation of the Swiss Watch Industry.
3 Donzé, *The Business of Time*, pp. 95 and 101–104.
4 Donzé, "The Transformation of Global Luxury Brands", p. 31.
5 Richon, *Omega Saga*, Chapter 4. Born in Zurich in 1915, René Bannwart began his career with Patek, Philippe & Cie in 1933. In 1955, he left Omega to take over the management of the family watchmaking workshop opened in 1924 in La Chaux-de-Fonds. Renamed Corum, the company grew from five employees in 1955 to ninety in 1992, thanks in particular to the launch of innovative watches, the most famous of which was the Golden Bridge.
6 Archives of the Longines Watch Company, B32.5, minutes of the Board of Directors, 30 November 1956.
7 Ibid.
8 Donzé, *Longines*, pp. 157–158.

5

Designing iconic products

Rolex showed strong organisational stability from 1945 to 1960, in line with the system in place during the interwar period – namely, the complementary relationship between two legally independent companies: Manufacture des Montres Rolex SA in Bienne (which produced movements) and Montres Rolex SA in Geneva (which took care of decoration, marketing, and sales). The relationship between the two companies was not merely supplier and buyer. Hans Wilsdorf, executive director of the Geneva-based company, sat on the Board of Directors of the Bienne-based company, and Emil Borer, CEO of the Bienne-based company, chaired the boards of both firms. The two companies also shared the same secretary: lawyer Fernand Lilla.[1] This interlocking of their governing bodies reflected the desire to manage Rolex as a single entity rather than as two independent companies. For this, good coordination between production and marketing was essential. Similarly, there were bound to be cross-shareholdings in the two companies' capital – although our lack of access to the archives means this hypothesis cannot be substantiated.

Rolex's marked institutional stability did not prevent creativity from expressing itself. Following the research conducted in the interwar years, Rolex launched new products with specific technical features, such as the Rolex Datejust, the Submariner, and the Cosmograph Daytona. Most of the product families that have made Rolex famous were developed in the years following the end of the Second World War.

Corporate governance

Despite the close collaboration between Wilsdorf and the Aegler family, each of the two companies retained its specific characteristics. The Bienne factory remained fundamentally a family business. When Hermann Aegler died in 1944, it was his son-in-law Emil Borer (1898–1967), a watchmaking technician by training, who took over the operational management of the firm and the chairmanship of the Board of Directors.[2] For more than two decades, Borer was the undisputed boss of the firm. However, unlike his father-in-law, he had little involvement in watchmaking politics or the community.[3] His primary involvement was with the Communauté d'intérêts des manufactures suisses d'horlogerie (CIM), an organisation founded in 1942 by major Swiss watch manufacturers such as Longines and Omega to strengthen their common interests vis-à-vis ASUAG AG and Ebauches SA.[4] Borer became vice-president of CIM in 1953 and president in 1957–1958, remaining on the committee until his death.[5] While he rarely spoke publicly, his company continued its paternalistic and social work internally. Like most of the country's major industrial companies in the years following the end of the war, it set up a foundation in 1953, the Hermann Aegler Foundation, to help its employees, workers, and their families in the event of old age, illness, accident, disability, or death.[6]

The organisation of the Bienne company was simple with a small Board of Directors (see Appendix, Table A.1). In addition to Borer, Wilsdorf, and Lilla, it included representatives of the Aegler family – Hans Junior (son of Hans Senior) and Emilie, Hermann's widow – as well as, for two years, Albert Kohler, chairman of a trust company in Bienne and member of the boards of several industrial companies.[7] Kohler probably played an advisory role in the development of Manufacture des Montres Rolex SA after Borer's appointment as executive director. He was not replaced on the board when he left in 1950.

The profile of these directors suggests that they had no operational responsibility for running the company. They represented the shareholders and oversaw the distribution of dividends. At the same time, Borer surrounded himself with a growing number of salaried managers. First and foremost, these were family members. Gertrud Hedwig Aegler (Hermann's daughter) and Hans Junior had been appointed authorised representatives in 1943, but these appointments were revoked in 1950 and 1954, respectively. During the 1950s, it was managers from outside the family who were appointed to such positions: Clara Lehnen-Habegger and Werner Keller.[8] These two people left no trace in the regional press or the archives consulted, so it has not been possible to identify their educational and professional background before their entry into the Rolex management team. However, their presence demonstrates that, since the early 1950s, meritocratic recruitment of managers has taken precedence over family considerations.

Montres Rolex SA, a Geneva-based company, was organised similarly, with a small Board of Directors (see Table A.2 in the Appendix) and an enlarged executive direction with salaried managers. The executive management was reorganised in 1945. Wilsdorf took on the title of executive director, supported by two directors: Werner Ryser and René-Paul Jeanneret. While Ryser oversaw the firm's administration until his death in 1964, Jeanneret (the son of the former director of Information Horlogère, a business intelligence organisation specialising in watchmaking and based in La Chaux-de-Fonds[9]) was a former advertising manager with the prestigious American agency J. Walter Thompson (JWT). Between 1934 and 1940, Jeanneret was director of the Antwerp agency in Belgium, which handled advertising in continental Europe for General Motors and other American multinationals.[10] The day before the German invasion in May 1940, he fled Belgium and took refuge in Normandy.[11] In July, he was still considering returning to Antwerp via Switzerland.[12] However, he finally settled in Switzerland, where he continued to work for JWT until 1945.[13] He was then poached by Wilsdorf and given responsibility for marketing at Rolex.[14] He held this position until 1975.[15] In addition, management was strengthened in the mid-1950s, with the appointments of André Heiniger (a former employee of the Ebel watch factory in La Chaux-de-Fonds, who had developed the South American market for Rolex in the early 1950s) as sales director (1955) and watch engineer Marc Huguenin as technical director (1956).[16] Also in 1956, Lucie-Cécile Huguenin was appointed assistant director.[17]

This extended direction was responsible for product development, marketing, advertising, packaging, and sales of watches. It was also responsible for the various companies founded by Wilsdorf, whose address was at the headquarters of Montres Rolex SA. These included the financial companies Rolex Holding (1946) and Invex (1947), as well as Montres Tudor (1946) and Marconi Watch (1948), the development of which is discussed below. Despite the creation of an extended operational management team, Wilsdorf also included members of his family in the management of Rolex. He had no children of his own, but nephews and nephews-in-law held certain positions in the company. For example, his nephew Diether Kübel, a German national who lived in Geneva, was appointed authorised representative in 1956, then director on the death of Hans Wilsdorf in 1960.[18] However, he played a secondary role and left the company in 1969.[19]

The organisational structure of the Rolex Group was completed in 1945 with the creation of the Hans Wilsdorf Foundation.[20] The main objective for Wilsdorf, then aged sixty-four, was to ensure the continued existence of Rolex, even though he had no direct descendants. Rather than sell the company to a group of investors, he decided to set up a foundation that would be entrusted with the ownership of Montres Rolex SA after his death. The deed of foundation makes no explicit mention of the watch brand but stipulates that its first two objectives are "to collect all the property assigned to it and to ensure its preservation, maintenance and profitability in accordance with the instructions and wishes of the donors" and "to allocate in the first instance all income and resources to the maintenance and development of the property belonging to the foundation".[21] Although the details of the deed of gift from Montres Rolex SA to the Wilsdorf Foundation are not known, the latter cannot, by its statutes, transfer this property. It must ensure the long-term management of the watch brand. This institutional arrangement was not exceptional in industry in general but extremely rare in the watch industry.[22] Today, there are many shareholder foundations in

Northern Europe and around a hundred in Switzerland, most of them founded after 1970.[23]

Foundation ownership has had two major consequences for the management of Rolex. Firstly, since Montres Rolex SA has no shareholders to reward with generous dividends (unlike the Bienne-based company, owned by the Aegler family), it can devote its profits to its own development and grow through self-financing, thus strengthening its financial independence. In fact, over the decades, the Wilsdorf Foundation has built up a veritable war chest (see Chapter 8). The main aim of this independence is to ensure the long-term continuity of the company and the jobs it provides. Geoffrey Jones emphasises the social responsibility that such an organisational form allows, described as a "steward-owned corporation".[24] Second, since Swiss law does not require foundations to detail their income, Rolex's business can be conducted behind closed doors. Given Hans Wilsdorf's discretion in the media and communication being limited to the brand's major advertising messages, the cult of secrecy became a veritable marketing paradigm after the 1960s (see Chapter 7).

It should be noted that the constitution of the Hans Wilsdorf Foundation is also entrusted with allocating donations to charities and grants to various institutions in Geneva, such as the Watchmaking School, the industrial arts section of the Ecole des Beaux-Arts and the Faculty of Social and Economic Sciences of the University, and the Laboratoire suisse de recherches horlogères in Neuchâtel. The philanthropic action includes allocating amounts to the founder's nephews and grandnephews, and their descendants. Although (with a few exceptions) Wilsdorf did not involve them directly in the operational management of Rolex, he did not forget to let his family benefit from his work.

The first Foundation Board was appointed by Hans Wilsdorf himself (see Appendix, Table A.3). Chaired until 1965 by Maurice Merkt, a business lawyer, tax adviser and director of Fiduciaire Suisse SA, it included Genevan notables (Gustave Martin, notary; Francis Guyot, director of Crédit Suisse), people close to Hans Wilsdorf (Alfred Chapuis and Eugène Jaquet, authors of the *Vade Mecum*) and executives from Montres

Rolex SA (Lucie Huguenin and Juliette Ihne). Subsequently, appointments were made by co-option, with the first renewal taking place in 1957. Montres Rolex SA family members and employees retired at that time. They made way for a relative of Wilsdorf (Robert Rauber) and members of the Geneva upper class (Emile Dupont, Conservative state councillor; Max Gamper, director of Crédit Suisse; Jean Malche, chairman of the Board of Directors of *Tribune de Genève*; Jean-Laurent Comtesse, director of Banque Romande).[25] The latter was responsible for administering the Wilsdorf Foundation until the beginning of the twenty-first century.

Boosting research and product-development activities

The years 1945 to 1960 marked a phase of intense research and development (see Figure 2.2, p. 37). A total of 185 patents were filed during this period, amounting to 30.5 per cent of all patents obtained by the Rolex Group from 1889 to 2019. What were the main areas of research conducted in Bienne and Geneva?

Rolex focused on four areas of activity. First and most important was the self-winding movement and its mechanism, for which it obtained thirty-four patents from 1945 to 1960. Despite obtaining the first patent for a self-winding movement in 1931 and launching Rolex Oyster Perpetual watches onto the market in the 1930s, self-winding technology was still not stable. Then, in the first part of the 1950s, it attracted the attention of the technical office – as a result, twenty-nine of the thirty-four patents were obtained between 1950 and 1954. After the Second World War, the automatic watch became the focus of fierce competition between the various brands and a symbol of watchmaking excellence. Omega (1943), Longines (1945), and Eterna (1948) successively marketed their own automatic watches, followed by many other manufacturers. The Japanese competitor Seiko, whose strategic objective was already to establish itself as the best watch manufacturer in the world, also launched an automatic model in 1959.[26] The growing competitiveness of the global market led Rolex to enhance the quality of its automatic movements through R&D.

Second, work on a water-resistant case and winding mechanism continued (twenty-three patents). The development of new types of cases made it necessary to adapt the technologies developed between the wars. A patent for a device to check the water resistance of cases was also obtained during this period. Water resistance was not the most important area of research, but Rolex worked to maintain the competitive advantage conferred by the Oyster model.

Third, a series of patents (totalling thirty-eight) related to the regulating organ (lever set, balance wheel, barrel, spring, etc.) The precision of the movement was an essential characteristic of a top-of-the-range watch until the 1980s, which explains the need for constant improvement. For example, Manufacture des Montres Rolex SA sought to control its own production of regulating organs to free itself from dependence on supplies from independent companies (see below, p. 117). The interest in watch precision also led Rolex technicians to develop an electric watch (four patents) and a control device for running watches (one patent).

Fourth and finally, new watch models became the principal area of innovation, along with automatic winding systems. Rolex obtained twenty-three patents for new wristwatches and fourteen others for various complications (calendar, hour and minute counters, world time and date). In addition, a total of eighteen patents were granted for the casing. Although Rolex sourced its bracelets and dials from independent partners, it did not remain inactive in the development of these components. The importance attached to aesthetics also explains why the Geneva company continued to register designs and models, although the number was lower than in the previous period. Between 1946 and 1960, Rolex registered a total of nine watch cases, six wristwatches (including several variations of the Submariner diver's watch), two hands, and one watch case bezel.[27]

Rolex's R&D activities during the years 1945–1960, therefore, focused on a few major elements that formed the basis of the brand's identity (water resistance, automatic winding movement, and precision), as well as a limited number of complications that enabled the launch of new models. Several of these models became emblematic of Rolex, and today remain the watches that best express the spirit of the brand. Like Omega

and Longines, Rolex launched collections distinguished by their functions and specific technical features. The Rolex Datejust, an automatic,
water-resistant chronometer wristwatch that displays the date in an aper-
ture at three o'clock on the dial, was launched in 1945 and became one
of the brand's iconic products (see Figure 5.1). It was developed into a
Day-Date in 1956, a model that became known as the "President's watch"
in the 1960s when President Dwight D. Eisenhower is said to have been
the first to wear one.[28]

In 1953, Rolex developed a second model to express the water resistance of its watches: the Submariner. Produced in partnership with Swiss
explorer Jacques Picard, this model was intended as a frontal attack on
Omega, which had enjoyed great success with its own Seamaster diver's
watch, launched five years earlier. This new type of watch attracted a great
deal of interest throughout the watch industry in the 1950s: Blancpain marketed its Fifty Fathoms (1953), Breitling a Superocean (1957), and Jeager-
LeCoultre its Deep Sea (1959). Rolex strengthened its presence in the diving
watch market with the launch of the Deepsea in 1960, developed to mark
Picard's dive into the Mariana Trench.[29] The launch of the Submariner was
part of a marketing plan to work with divers around the world. Numerous
models were offered to sports divers, explorers, diving club directors, as
well as British military personalities such as Admiral Mountbatten and
the US Navy.[30] The J. Walter Thompson (JWT) advertising agency oversaw promotion, seeking to incorporate technically innovative products
into a discourse on personal success (see Chapter 6). In the year following
its launch, the first sales of the Rolex Submariner were concentrated in
the United States (500 pieces), far ahead of Italy (thirty-three), Canada
(thirty), Switzerland (twenty-eight), and Hong Kong (twenty-four).[31] The
Submariner became an icon in the 1960s, thanks in particular to the actor
Sean Connery, who wore this model in several James Bond films during
that decade,[32] inspiring numerous imitations by Swiss watch companies
and making it one of the most counterfeited watch models.

The other major models launched during this period were the
Rolex Explorer, made to mark the ascent of Mount Everest (1953), the
GMT Master, a watch with a second time-zone display, developed in

Figure 5.1 Rolex Datejust, 1953

Note: The Rolex Datejust is an expression of the new product development strategy that emerged after the Second World War, aimed at making the Oyster an iconic model. Rather than launching completely new models for its technical innovations (here, the three o'clock date), Rolex integrated them into variations of the Oyster model.

Source: The Eastern Jeweller and Watchmaker, 1953, no. 18, p. 148. © Europa Star Archives.

113

collaboration with the American airline Pan Am (1954), and the Rolex Cosmograph, a chronograph watch that would become known as the Daytona (1963). All these models were aimed at men. Rolex's masculinity in the post-war years was essential, as it was accompanied by a discourse on individual success and the exceptionality of personal destinies, which appealed mainly to men at the time. In fact, in 1953, JWT suggested that ladies' watches should be given greater prominence in the brand's communications (see boxed text below). This led to the launch of a ladies' version of the Datejust in 1957. JWT also launched several advertising campaigns aimed at women, including a famous series of advertisements in the early 1960s featuring a black cat (see Figure 5.2).

Advice on ladies' watches from the J. Walter Thompson advertising agency

Some of the Rolex ladies' models are amongst the finest watches made by any watchmaker. Yet we know that a Rolex is not a lady's watch. The Oyster, the Oyster Perpetual, the Oyster Datejust have determined the personality of the Rolex – and here surely you have good reason to be satisfied and even proud. From a merchandising and advertising point of view the very success of these watches, which defy the elements, whose performance is backed by almost unbelievable testimonials, makes Rolex primarily and unquestionably a man's watch. Yet this should not mean that you must write off filling orders for ladies' watches as they come. Surely you should attack those sectors of the ladies' market where the Rolex name, its matchless performance, its chronometer accuracy (the red seal story) are assets justifying the premium price demanded for any Rolex watch.

The Rolex ladies' Oyster and Oyster Perpetual models are ideal watches falling into the following categories:

a) Women who are competing with men in business or the professions.
b) Women interested in and practicing sports.
c) Women whose eye-sight compels them to wear watches with visible markings.

We suggest that a decision in this matter is urgent. This memorandum is not the place to hint at the copy and presentation of advertising directed to women. We merely want to state that we would not propose making these advertisements "masculine". They would be unmistakably taken feminine, with a definite appeal to women who can spot real value and elegance, who demand accuracy in their watches and also can afford to pay for these qualities.

[...] We therefore recommend that you give top priority to the designing of some six to ten basic models, so that we can offer a real selection to women, and, what is more important, plan the packaging, advertising, literature and window displays simultaneously.

Just as in every other field, we understand that you are rightly not interested in putting ladies' watches on the market on a price appeal. You actually want to sell quality watches to women interested in style and accuracy. It is, therefore, essential that you have a story to tell, and for that careful planning is essential. We think that the closest liaison between your designers and our own Group is essential.

Source: HAT, JWT, HAT50/1/154/1, review of Rolex advertising activities, 8 January 1953.

Transforming the production system

One can estimate that Rolex's production volume doubled in the fifteen years following the end of the Second World War. In 1946, Manufacture des Montres Rolex SA deposited a total of 16,725 movements at the Bienne Watch Control Office.[33] The bulk of its deposits were made there, so this figure corresponds closely to the volume of chronometers produced by Rolex that year. However, not all watches sold under the Rolex brand had a chronometry certificate at the time. The company's sales volume was, therefore, higher. The number of chronometry certificates reached a total of 41,536 in 1961.[34] In 1960, according to statistics provided to JWT, sales by Rolex and its second brand, Tudor, totalled around 163,000 pieces (see Table 7.2, p. 177). This means that chronometers represented only around a quarter of production and sales volume.

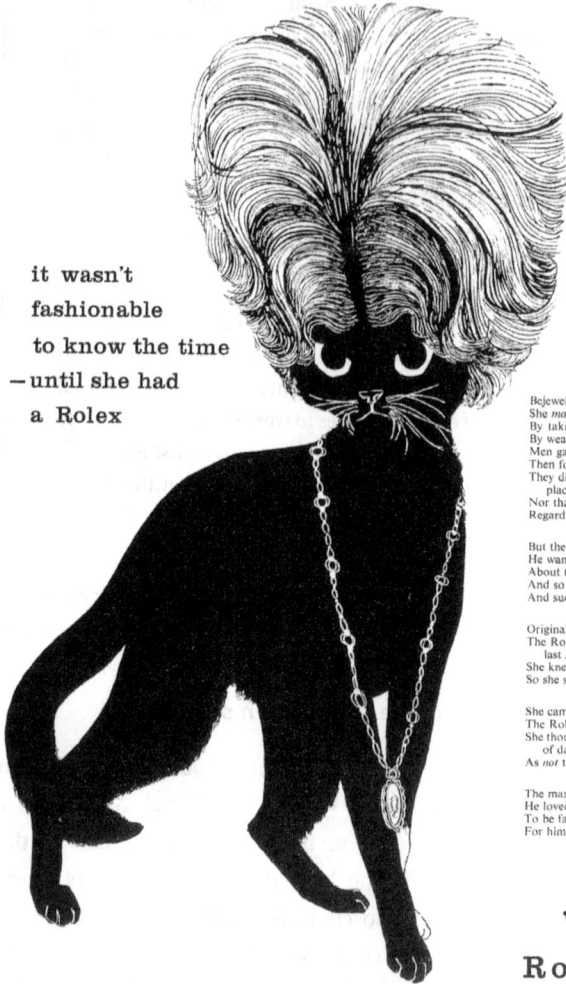

it wasn't
fashionable
to know the time
—until she had
a Rolex

Bejewelled or just casually exotic,
She *made* fashions—
By taking panthers to a glittering first night
By wearing diamonds to the beach . . .
Men gasped, adored,
Then followed, devastated, in her wake.
They didn't mind how long she took to
place one gorgeous strand of hair,
Nor that she was nearly always late,
Regarding time, in fact, as rather démodé

But then she met a different man—
He wanted her to care
About the time
And so he brought a Rolex watch—
And suddenly time was *fashionably* right

Original and absolutely perfect,
The Rolex had a special beauty that would
last . . .
She knew she'd always want to wear it
So she simply changed her attitude to time

She came à l'heure to lunch à deux,
The Rolex shining subtly on her wrist.
She thought it odd that anyone could be out
of date
As *not* to know the time.

The man just smiled.
He loved her
To be fashionably in time
For him.

Rolex

THE ROLEX WATCH COMPANY LIMITED *(H. Wilsdorf, Founder)* GENEVA, SWITZERLAND; 1 GREEN ST., MAYFAIR, LONDON, W.1

Figure 5.2 Rolex advertisement aimed at women, 1961

Note: The first Rolex advertisements aimed at women had a different style from the campaigns aimed at men. The gender distinction ceased after 1970, with JWT preparing ads featuring both men and women within a similar aesthetic and narrative framework.

Source: Europa Star, 1961, no. 11, p. 7. © Europa Star Archives.

The situation was similar for Omega – in 1960, Omega sold more than 630,000 movements but obtained only 47,209 chronometry certificates.[35]

Therefore, Rolex experienced increased production from 1945 to 1960, although growth remained relatively limited. It was mainly after 1960 that the company entered a phase of rapid expansion. The sources available to measure this development are rare for this period. However, thanks to bureaucratic control of the activities of watch factories by the federal government under the cartel regime, it is possible to highlight a few elements.[36]

First, production capacity at the Bienne factory did indeed increase. In 1948, Manufacture des Montres Rolex SA obtained permission from the federal authorities to enlarge its buildings. The number of workers rose from 223 in September 1946 to 323 by October 1954.[37] By then, the company had reached its maximum quota of authorised workers.[38] In 1960, however, it sought to increase its workforce further by hiring foreign nationals because of the difficulties in recruiting Swiss citizens.[39]

Second, as the nature of the patents filed during this period has shown, Borer sought to verticalise several operations, which led to long and difficult negotiations with component suppliers, as had been the case with the manufacture of springs during the 1930s (see pp. 60-61). In 1954, for example, Manufacture des Montres Rolex SA requested authorisation to carry out the silvering of its movements in-house because it was not satisfied with the work carried out by a dozen independent silverers. This request was vehemently opposed by these artisans, supported by their trade association, Union des branches annexes de l'horlogerie (UBAH), which appealed to the federal authorities. It was only in August 1956, after two years of negotiations, that Manufacture des Montres Rolex SA obtained authorisation from the government to silver its own movements, up to a maximum volume of 200 per week.[40] This represented an annual volume of around 10,000 movements but only a small proportion of total production if the above figures are anything to go by. Until 1960, the verticalisation of activities came up against the protectionism of the cartel regime.

As for the Geneva company Montres Rolex SA, its development during the years 1945–1960 is not documented. No files have been found in the Federal Archives that would allow us to identify the conditions of its expansion. However, insofar as its activities were linked to those of the Bienne factory, it probably underwent a similar development that brought it to the limits of its quota of workers.

Conclusion

By the end of the Second World War, Rolex was in a strong position. It was able to face up to major difficulties (such as the loss of the British market) and challenges (its repositioning in the United States), and had invested massively in the in-house design of finished watches – expressed by numerous model registrations and the acquisition of a stake in the case factory Genex SA. After years of transition and restrictions due to the world conflict, Rolex was able to create new types of watches. The years 1945–1963 were highly productive in terms of product development. It was during this period that almost all of Rolex's iconic models, which remain the hallmark of the brand today, were created and brought to market. The company created a series of watches with strong aesthetic qualities (tangible design), which became iconic and formed the material basis on which Rolex continues to develop today. It was also on this basis that Rolex built a new discourse, one no longer solely about precision but also about power and individual success, thanks to the collaboration explored in the next chapter.

Notes

1 *FOSC*, various years and volumes.
2 Hebeisen Philippe, "Borer, Emile (1898–1967)", *Dictionnaire du Jura (DIJU)*, https://diju.ch/f/notices/detail/1003913-borer-emile-1898-1967 (accessed 3 February 2023).
3 *Bieler Tagblatt*, 18 March 1967.
4 The control over the production and trading of watch components established within the framework of the watch cartel between the 1920s and the early 1960s was the subject of heated exchanges between the watch

manufacturers (who defended, in particular, the in-house production of components and the possibility of selling them to other companies) and the component manufacturers (who defended monopolistic production and price control). See Boillat, *Les véritables maîtres du temps*, and Pasquier, *La "Recherche et Développement" en horlogerie*, p. 181.

5   *FOSC*, 1953–1967.

6   *FOSC*, 1963, p. 3156.

7   Kohler was a former finance inspector who founded his own company, Fiduciaire Kohler SA, in Bienne. Between the wars, he was a member of the boards of directors of Fabrique de La Glycine, Bourquin Frères SA, Société des Produits Houghton SA, all three in Bienne, and Léon Charpilloz SA in Moutier. *FOSC*, various years.

8   *FOSC*, 1954, p. 1578, and 1955, p. 3335.

9   *L'Impartial*, 25 October 1963. Paul-César Jeanneret.

10   The archives of the Antwerp branch do not list Rolex or any other Swiss watchmaker among Jeanneret's clients. Duke University, Rubenstein Library, J. Walter Thompson Papers (JWT), Treasurer's Office Records, Correspondence with JWT Antwerp, 1930–1947.

11   Duke University, Rubenstein Library, J. Walter Thompson Papers (JWT), Treasurer's Office Records, Box 4, Letter from J.H. Cerny, JWT Antwerp, to S. W. Meek, JWT New York, 21 August 1940.

12   Ibid; letter from Paul C. Jeanneret, director of Information Horlogère in La Chaux-de-Fonds, to S.W. Meek, JWT New York, 29 July 1940.

13   Ibid; letter from René Jeanneret to Myron, JWT Antwerp, 25 June 1942. The nature of his work between May 1940 and June 1942 is unknown. See also Pouillard, *La publicité en Belgique*, pp. 333–337. René Jeanneret has been based in Geneva since at least 1943 when he acquired a stake in the Zurich press company Zeitungslupe GmbH. *FOSC*, 19 April 1943.

14   Duke University, Rubenstein Library, J. Walter Thompson Papers (JWT), Treasurer's Office Records, Box 4, letter from G. Noeninckx, Fiducia Anversoise, to JWT Antwerp, February 1946.

15   *FOSC*, 29 July 1975.

16   *Le Temps*, 6 January 2000.

17   *FOSC*, 1955, p. 106.

18   *FOSC*, 1956, p. 2493, 1960, p. 2368, and 1969, p. 2261.

19   *FOSC*, 1969, p. 2261. He continued his career at the head of various companies in French-speaking Switzerland until the 1990s.

20   *FOSC*, 1945, p. 2204.

21   Ibid.

22 Victorinox AG also belongs to two foundations.

23 Bottge, *Les fondations actionnaires en Suisse.*

24 Jones, *Deeply Responsible Business*, pp. 335–341.

25 *Journal de Genève*, 10 February 1976, 7 December 1974, and 12 May 1978.

26 Donzé, *History of the Swiss Watch Industry*, p. 116.

27 *FOSC*, 1946–1960.

28 Brozek, *The Rolex Report*, p. 63.

29 *The Millennium Watch Book.*

30 History of Advertising Trust (HAT), Collection J. Walter Thompson, (JWT), HAT50/1/154/1, note, 20 October 1954.

31 HAT, JWT, HAT50/1/154/1, sales of Rolex Submariner, undated [1954]. The other countries are less than twenty pieces.

32 Izuishi, *Rorekkusu no himitsu*, pp. 160–161.

33 *La Fédération horlogère suisse*, 30 January 1947.

34 Annual report of the Swiss watch control offices, 1961.

35 Pasquier, *La "Recherche et Développement" en horologerie*, p. 443.

36 AF, 7004#19727#8.

37 SFA, E7004#19727#8, letter from the Federal Department of Public Economy to the CSH, 23 September 1946 and 6 October 1954.

38 Watchmaking companies were allocated maximum quotas of workers under the cartel scheme.

39 SFA, E7175B#1976197#883, letter from the City of Bienne to the Federal Office for Industry, Trade and Labour, 3 March 1960.

40 SFA, E7004#19727#8, letter from the Federal Department of Public Economy to Rolex-Aegler AG, 31 August 1956.

6

The start of a fruitful collaboration

Since the 1930s, Rolex has established itself as one of Switzerland's leading watch manufacturers based on the precision and quality of its products. Moreover, the launch of the Rolex Oyster in 1926, a model that became iconic for its embodiment of the brand's values, represented a striking innovation in terms of design. Other companies did not adopt such a strategy until much later, in the 1940s, with the development of specific collections. Rolex continued in this direction from 1945 to 1963 with the launch of a series of new product families. Technical excellence was the key to the brand's success in the face of major manufacturers such as Omega and Longines.

However, Rolex's originality lay in not limiting its discourse to the performance of its products. Although the technical excellence and beauty of its products remained at the heart of the brand's communications until 1960, as was the case with all its competitors, a new dimension emerged in the early 1950s: the discourse on power and individual success. Rolex no longer merely expressed Swiss technical and industrial excellence but also the exceptional destiny of those who wore it. This major design innovation made the watch an object of social distinction for the first time. Success was made possible by collaboration with the J. Walter Thompson advertising agency.

Continued emphasis on technical excellence

In parallel with the development of a series of new products, the management of Montres Rolex SA pursued a communications strategy aimed at establishing its brand as the expression of Swiss watchmaking excellence. In 1947, it called on the services of the London agency of the American company J. Walter Thompson (JWT), the world's largest advertising agency.[1] Two years earlier, it had recruited a former JWT manager, René-Paul Jeanneret, to take charge of Rolex's marketing department, and he was clearly the intermediary in this relationship.

JWT's origins lie in a small advertising agency, Carlton & Smith, founded in New York in 1864, which the young James Walter Thompson joined four years later. Thompson bought the company from his employer in 1877 and renamed it after himself. It opened its first foreign branch in London in 1899. However, it was mainly during the interwar years (1918–1939) that the company expanded internationally, thanks to its collaboration with several major American companies, including General Motors, for whom it ran advertising campaigns across the globe. As a result, JWT became the world's largest advertising company with a strong belief in its ability to create advertising that transcended national and cultural differences. It transferred new advertising know-how around the world (the creation of a global message broadcast worldwide through the foreign editions of the American media, widespread use of market analysis, and the establishment of long-term relationships between agents responsible for a brand and the brand's management). Advertising was not seen as a creative activity but the result of rigorous and scientific data analysis.[2] By adapting to the needs of non-American clients and responding more effectively to different local realities, the company was able to expand its client network outside the United States.[3] Montres Rolex SA was one of its clients.

Cooperation with JWT's London agency was essential to reviving sales in Britain and the British Empire. JWT insisted on establishing Rolex as a watch for the upper and upper-middle classes. In a report in the mid-1960s, JWT managers recalled Rolex's position at the start of their collaboration:

Rolex came to Thompson immediately after the war. They were a small company with a superb product – and their problems were many. A complex distribution system, a number of subsidiary companies haphazardly developed, a market strongly influenced by political ups and downs, tariffs and embargos. Furthermore, Rolex at that time were determined to reach the heights with their very limited appropriation. This ruled out thin advertising in world markets. A precise approach in a sure-fire medium was the only answer.[4]

JWT, therefore, proposed that Montres Rolex SA target a range of conservative newspapers for its advertising, including *The Times* and *Daily Telegraph*, the satirical newspaper *Punch*, and the upper-class fashion magazines *Tatler* and *Vogue*.[5] Outside the UK, the initial aim was to target American citizens, both civilian and military, living and travelling around the world, through the international editions of major American magazines. In 1953, JWT explained: "Although we do not have detailed statistics we are inclined to believe that purchases made by American servicemen and civilians account for a large part of the sales in this area as they do in the European theatre."[6] Rolex needed to target this high-income clientele for growth.

The use of JWT's services was soon extended to the other major markets in which Rolex was present. Contracts were signed with local JWT agencies in Belgium (1947), Mexico (1948), Argentina (1950), France (1951), Germany (1954), Japan (1959), and Brazil (1960).[7] The activities of these various agencies were coordinated from London so that Rolex advertising in Europe, Asia and Latin America was largely uniform. Apart from the Middle East and Africa, which were secondary markets at the time, the main country not controlled by JWT was the United States. Rolex's American subsidiary, which apparently enjoyed a great deal of autonomy, had been working with an independent advertising agent, Louis De Garmo, since 1950 (see p. 141).

The collaboration between Montres Rolex SA and JWT was, therefore, expressed by a massive investment in advertising. In 1959, publications in the international press amounted to more than $139,000 (see Table 6.1; approximately $1.3 million in 2022). At that time, according to a JWT study, the amount the Rolex brand spent on advertising was second only to Omega, which remained well ahead. Longines followed in third place, just a few thousand francs behind Rolex.[8] These three manufacturers were well ahead of the other Swiss manufacturers. Between them, they accounted for more than half of all advertising expenditure by Swiss watch companies.

However, the value of advertising depends on more than the volume of expenditure. Content is important: What should be communicated? What message should be sent to the consumer? In 1953, René-Paul Jeanneret, who was in charge of advertising, explained the objective of advertising communication: "In our advertisements, we relate dramatic and authentic events that prove the qualities of resistance and precision of Rolex watches."[9] The two main ways for showcasing the precision and quality of Rolex watches were, as in the interwar period, by obtaining bulletins from official watch control offices and by participating in the exploits of explorers and sportsmen and women.

Table 6.1   *Advertising expenditure by Swiss watch companies in the international press, 1959*

Company	Expenses in dollars	Percentage
Omega Watch	253,231	27
Rolex Watch	139,478	15
Longines Watch	126,585	14
Cyma Watch	73,804	8
Mido Watch	64,677	7
Watchmakers of Switzerland	60,825	6
Movado Watch	39,201	4
Breitling Geneva Watch	33,423	4
Certina Kurth Frères	27,275	3
Tissot & Fils	26,850	3
Universal Watch	23,677	2
Marvin Watch	17,805	2
International Watch Co (IWC)	16,475	2
Roamer Watch	15,642	2
Enicar Watch	10,380	1

Source: HAT, JWT, HAT50/1/154/1, expenditures by all competitors, 4 May 1960.

First, the purpose of depositing watches in the control offices was no longer to use the services of this institution as a quality-control body for developing new watches, as was the case during the interwar period. The main objective was promotion. Mass certification arose from a desire to position itself in the marketplace as an industrial manufacturer of high-precision watches. The pursuit of participation in observatory chronometry competitions shared the same goal. In 1947, Rolex is said to have decided to adopt the English designation *chronometer* for all its watches, although the French designation *chronomètre* had also been used.[10] If this assertion is correct, the total number of bulletins obtained from control offices after the Second World War corresponds fairly well to Rolex production. However, the figures presented above contradict this assertion (see p. 115). The name was subsequently changed to *certified chronometer* (1948) and then to *officially certified chronometer* (1949), accompanied by a red seal that could be seen in retail shop windows and advertisements. Hans Wilsdorf would have demanded that his engineers develop movements capable of systematically obtaining the "particularly good results" awarded by the inspection bodies at the time, asserting that "this is how Rolex's prestige will increase".[11] Finally, in 1957, Rolex introduced a series of tests to complement the watches certified by the inspection bodies, enabling it to use the *superlative chronometer* label.

After the Second World War, the competition between Omega and Rolex had two main effects. First, it led to an explosion in the number of depots. In Bienne, they rose from 20,288 pieces in 1944 to more than 80,000 in 1960. The city's two main factories had a virtual monopoly on the institution, together accounting for 89.6 per cent of all Bienne chronometers from 1953 to 1958. Second, the limited capacity of the Bienne office to meet the growing demand for certification from these two companies led them to hand in their watches at other offices from the end of the 1950s. It was in particular the case in Geneva, where they were also established.[12] Omega was a latecomer to the mass certification of chronometers, but it established itself as the leading producer during the 1950s. Competition between the two firms intensified in the 1960s.

Figure 6.1 Advertisement for Rolex, 1950

Note: In the years following the end of the Second World War, winning distinctions in chronometric competitions remained a prime objective in building a top-of-the-range watch brand that expressed precision. It was during the 1950s that Rolex's discourse gradually shifted towards social distinction.

Source: Journal de Genève, 15 September 1950.

The start of a fruitful collaboration

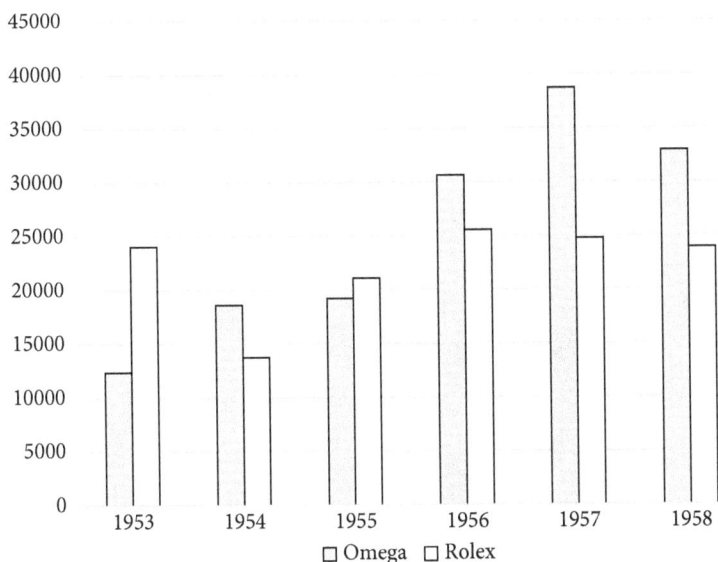

Figure 6.2 Chronometer bulletins issued to Omega and Rolex by the Bienne Watch Control Office, 1953–1958
Source: COSC archives, annual report of the Bienne Watch Control Office, 1953–1958.

Rolex's involvement in sporting and scientific exploits continued and expanded during the 1950s. Rolex was notably associated with the first ascent to the summit of Mount Everest (1953) and the dive into the Mariana Trench (1960), as well as the first transcontinental flights during the 1950s. These various collaborations provided the opportunity to develop a series of new watch models corresponding to the conquest of the sea (Submariner), land (Explorer), and air (GMT Master), which express the high quality and resistance of Rolex watches when subjected to extreme natural conditions. Although collaboration with explorers and sportsmen and women was nothing new, Rolex broke new ground in 1953 by taking direct testimony from Sir John Hunt, who led the expedition to the summit of Mount Everest. Until then, it had been the brands themselves that produced the stories, as in the case of Mercedes Gleitze's swimming the English Channel in 1927 (see pp. 80–83). The direct testimony of a celebrity lends higher value to the collaboration. This innovation was realised by

Figure 6.3 Rolex advertisement, 1952

Note: Following the example of a professor at the University of Milan who was a keen diver, some Rolex customers sent testimonials to the Geneva head office. These were then used in advertising to demonstrate the extreme resistance of these watches. This type of communication continued at least until the 1970s. In 1970, an advertisement for an American magazine featured a Swiss gold bar, explaining that it would be cut up to form an "almost indestructible" watch case (Duke University, Rubenstein Library, J. Walter Thompson Collection, Advertising Collection, 1970).

Source: The Eastern Jeweller and Watchmaker, *vol. 10, 1952, p. 11. © Europa Star Archives.*

JWT, whose London offices suggested to their Bombay subsidiary that they try to collect testimonials for Rolex watches and Braemar Sweaters underwear, which were also produced by their clients.[13] A similar operation was carried out in 1955 on the occasion of new British and French expeditions to the Himalayas.[14] Obtaining testimonials gave greater credibility to the advertising carried out in the years that followed.[15]

Rolex's advertising in the 1950s was based on these exploits. In addition, to reinforce the link between the watch used on exceptional occasions by extraordinary adventurers and the timepiece worn daily by a wide variety of consumers, Rolex launched a major advertising campaign featuring true anecdotes told by customers to illustrate the exceptional resistance of Rolex watches. These included a professor at the University of Milan with a passion for scuba diving (see Figure 6.3), a Royal Air Force pilot who survived the crash of his plane, and an English traveller who explored the Amazon rainforest in search of diamonds. Correspondence sent to the Geneva headquarters, which the advertisements claim to make available for verification, attests to the robustness and quality of Rolex watches in the most diverse situations. It is essentially their water resistance that is highlighted in this campaign.

The second major theme in the advertising of this period relates to another of Rolex's great innovations: the automatic movement. Here, it was not the high quality of the watch that was highlighted but the company's contribution to watchmaking history. Rolex presented itself as the company that put an end to technical research dating back at least to the end of the eighteenth century. Several advertisements and subsidised articles in the watchmaking and general press emphasised this historical role (see Figure 6.4). In the early 1950s, the company financed two books that offered a teleological reading of watchmaking history and saw the Oyster Perpetual as the end of a centuries-long evolution. The first is an English-language book, *The Anatomy of Time*, undoubtedly aimed at the American market. It provides a general account of the history of time measurement, from sundials and Egyptian water clocks to Wilsdorf's waterproof self-winding watch, via Galileo and Breguet. Second, Hans Wilsdorf financed the publication of a book on the history

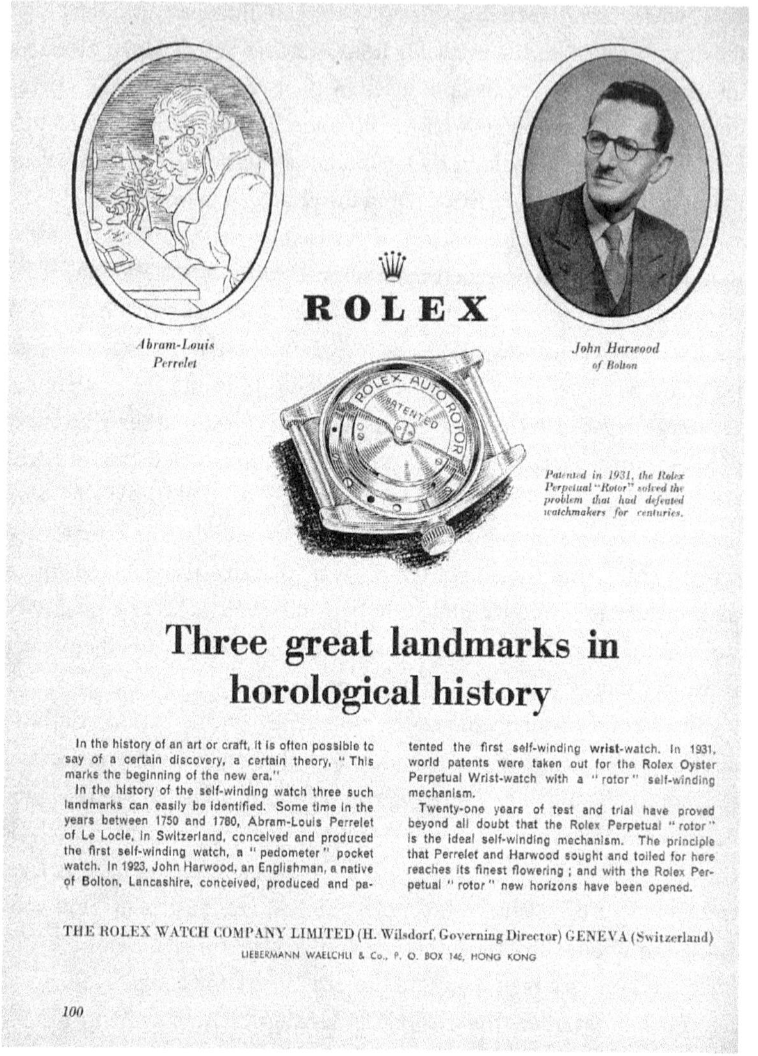

Figure 6.4 Rolex advertisement, 1953

Note: *The collaboration with two historians prominent in watchmaking circles enabled Rolex to offer a discourse on its contribution to the technical evolution of watchmaking. It stands out as the brand that succeeded in creating a high-quality automatic wristwatch for industrial production.*

Source: *The Eastern Jeweller and Watchmaker, vol. 18, 1953, p. 114, © Europa Star Archives.*

of the automatic watch, published in 1952 by two of the leading watch historians of the day, Alfred Chapuis and Eugène Jaquet.[16] The book covers the origins of the automatic movement in the eighteenth century, its development in the nineteenth century, and its revival with the development of wristwatches. After more than 200 pages of discussion, the book concludes with the development of the Rolex automatic watch. Asserting that it was necessary to solve the problem of the watch's water resistance before that of automatic winding, our two historians can thus conclude that:

> Mr. Wilsdorf can be considered the first producer of the waterproof automatic wristwatch built in series [...]. The problem of the waterproof watch and that of the self-winding watch was, as we have said, complementary, since the waterproof watch could offer the mechanism much greater protection than an ordinary watch.[17]

The Rolex Oyster was thus the end of history.

The emergence of a discourse on power and individual success

Alongside the discourse on technical excellence, which was very similar to the narrative of other watch manufacturers of the time, a new communication theme emerged in the mid-1950s: Rolex as an expression of power. Rolex was no longer just an exceptional watch, but the watch worn by the world's great and good, from political decision-makers to the military. The advertising campaigns of the second half of the 1950s, produced by JWT, featured men of power in various situations, particularly in front of the press or at meetings. However, the personalities were anonymous (see Figure 6.5). They embody general representations of power. An advertisement published in 1956 explains the relationship between Rolex and these personalities:

> Wherever historical decisions are made, at top-level conferences, in Cabinet meetings, at strategic discussions, you will find these men. Not day passes without some reference to them in newspapers, on radio or

television. Their fame is the measure of their importance – to each of us and to the world.

We cannot mention their names or picture them. It would not be fitting to do so – for they include royalty, heads of States, great service chiefs and statesmen. But when next you see them or their picture, look at something you might not normally notice: the watch on their wrists. That watch will most likely have been made by Rolex of Geneva.

These men expect accurate and reliable service, yet even they are amazed at the efficiency of their Rolex watches. Rolex are proud that they so soon take it for granted.[18]

Rolex as an expression of power and individual success is a concept that dates back to the mid-1950s. It was refined during the 1960s in collaboration with JWT's US headquarters (see Chapter 7) and has remained at the heart of Rolex's communications strategy to the present day.

This discourse on the "man of power" enabled Rolex to add an emotional dimension to its narrative on technical excellence, as well as to its message on the elegance and beauty of watches. It was no longer merely a precision instrument that measured time accurately but also an object that expressed power and individual success. Rolex became a concept, much more than a product. This was the first time a leading watchmaking company had ceased to focus on the intrinsic qualities of its watches (their technical and aesthetic characteristics). There are, of course, a few other exceptions, such as Vulcain, which gave watches to US presidents Truman and Eisenhower in the 1950s, but these gifts were not part of the construction of a new narrative about the brand's exceptionality, unlike with Rolex.[19]

It should be stressed, however, that there was no break between the traditional discourse and this new narrative. Both overlapped during the 1950s. Moreover, the discourse on social distinction was limited to men's watches, which dominated the Rolex catalogue. Ladies' watches remained, as with rival brands, a fashion accessory characterised by an elegant and discreet aesthetic.

Finally, as JWT did not hold the contract for the American market, advertising and communication in this market was carried out alongside

Men who guide the destinies of the world wear Rolex watches

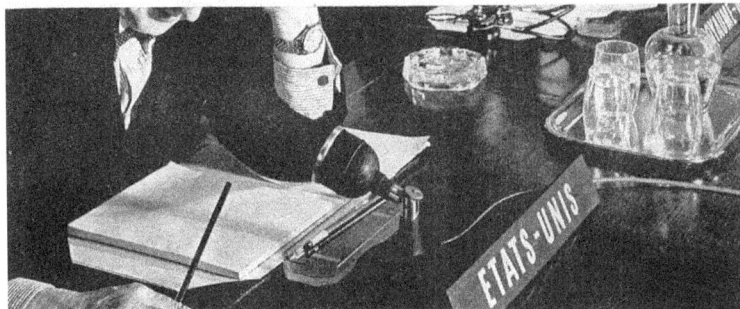

Wherever historical decisions are made, at top-level conferences, in Cabinet meetings, at strategy discussions, you will find these men. No day passes without some reference to them in newspapers, on radio or television. Their fame is the measure of their importance—to each of us and to the world.

We cannot mention their names or picture them. It would not be fitting to do so—for they include royalty, the heads of States, great service chiefs and statesmen. But when next you see them or their pictures, look at something you might not normally notice—the watch on their wrists. That watch will most likely have been made by Rolex of Geneva.

These men expect accurate and reliable service, yet even they are amazed at the efficiency of their Rolex watches. Rolex are proud that they so soon take it for granted.

The Rolex Oyster Perpetual Datejust, the most remarkable achievement in watchmaking. Every Datejust is awarded an Official Timing Certificate by a Swiss Institute for Official Timekeeping with the mention "Especially good results." This accuracy is protected by the famous Oyster case. Thirty years ago the Oyster case won fame as the first waterproof watch on the wrist of a Channel swimmer. In 1953 it withstood the rigours of the successful British Everest Expedition. It protects the movement from all hazards. The watch is self-wound by the Perpetual "rotor" mechanism, another Rolex invention, that makes for even greater accuracy. The date is shown on the dial, changing automatically every midnight, and magnified by the "Cyclops" lens for easy reading.

ROLEX

A landmark in the history of Time measurement

A ROLEX
RED SEAL
CHRONOMETER

THE ROLEX WATCH COMPANY LIMITED *(H. Wilsdorf, Founder and Chairman)*, GENEVA, SWITZERLAND, *and* 1 GREEN STREET, MAYFAIR, LONDON, W.1, *and* THE AMERICAN ROLEX WATCH CORPORATION, 580 FIFTH AVENUE, NEW YORK

Figure 6.5 Rolex advertisement, 1956

Source: The Eastern Jeweller and Watchmaker, *1956, vol. 36, p. 9.* © Europa Star Archives.

the campaigns launched by JWT on a global scale. This had an impact on Rolex's image in this market. Thus, in the early 1960s, in parallel with the discourse on precision, De Garmo developed an advertising campaign on the Rolex watch as a fashion accessory, particularly for women, based on cooperation with American designers such as Bill Blass, Rudi Gernreich, and Oleg Cassini. An advertisement dated 1967, for example, states: "As Gernreich himself puts it, *A woman is beautiful when she looks like what she is. A woman.* In the same way, a Rolex is beautiful because it looks like what it is. A watch."[20] Such autonomy was clearly at odds with the desire to create a strong and coherent global luxury brand. André Heiniger put an end to it after taking over at Montres Rolex SA.

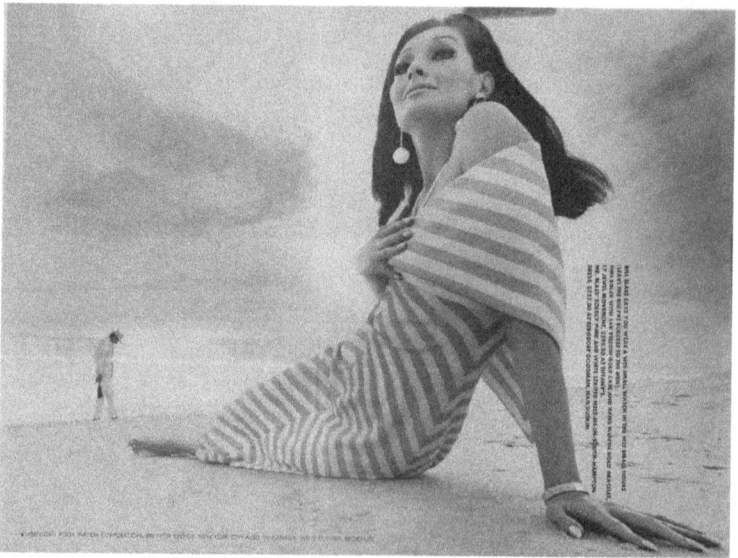

Figure 6.6 Rolex advertisement for the American market, 1966

Note: The De Garmo agency developed advertising campaigns specifically for the American market between 1950 and 1967. The risk of inconsistency with the global strategy and the desire to exercise direct control over advertising worldwide led André Heiniger to entrust the American market to JWT in 1967.

Source: Duke University, Rubenstein Library, J. Walter Thompson Collection, Domestic advertisements collection RO1, Harper's Bazaar, June 1966.

The start of a fruitful collaboration

While Omega, Longines, Zenith, Breitling, Audemars Piguet, and all the other big names in Swiss watchmaking were talking about technical performance and elegance, Rolex was adopting an innovative approach based on social distinction and individual success. However, this clever marketing innovation did not break with traditional communications. The message about social status ran alongside advertising about technical excellence and fashion. It was during the 1960s that Rolex gradually focused the whole of its brand identity on social distinction and had it embodied by specific, rather than anonymous, personalities who reinforced the brand's exceptional character (see Chapter 7).

Tudor and the management of a brand portfolio

Although Wilsdorf based the core of his strategy on enhancing the Rolex brand through a strong identity and clear positioning, he continued after 1945 to use secondary brands aimed at the lower segments. The aim was to concentrate Rolex on the high-end market and not to market watches with the same brand name at lower prices. This strategy was not unique to Wilsdorf. Since its foundation in 1930, the Société Suisse pour l'Industrie Horlogère (SSIH) has had two main brands: Omega for the top end of the market and Tissot for the mass market. However, until the 1960s, most watch manufacturers relied on a single brand, which they used for their entire production. This was the case for Longines, Patek Philippe, Vacheron Constantin, and Zenith, which represented Swiss watchmaking excellence alongside Rolex and Omega, as well as the Japanese manufacturer Seiko. The strategy of creating a portfolio of brands was therefore not limited to Rolex, but it remained rare in the watch industry.

According to the database of the World Intellectual Property Organization (WIPO), Rolex registered a total of thirty-seven trademarks during the years 1945–1960.[21] The overwhelming majority were registrations of various graphic versions of the Rolex brand and crown symbol, as well as the main collections (Day-Date, Explorer, GMT Master, Lady Datejust, Oyster Perpetual, Submariner, etc.). There were also a few names that had not been used, or only for short periods, and whose legal protection had not been sought. The only two perfectly distinct Rolex brands were Tudor Prince and Tudor Princess, both registered in 1951 – they sought legal protection for use of the name Prince. These two brands were registered jointly with Montres Tudor SA, which also registered its own Tudor brand in 1949.[22]

The legal protection of brands is an excellent expression of the marketing strategy implemented by Wilsdorf during this period. The focus was first and foremost on exploiting the Rolex brand. It also used two other brands, positioned in distinct price segments: Tudor and Marconi. Although they had been in use since the interwar years, Wilsdorf institutionalised their existence by creating ad hoc companies after the end of the Second World War.

In 1946, Montres Tudor SA was founded with capital of 250,000 francs. Its Board of Directors comprised Hans Wilsdorf and two of his close friends: the business lawyer Fernand Lilla, who was chairman and also sat on the Board of Montres Rolex SA, and Francis Guyot, executive director of Crédit Suisse in Geneva and a member of the Board of the Hans Wilsdorf Foundation. Thus, the Boards of Directors had no executive function, their tasks limited to financial oversight. As for operational management, it was occupied by the two directors of Montres Rolex SA: Werner Ryser and René-Paul Jeanneret.[23]

Marconi Watch SA was founded two years later, in 1948, also in Geneva, but with a capital of 50,000 francs. Its Board of Directors did not include Wilsdorf. The chairman was Geneva lawyer Maurice Merket, who was also chairman of the Hans Wilsdorf Foundation, while Ryser and Jeanneret were appointed executive directors, taking charge of the firm's operational management.[24] Marconi did not register any trademarks between 1945 and 1960.

The composition of the boards of Tudor and Marconi at the time of their foundation perfectly illustrates their complete integration into the parent company, Montres Rolex SA, whose office they also shared. The same team of directors managed all three brands. What did they have in common, and what were their differences?

The start of a fruitful collaboration

First of all, as far as Tudor is concerned, it is worth emphasising the close relationship with Rolex. Tudor watches used Rolex's major innovations (waterproof and automatic movement) and focused on the latter's successful models, particularly diving watches and chronographs. In the early 1950s, some advertisements made no distinction between the two brands. For example, one of them, published in the *Journal de Genève* in 1952, stated: "If you demand perfection, you will find it in a Rolex or a Tudor Oyster."[25] The watches were sold by the same retailers, notably in Switzerland, Latin America, and the Far East.[26] The JWT advertising agency insisted on the need to distinguish the two brands. In 1951, it explained that the launch of the Tudor Prince in Great Britain "may well have serious repercussions on Rolex sales in this country".[27] Two years later, it repeated that, although the aim was to counter Omega's expansion on the world market, cannibalisation had to be avoided: "We shall have to be very careful to see to it that Tudor takes customers away from competitors and not from Rolex. We therefore reiterate our recommendation to keep the Tudor Oyster line in the stainless-steel field, as gold Tudors would inevitably compete with Rolex." [28] Advertising began to make a real distinction between Rolex and Tudor after the 1960s. As part of the collaboration with JWT on the UK market, sales director Heiniger initially asked that the entire advertising budget for 1962 be concentrated on Rolex and that nothing be allocated to Tudor: "Mr. Heiniger expressed the view which was endorsed by all present, that the policy of Rolex in the UK should be to sell more of the expensive pieces (thereby creating higher turnover), and not to increase sales of the cheaper movements."[29] Two years later, in 1964, advertising budgets for Tudor were again accepted but for less exclusive magazines than those chosen for Rolex, such as *Reader's Digest* and the *News of the World*, two publications aimed at the general public.

As for Marconi watches, their volume was low after 1945. Advertisements in the *Europa Star* database suggest their presence in Latin America during the 1950s, but their visibility faded thereafter. Thus, although Montres Rolex SA has maintained the company's existence to the present day, this is apparently for financial or tax reasons.[30] Its watchmaking activities soon disappeared.

The global expansion of sales

After 1931, falling sales in Great Britain forced Hans Wilsdorf to diversify his markets, with the United States becoming the main target of Rolex's commercial redeployment. However, the various restrictions during the Second World War made it difficult to implement this new strategy (see Chapter 4). Gradually freed from these restrictions, Rolex experienced strong international expansion from 1945 to 1960. It was during this period that it became a truly global brand. The conditions of this development remain almost impossible to establish without access to archival sources that would make it possible to quantify the growth in sales in the main markets.

However, the JWT archives contain a few rare documents relating to the volume and value of sales by market. These are figures provided by Montres Rolex SA. In 1960, sales of Rolex and Tudor watches (details by brand unknown) totalled 38.4 million francs for a volume of 163,663 watches.[31] Table 6.2 shows the share of the main markets, as defined in the document provided to JWT. It highlights four main characteristics of the presence of Rolex and Tudor.

First, the importance of the Swiss market. The collaboration with Bucherer bore fruit, and the presence of the latter's boutiques in luxury tourism hotspots benefited Rolex. In fact, it is in the Swiss market that the average value of a Rolex was the highest (342 francs, compared with 235 francs worldwide), demonstrating the relevance of the collaboration with Bucherer.

Second, the dominance of the UK and areas under British influence. Details of the European market are not known, but the UK undoubtedly accounts for a large share. In fact, it was the London subsidiary of JWT, and not another subsidiary, that Montres Rolex SA contacted after the Second World War, illustrating its desire to return to the market where it had enjoyed an excellent reputation. In March 1947, it placed an advertisement in *The Times* informing the British public that "the Rolex Oyster again comes to England".[32] Trade was liberalised, and the company was once again able to supply its British retailers. Numerous advertisements appeared in *The Times* throughout the 1950s.[33] Moreover, in 1953, JWT

Table 6.2   *Rolex and Tudor sales by market, value and volume in %, 1960*

Market	Value (%)	Volume (%)
Switzerland	13.8	9.5
Europe	15.4	20.9
Africa	1.3	1.1
Middle East	10.7	7.5
India and Asia	34.8	33.9
North America	7.4	10.9
Central America	2.7	2.0
South America	4.3	3.1
Australia and New Zealand	1.4	3.7
Armies	8.3	7.5
TOTAL	100	100

Source: HAT, JWT, HAT50/1/154/2/1-5, Rolex Tudor exports, n.d.

explained in a report that Great Britain should be Rolex's priority because of the country's size and high standard of living.[34] Six years later, in 1959, the advertising agency insisted on the need to react to "the aggressive campaign by Omega". It proposed to "modernise one or more shops in London so that Rolex products may be found in a setting worthy of their quality".[35] Apart from Great Britain, the main European country to show strong growth during the 1950s was Italy. In 1953, JWT explained the reasons for this success:

> Due to the outstanding ability and know-how of your sales representative there you have achieved and maintained a volume which defies statistical analysis. All we need say is that your performance in Italy has demonstrated that even seemingly "closed" and "poor" markets can produce results if the right person is found to apply the correct methods and remedies.[36]

Third, access to the Eastern markets. India and Asia accounted for around a third of sales, while the Middle East amounted to over 10 per cent. Access to Eastern markets was generally through independent trading companies that acted as intermediaries between Montres Rolex SA and local retailers. In Thailand, for example, Rolex cooperated with Société Anonyme Belge, a trading company founded in Bangkok in 1907, headed by a Swiss national and controlling an extensive jewellery network throughout the country.[37] British trading company Borneo Company was Rolex's representative in Singapore, and Swiss firm Liebermann Waelchli & Co. in Japan and Hong Kong.[38]

Fourth, the market share of the Americas. The Americas still had a relatively small market share: 7.4 per cent of sales for North America (with an average value of just 159 francs) and 7 per cent for Latin America (Central and South). The United States still appeared to be only a secondary market for Rolex. However, appearances can be deceptive: the strength of the dollar meant that many American customers bought their luxury watches at reduced prices outside the country, particularly in Europe and Asia.[39] This included the military, which was a major target for Rolex (see p. 123). Thus, if we add the market share of the armed forces to that of North America, we obtain one of the largest markets after India and Asia, which includes sales to visiting American citizens, as is the case in Hong Kong and Japan. It should also be remembered that sales in North America were virtually non-existent in the 1930s. From this perspective, the growth was remarkable, and the management of Montres Rolex SA was clearly aware of the potential offered by this market. The company's presence in the US was reorganised in 1948. The New York subsidiary became a company registered in the United States under the name The American Rolex Watch Corporation.[40] Its management was entrusted to René P. Dentan, a Swiss national who had been living in New York for around ten years. Born in Lausanne in 1912 and a graduate of the University of Lausanne, he moved to New York in 1937, where he held various positions in finance and sales, working for Patek, Philippe & Cie before taking over as head of the new Rolex's subsidiary.[41] He spent his entire career with the company. Well-integrated into the American management elite, he spent his entire life in the United States until his death in 1990.[42] He certainly had to face up to some difficulties, such as the use of radioactive strontium in certain models sold on the American market and the accusations of anti-competitive behaviour made by the American authorities against Swiss watchmakers.[43] However, the bulk of his activities lay in expanding sales in New York – notably in collaboration with the jeweller Tourneau – and throughout North America. In 1953, the London office of JWT expressed its admiration for the work carried out in the United States: "Your American organisation is impressive. We believe that it has done a remarkable job in a market where it is notoriously difficult to establish quality goods without very heavy advertising and promotion expenditures."[44] The importance of this subsidiary and the United States was not just in boosting sales in this market. It also played a fundamental role in the new communications strategy implemented at this time, which contributed to making Rolex not only a watch with exceptional technical qualities but also a brand representing individual success and social exclusivity.

In 1950, the American Rolex company signed a contract with the advertising agency De Garmo Inc.[45] It was headed by Louis de Garmo, a former manager of the Albert Woodley Company, a small firm specialising in public relations and advertising. De Garmo helped develop the discourse of social distinction, which became an important message for Rolex in the United States. He made Rolex the watch of the presidents in the 1960s (see Chapter 7).

Conclusive remarks

The years 1945–1960 marked an important transitional phase during which Rolex succeeded in establishing itself as one of the great names in Swiss watchmaking, alongside historic manufacturers such as Longines, Omega, and Zenith. However, Rolex was not yet recognised as the brand that single-handedly expressed Swiss technical excellence. It remained in a fiercely competitive position with Omega as the embodiment of Swiss watchmaking on world markets. Statistics on chronometer registrations at the Bienne Watch Control Office show that Omega continued to dominate the precision watch market. Rolex had certainly distinguished itself with an innovative product – the waterproof automatic watch – but it was not alone in mass-producing high-quality watches. Similarly, the construction of global brands for collections that initially embodied a technical specificity, such as Omega's Seamaster or Rolex's Datejust, was the subject of fierce competition between the two manufacturers. Until 1960, neither manufacturer was able to impose itself on the other.

However, it was at the heart of Rolex's marketing strategy that the original elements that would enable the company to experience extraordinary growth over the following decades emerged. The first was the use of direct testimonials from explorers, sportsmen and women, and ordinary customers. Rolex went beyond sponsoring major sporting events, such as the Olympic timekeeping of Longines and Omega. It engaged in a dialogue with extraordinary people that enabled direct communication with the public. Rolex also began to develop a discourse on the social distinction associated with the use of its products. The Rolex Oyster watch was no longer just a high-quality timepiece that could withstand the harshest environments but also an object that embodied a privileged social status. The discourse on men of power was a radical innovation in terms of watchmaking marketing: Rolex stopped talking about its products and started talking about its consumers.[46] These innovations were made possible by cooperation with the advertising agencies JWT and De Garmo, and the appointment of one of their former managers, René-Paul Jeanneret, as marketing director of Montres Rolex SA.

Finally, from a design management perspective, the years 1945–1960 were a time of consolidation and openness. On the one hand, tangible design (the shape, colour, and style of watches) was strengthened with the creation of special collections that embodied a specific technical feature. These activities were directly controlled by Rolex, which continued to verticalise the production of components (Manufacture des Montres Rolex SA) and directly controlled the design and manufacture of cases (Montres Rolex SA). Iconic products were developed to embody the brand, and the company concentrated on these models, abandoning the wide variety of products that had characterised it until the Second World War. In addition, Rolex's directors were determined to develop a truly global brand and not adapt to the specific characteristics of different markets. In 1959, for example, when JWT asked André Heiniger to carry out a market study in the UK to gain a better understanding of the profile of the male clientele, Heiniger accepted but warned his publicist that "in no event would special models be made for the English market".[47] There was also an early desire to protect these iconic products and combat imitations (see Figure 6.7).

MISE EN GARDE

Nous portons à la connaissance des inté-
ressés que nous poursuivrons avec toute
la sévérité de la loi les maisons ou
personnes qui, dans la fabrication ou la
vente des montres, feront usage sur les
cadrans, mouvements et écrins, de
marques susceptibles d'être confondues
tant au point de vue visuel que phoné-
tique avec les marques que nous avons
déposées dans le monde entier.

MONTRES ROLEX S. A., GENÈVE

AEGLER S. A., BIENNE

Figure 6.7 Advertisement in the Swiss watchmaking press, 1947
*Note: The decision to focus Rolex on iconic models goes hand in hand with a desire to protect
the brand's aesthetic identity.*
Source: La Fédération horlogère suisse, *20 February 1947.*

On the other hand, the collaboration with JWT enabled an emotional dimension to be added to the Rolex brand, with the emergence of a discourse on men of power, although the general narrative remained centred on the technical qualities of the watch. Design activities thus began their transition towards an intangible dimension: Rolex was no longer just a precision instrument but an expression of social success. This transformation was completed in the 1960s.

Notes

1   HAT, JWT, HAT50/1/154/1, review of Rolex advertising activities, 8 January 1953.
2   Frank, *The Conquest of Cool*.
3   On JWT, see in particular Rhiannon, "Negotiating Local and Global Knowledge and History"; Hultquist, "Americans in Paris"; Pouillard, "American Advertising Agencies in Europe"; West, "From T-Square to T-Plan".
4   Duke University, Rubenstein Library, J. Walter Thompson Collection, Samuel W. Meek papers, Rolex Watches, undated report [mid-1960s].
5   Izuishi, *Rorekkusu no himitsu*, p. 21.
6   HAT, JWT, HAT50/1/154/1, review of Rolex advertising activities, 8 January 1953.
7   Duke University, Rubenstein Library, J. Walter Thompson Collection, Joseph O'Donnell Papers, *The Rolex Oyster: 40 Years of Advertising*, 1986.
8   On advertising at Longines, see Paratte, *Marketing et publicité dans l'horlogerie*.
9   *L'Illustré*, 20 October 1953, p. 56.
10 Brozek, *The Rolex Report*, p. 193.
11 According to a Rolex press release published by the Swiss Watch Federation in April 2016, www.fhs.swiss/fre/2016_04_28_01_Rolex.html (accessed 20 August 2020).
12 Donzé, *Histoire sociale et économique de la chronométrie*, p. 104. Rolex had also made a few unsuccessful attempts with the Bureau facultatif de contrôle des montres de Genève (Poinçon de Genève) at the end of the 1940s (deposit of six watches in 1948 and 35 in 1949). Source: Timelab Foundation, Poinçon de Genève archives, deposit registers.
13 Duke University, J. Walter Thompson Company Newsletter Collection, vol. 10, no. 31, 1 August 1955.
14 Ibid.

15 *New York Times*, 4 October 1953.

16 Chapuis and Jaquet, *La montre automatique ancienne*.

17 Ibid., p. 222.

18 *The Eastern Jeweller and Watchmaker*, 1956, vol. 36, p. 9.

19 Moreover, it was mainly in the second half of the 1960s, when Rolex enjoyed great success, that Vulcain began to exploit its donations of watches to presidents. See for example *Europa Star*, 1967, no. 48, pp. 80–81.

20 Duke University, Rubenstein Library, J. Walter Thompson Collection, Domestic advertisements collection RO1, unidentified press cutting, 1967.

21 World Intellectual Property Organization (WIPO), www3.wipo.int/madrid/monitor/fr/# (accessed 29 October 2021).

22 Ibid.

23 *FOSC*, 1946, p. 767.

24 *FOSC*, 1948, p. 2753.

25 *Journal de Genève*, 6 December 1952.

26 *La Revista Relojera el Orfebre*, 1947, vol. 63, p. 62; *The Eastern Jeweller and Watchmaker*, 1952, vol. 10, p. 72; *Journal de Genève*, 21 February 1957.

27 HAT, JWT, HAT50/1/154/1, *Proposals for the Future Advertising Policy on Rolex and Tudor Watches*, November 1951.

28 HAT, JWT, HAT50/1/154/1, review of Rolex advertising activities, 8 January 1953.

29 HAT, JWT, HAT50/1/154/1 Rolex, reports of meetings, 23 January 1962.

30 In 1965, following the death of Werner Ryser, André Heiniger was appointed to the Board of Directors. Marconi Watch SA was renamed Marconi Investments SA in 1987. Its purpose was to manage property assets. Its directors to this day include personalities involved in the management of Montres Rolex SA, such as André and Patrick Heiniger, and Nicolas Brünschwig. *FOSC*, 22 December 1987 and Geneva Commercial Register. *FOSC*, 1965, p. 2904.

31 HAT, JWT, HAT50/1/154/2/1-5, Rolex Tudor exports, n.d.

32 *The Times*, 6 March 1947.

33 A total of sixty-eight advertisements for the whole of the 1950s. Source: Gale Primary Sources, The Digital Times Archives (consulted on 10 August 2023).

34 HAT, JWT, HAT50/1/154/1, review of Rolex advertising activities, 8 January 1953.

35 HAT, JWT, HAT50/1/154/1, report of a meeting held in Geneva on 28 August 1959.

36 HAT, JWT, HAT50/1/154/1, review of Rolex advertising activities, 8 January 1953.

37 *Eastern Jeweler and Watchmaker*, vol. 3, 1951, p. 89.

38 *Eastern Jeweler and Watchmaker*, vol. 20, 1953, p. 2.

39 HAT, JWT, HAT50/1/154/1, review of Rolex advertising activities, 8 January 1953; *New York Times*, 18 December 1959.

40 MIH, CSH, letter from CSH to Rolex Watch, 2 February 1948.

41 *Belles Lettres de Lausanne: Livre d'or du 175 anniversaire, 1906–1981*, Lausanne: Belles Lettres, 1981, p. 339; *New York Times*, 17 March 1948; Duke University, Rubenstein Library, J. Walter Thompson Collection, Account files, RO1, *Modern Jeweler*, February 1983, p. 53.

42 *New York Times*, 9 February 1990.

43 HAT, JWT, HAT50/1/154/1, review of Rolex advertising activities, 8 January 1953; *New York Times*, 18 December 1959.

44 HAT, JWT, HAT50/1/154/1, review of Rolex advertising activities, 8 January 1953.

45 *New York Times*, 31 January 1950.

46 Rolex's emerging strategy was an early one, as it was generally during the 1960s that this break with the past appeared in large American consumer goods companies. Alan Pottasch at Pepsi Cola, for example, launched the "Pepsi Generation" campaign in 1963. See Nourrisson, *L'Amérique en bouteille*, pp. 193–194.

47 HAT, JWT, HAT50/1/154/1, report of a meeting held in Geneva on 28 August 1959.

Part III

Embodying individual success (1960–2020)

Hans Wilsdorf died on 6 July 1960.[1] However, there was no major break in the decades that followed. The new directors of Rolex continued and developed the strategy put in place after the war. By the early 1960s, Rolex had established itself as one of the most renowned Swiss watch brands. However, it was not considered the undisputed leader of the industry and faced stiff competition from a number of other manufacturers, notably Omega and Longines. It also had to distinguish itself from the Geneva-based manufacturers of luxury watches, in particular Patek, Philippe & Cie, which flourished after the war.

However, during this decade, Rolex underwent a profound change in its strategy. Although it continued to produce high-quality chronometer watches on an industrial scale, it radically transformed its communication, presenting itself as a brand that expressed individual success, professional excellence, and social distinction. Rolex was soon no longer a watch: it became a status symbol. This new positioning enabled Rolex to weather the crisis of 1975–1985 almost unscathed, at a time when Omega and Longines were facing existential difficulties, and to establish itself as the new number one in Swiss and world watchmaking. This third part analyses how Rolex's new strategy was implemented and pursued after 1960.

Note

1   *Journal de Genève*, 8 July 1960.

7

Rolex becomes world number one (1960–1990)

In 1977, at a time when the Swiss watch industry was in deep crisis, Rolex bought a building in the centre of New York for $15 million.[1] This anecdote starkly illustrates the gap that existed between Rolex and its competitors at the time. SSIH, which owned Omega, was facing insurmountable financial problems because of poor strategic choices characterised by massive investment in the mass production of inexpensive Roskopf watches, sales of which collapsed with the advent of quartz.[2] As for Longines, it had suffered from a chronic lack of investment since the 1950s. It was a family business whose shareholders wanted to retain control but no longer had the means to develop the company alone. Improvements to production capacity and the launch of a second brand suffered from this lack of financial resources, with the result that the company was bought by ASUAG in 1971.[3] Finally, Omega and Longines opted for the technological transition to quartz, which would enable the development of watches with excellent precision, but they encountered great difficulties in industrialising this product, unlike their Japanese competitor, Seiko.[4] The crisis led to the merger of SSIH and ASUAG to form Société Suisse de Microélectronique et d'Horlogerie SA (SMH, Swatch Group since 1998) in 1983. At the same time, many watchmaking companies disappeared (1,618 firms in 1970 and 634 in 1985), while employment in the industry fell from nearly 90,000 in 1970 to around 33,000 in 1985.[5]

Table 7.1   *Rolex and Omega sales, estimated in millions of current francs,*
1960–1987

	1960	1970	1980	1987
Rolex	38	100	470	1,000
Omega	30	65	370	530

Sources: HAT, JWT, HAT50/1/154/2/2/1-5, Export Rolex Tudor, n.d. (Rolex 1960 and 1970); Pasquier, La "Recherche et Développement" en horlogerie, p. 443 (Omega 1960 and 1970); New York Times, 19 October 1980 (Omega and Rolex 1980); L'Hebdo, 16 June 1988 (Rolex 1987); SMH, Annual Report, 1987 (Omega estimated to account for 35 per cent of watch sales).

While its competitors were looking for a way out of the crisis, Rolex established itself as the world's leading watch brand. It was in sales that its dominance was visible. As the company does not publish any financial data, we must rely on estimates quoted in the press or made by banking analysts, or figures mentioned in rare archive documents. These are often very rough estimates, but they do have the merit of showing a long-term trend. They highlight Rolex's strong growth during the crisis years, enabling it to outstrip its rival, Omega (see Table 7.1). The available figures show that Rolex was already ahead of Omega in 1960 and 1970. However, the figures for Rolex include its second brand, Tudor, whereas Omega's sales figures do not include the other SSIH brands, such as Tissot. The two brands were undoubtedly extremely close, as the statistics for chronometer registrations during these years suggest (see Figure 7.3, p. 160). It was during the 1970s and, above all, 1980–1987 that Rolex largely outstripped Omega. In 1987, its turnover was almost double that of its main competitor.

At the end of the 1980s, Rolex enjoyed unrivalled prestige. It embodied the industrial excellence of the Swiss watchmaking industry and the genius of an innovative marketing strategy that made watches the expression of individual success. This chapter analyses the sources of this transformation.

Changes in Rolex's governance

The organisation of the Rolex Group underwent no major changes between 1960 and 1990. The system put in place during the previous period ensured perfect organisational continuity. Its governance was still based on three main organisations: Manufacture des Montres Rolex SA, Montres Rolex SA, and the Hans Wilsdorf Foundation.

Bienne-based Manufacture des Montres Rolex SA remained a family business owned and run by the Borer–Aeglers families. Emil Borer oversaw operations until his death in 1967, and then his son Harry did so until 2001. Several other members of the family were involved in management positions, including Alfred Aegler, Hermann Müller-Aegler, and Hans Sautter-Borer. It is also remarkable that there were only nine appointments to the Board of Directors between 1960 and 1990 (see Table A.1, pp. 234–235). Of these new directors, only three were from outside the family: two notables from the canton of Berne (former Berne state councillor and chairman of the Berne Cantonal Bank Ernst Jaberg and Willy Meier, a notary and company director in Berne) and André Heiniger, executive director of Montres Rolex SA in Geneva. While Heiniger's presence is clearly intended to ensure good business coordination between the two Rolex companies, the appointment of Jaberg and Meier illustrates the desire to maintain good relations in local and regional economic circles. Manufacture des Montres Rolex SA remained a purely family-owned company.

Montres Rolex SA in Geneva was also undergoing changes at the top. Following the death of Hans Wilsdorf in 1960, the Board of Directors initially did not appoint an executive director. Board members Emil Borer, Fernand Lilla, Victor Maerky, and Jean Malche were given joint signing authority, although until then they had not had the power to bind the company. At the same time, Diether Kübel-Wilsdorf, the authorised representative and nephew of the late Hans Wilsdorf, was elevated to the status of director.[6] He ran the company alongside four other men: Heiniger (sales director), Huguenin (technical director), Jeanneret (product and marketing director), and Ryser (administrative director). The absence of an executive director at the head of Montres Rolex SA suggests that the successor appointed by Hans Wilsdorf, his nephew Dieter Kübel, was not to the satisfaction of Rolex's new owners, the Wilsdorf Foundation.[7] Born in Germany in 1930, Kübel moved to Switzerland in 1948. After attending the School of Commerce in Neuchâtel and the Watchmaking School in Le

Locle, he joined Montres Rolex SA in 1952, which sent him on internships at the Fabrique d'Ebauches in Fleurier and the Manufacture des Montres Rolex SA in Bienne. He was appointed director of Montres Rolex SA in 1960, at the age of twenty-nine. At his uncle's request, he had "Wilsdorf" added to his name.[8] There was a period of uncertainty at the head of the Geneva company. It was not until the death of Werner Ryser in 1964 that the management was reorganised.[9] André Heiniger was appointed executive director, a position he held until 1992. One of the first significant measures he took after his appointment was to regain control of the American subsidiary, which had become increasingly important as sales in the United States grew. It had enjoyed autonomy in terms of an advertising and marketing strategy that conflicted with the desire to build a global luxury brand. Changing advertising agencies is often used by new managers as a way of establishing their legitimacy at the head of the company once they have taken office. This is exactly what Heiniger did in the United States in 1966 when he decided to entrust advertising and public relations to JWT. Similarly, Montres Rolex SA appointed a new advertising director at The American Rolex Watch Corporation, who came from JWT.[10] It is also likely that it was Heiniger who put an end to the casing of ladies' watches in the United States. Until the end of the 1960s, Montres Rolex SA exported around 10,000 bare movements for ladies' watches to New York each year. They were cased in the US, probably by local subcontractors, under the responsibility of the American subsidiary.[11] There is no mention of this practice after 1970. The assumption of power by the Geneva headquarters over the New York subsidiary led to a few conflicts. An internal JWT report in 1973 laconically states: "There is still a philosophical conflict between US Rolex and Geneva in advertising strategy [...]. This has not been resolved, and could result in serious account difficulties which are compounded by other political and personal conflicts within the Rolex organization."[12] Between 1960 and 1964, after Wilsdorf's death, Heiniger's undoubtedly long-term, global vision for the brand, his ability to assert himself in a conflict-ridden environment, and his desire to centralise power in Geneva made him the best candidate for the general management of Montres Rolex SA. For nearly thirty years, he implemented the strategy that enabled Rolex to become the world's leading watch brand.

Probably disappointed not to have succeeded his uncle, Diether Kübel-Wilsdorf left Rolex in 1969 and took over the general management of the Manufacture des Montres Universal Perret Frères SA in 1970.[13] Despite this departure, there was a great deal of continuity under André Heiniger, who retained the men with whom he had worked since the 1950s. Marc Huguenin was technical director until 1972, and René-Paul Jeanneret was marketing director until 1975.[14] They were then replaced by a growing number of directors and representatives, particularly in the sales, finance, and marketing departments. In 1975, for example, six new deputy directors and two new authorised representatives were appointed.[15] One of Heiniger's lieutenants was René Le Coultre, who headed the technical department between 1972 and 1987.[16] Considered the "father of the quartz watch", he played a major role in the acquisition of this technology in the 1970s (see pp. 186–187).

In comparison to the growing power of the management of Montres Rolex SA under André Heiniger, the company's Board of Directors played a minor role, as the profile of the sixteen people appointed between 1960 and 1990 shows (see Appendix, Table A.2, pp. 236–237). Except for André and Patrick Heiniger, and Harry Borer, who ran the Rolex companies in Geneva and Bienne, Genevan notables were chosen as directors. There were seven directors of Geneva companies, three business lawyers, among whom Bertrand Gros, Patrick Heiniger's partner, and a major Rolex executive after 1990, two professors from the University of Geneva, and a former ambassador. The Board therefore played no role in the strategic direction of the company. Moreover, recruitment was purely local. Montres Rolex SA was not part of the network of directors who ran the major Swiss companies and banks at the time.[17] The rare exceptions were Claude Barbey, executive director of the trading company Cosa Liebermann and director of Swissair, and Paul Waldvogel, executive director of Ateliers des Charmilles SA and member of the Vorort committee. Apart from these two men, the board members of Montres Rolex SA were, above all, Geneva elites, part of essentially local networks on the fringes of the Swiss elite. The Hans Wilsdorf Foundation, which had owned Montres

Figure 7.1 André Heiniger

Note: André Heiniger, CEO of Montres Rolex SA from 1964 to 1992, was the man who made Rolex a global luxury brand that embodies individual success. In collaboration with the JWT advertising agency, he built a powerful concept based on the exceptional nature of the Oyster watch, its designer Hans Wilsdorf, and its customers around the world. He had the intelligence to take a back seat in the communication of his brand and make Wilsdorf a legendary figure.

Source: © Rolex/Christian Poite.

Rolex SA since 1960, was clearly seeking to maintain its control over the company by recruiting directors from a similar social background.

The renewal of the Hans Wilsdorf Foundation's Board between 1960 and 1990 continued the principles adopted in 1957 – namely, the presence of a representative of Hans Wilsdorf's descendants, who were entitled to allowances, as well as representatives of Geneva's upper class. The ten people appointed during this period comprised two of Wilsdorf's descendants, three university professors, two notaries and a lawyer, a former Christian Democrat member of the Council of State, and a bank manager, all of whom lived in Geneva apart from one German professor. The Foundation Board, responsible for managing Rolex's profits, distributed various forms of social aid and subsidies to many institutions. One of the first major donations made after Wilsdorf's death was a sum of 100,000 francs granted in 1965 to the Geneva Cantonal Hospital for the construction of a laboratory for Professor Georges Bickel.[18] This type of donation increased in the years that followed. The accumulated fortune of the Hans Wilsdorf Foundation was also to contribute to the development of Rolex. However, there are no accessible documents to help us understand how the Rolex Group's investment strategy worked. Montres Rolex SA does not depend entirely on the Wilsdorf Foundation to finance its growth. It holds its own reserves and uses Rolex Holding to carry out various stock market and financial transactions (see p. 204).

Innovation and product development

Rolex's extraordinary growth between 1960 and 1990 was not based on the development of new products. For the most part, it exploited the models developed in the post-war period. The main model launched on the market after 1960 was the Cosmograph chronograph, which went on sale in 1963. Originally intended for American astronauts, this watch was transformed into a racing driver's watch after the failure of the collaboration with NASA (National Aeronautics and Space Administration). It enjoyed phenomenal success under the name Cosmograph Daytona.[19] The company also strengthened its presence in the luxury jewellery watch market with the Cellini collection, launched in the 1960s.[20] These were initially watches that were neither water-resistant nor automatic and therefore contradicted Rolex's positioning. They did not appear in the company's general catalogue during the early years but in a catalogue of their own.[21] They adopted the main codes of the jewellery watch of the time – namely, an ultra-flat shape and the use of precious materials, following the example set by Piaget.[22] Until the 1990s, Rolex did not communicate much about this collection because of its marginal positioning.

For the most part, Rolex concentrated on a dozen models developed between 1945 and 1963, available in various styles. Among them, the Oyster Perpetual concept (a waterproof automatic chronometer) perfectly embodied Rolex's values. In 1987, it accounted for around 90 per cent of the volume of watches sold by Rolex.[23] This unique product strategy was championed by André Heiniger, who, in 1980, told the *New York Times*, "We've always avoided trends toward quantity and toward fashion".[24] In the 2000s, luxury management gurus Jean-Noël Kapferer and Vincent Bastien explained that developing products without taking consumers' desires into account was one of the basic principles of luxury marketing: the brand must totally dominate its customers.[25] This is exactly what Heiniger did at Rolex.

Against this backdrop, what room was left for innovation? What research activities were developed by Rolex engineers between 1960 and 1990? The patents filed by Rolex during these three decades reveal a real stagnation in research. Only fifty-four patents were obtained, an average of 1.7 per year. Compared with the 1930s (4.7 patents per year) and the 1950s (16.6 patents per year), marked respectively by the development of the water-resistant watch and the automatic movement, the decades of strong growth appear to have been relatively poor in terms of research (see Figure 2.2, p. 37). The technologies used were stable and did not require any particular research effort. Only six patents relating to the water resistance of the case and two relating to the automatic movement were filed between 1960 and 1990. Similarly, although precision remained a major issue in terms of marketing positioning, the mechanical movements developed in previous years met this need perfectly. Only a few detail operations

A la gloire de Cellini

Lors de l'une de ses récentes visites au Siège Central de Rolex à Genève, Hélène Stewart, épouse du coureur automobile Jacky Stewart, présente l'une des dernières créations de la Collection

Cellini : une montre en platine sertie de 314 diamants tailles spécialement pour ce modèle. De lignes harmonieuses. cette pièce créée pour la Foire de Bâle 1969 coûtera quelque 80.000 francs.

39

Figure 7.2 Advertisement for Rolex Cellini, 1969

Note: The Cellini collection allowed Rolex to develop jewellery watch models, particularly for ladies, without following the aesthetic codes and concept of the Oyster. However, the positioning remained that of luxury.

Source: Europa Star, no. 56, 1969, p. 39. © Europa Star Archives.

made it possible to improve certain parts of movements (nine patents) and regulating organs (five patents). However, although the number of patents relating to movement precision was relatively low, it remained vital to the Group's management. Around 1960, Rolex hired André Zibach, the former star timer at Patek, Philippe & Cie. As it had stopped taking part in competitions at the Observatories in Geneva and Neuchâtel at the end of the 1950s, Rolex did not hire Zibach to prepare special timepieces for chronometric concours but to work on improving the quality of ordinary wristwatches. He is mentioned as the inventor of several patents after 1960.[26]

Furthermore, the lack of development of new models can be seen in the patents filed. Rolex obtained only three patents for wristwatches, one patent for a diver's watch, and two for a watch case. While it is true that the finishing of external parts was subcontracted to independent companies, which developed their own components in accordance with Rolex's requests, from 1960 to 1990, these suppliers filed few patents. The bracelet manufacturer Gay Frères and the case manufacturer Genex were absent from the Espacenet patent database. Crown manufacturer Boninchi was the exception, with a total of fifteen patents during this period. As crowns play an essential role in ensuring that watches are water-resistant, it is in this area that most of the company's research activities were focused. Dial manufacturer Beyeler registered eight patents relating to industrial production methods for this component.[27] Finally, Rolex obtained four patents for tooling and two patents for instruments other than watches (a racing chronometer and a device for measuring blood circulation).

These data reveal a company that had largely abandoned research into mechanical watchmaking. Rolex exploited the high-quality products and industrial apparatus developed over previous decades, concentrating its efforts on promotional and commercial activities. However, it is worth highlighting the considerable effort made in the field of electrical, electronic, and liquid crystal display technologies. Rolex obtained a total of twenty patents in these fields. This enabled it to master quartz technologies as they emerged and to launch a few electronic models when the market was in a recomposition phase (see below, p. 187).

Evolution of the production system

Compared with R&D, which remained stable from the 1960s to the 1990s, the production system expanded to become a key factor in Rolex's rise to the world's leading watch brand. The group embarked on a veritable race to mass-produce quality watches. Although Rolex does not publish data on the volume of its production, the annual reports of the watch control offices (1961–1973) and the Contrôle officiel suisse des chronomètres (COSC, 1973–2015) provide a fairly accurate assessment of the general trend in Rolex production. After the Second World War, most of the watches produced and sold by Rolex were chronometers subject to official control (see Figure 7.3). What can we learn from these statistics?

For the period in question, three elements stand out. First, Rolex experienced a sharp increase in production, with the number of certifications obtained rising from 41,836 in 1961 to 583,108 in 1990. The Group's production capacity increased at least tenfold during these years. Second, Rolex was a company on which the crisis had a violent but extremely short-lived effect: it was a cyclical episode. The number of certifications fell sharply between 1974 (230,341 chronometers) and 1976 (135,501 chronometers), but the number of certifications began to rise again in 1977, and the 1974 record was surpassed in 1980. This momentum was remarkable, given that the Swiss watch industry, as a whole, was then facing a veritable existential crisis marked by the disappearance of two-thirds of watchmaking jobs.[28] The reasons for this resilience are discussed below (pp. 183–188). Third, the crisis was an opportunity to establish itself as the world's most important watch brand in the face of Omega. Chronometer statistics highlight the strong competition between the two brands, with Omega slightly ahead of its rival during the 1960s. Together, they had a virtual monopoly on chronometry (86.6 per cent of certificates in 1961–1973). However, the difficulties of the SSIH group, to which Omega belonged, led the company's management to abandon high-precision mechanical watchmaking and refocus on electronics.[29] This strategic choice led to a sharp drop in the overall activity of the COSC offices. Rolex became the absolute leader in the production of chronometers. Its share of total certifications rose from 50.9 per cent in 1975 to 81.3 per cent in 1980 and 94.2 per cent in 1990.

Mass production of chronometers was carried out within the Rolex Group based on the organisation established during the interwar period – that is, a division of tasks between Manufacture des Montres Rolex SA, in Bienne, which concentrated on the production of movements, and Montres Rolex SA, in Geneva, which was responsible for the final assembly and marketing. However, although the organisational basis remained the same, there was a significant difference between the two partners, with the Bienne-based company committing more and more capital to its suppliers, while the Geneva-based company pursued a policy of legal and financial independence.

In Bienne, the movement manufacturer first developed its production capacity. In 1969, it opened a branch in Le Locle, co-financed with its

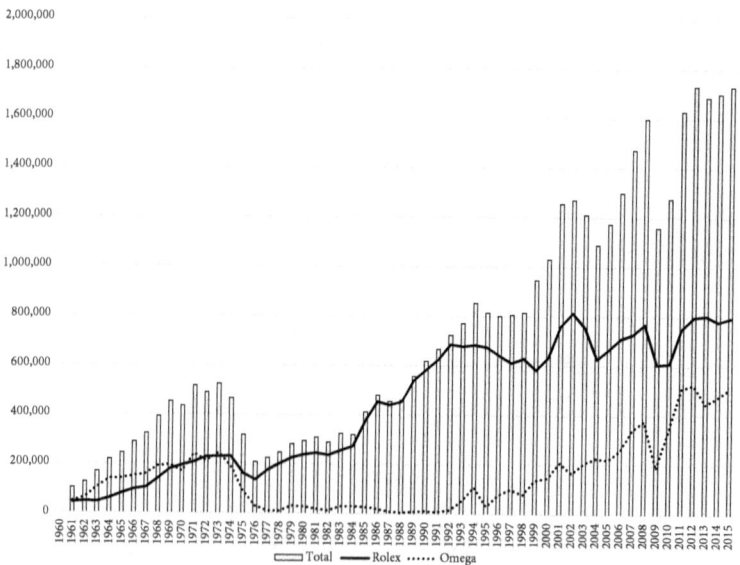

Figure 7.3 Official chronometer certificates issued in Switzerland, 1961–2015
Note: Details by brand have not been published since 2016.
Source: COSC.

partner in Geneva.[30] Three years later, in 1972, it bought the buildings of the Gruen factory in the town of Bienne, renamed Rolex II, for around a million dollars[31] and set up a machining department and some research laboratories there.[32] It also acquired majority stakes in a number of its subcontractors, including the gilding, nickel-plating, and silver-plating workshop Doniar SA (founded in Bienne in 1959), the machine-tool manufacturer Dynafer SA (La Chaux-de-Fonds, 1982), and the stamping factory Silexa SA (Bienne, 1985).[33] In 1979, Harry Borer also founded Micrométal SA in Bienne, a company specialising in the manufacture and sale of precision instruments.[34] In addition, to manage these assets and various investments, the Borer family set up several financial companies, including Vinetum (1974) and Geocent SA (1982).[35] These various investments reflect the Borer family's desire to exercise control over the production system.

In Geneva, on the other hand, Montres Rolex SA pursued a policy of subcontracting to a group of independent manufacturers who supplied the company with cases, bracelets, and dials. According to Laurence Marti, it was the desire to preserve competition that explains the absence of verticalisation.[36] However, the example of the watch-case manufacturer Genex SA, in which Montres Rolex SA had a stake (a representative has sat on the Board of Directors since it was founded in 1940, and Rolex owns the Genex watch brand), reveals a close relationship between the two partners, similar to that between Montres Rolex SA and its movement supplier. In 1971, when Genex inaugurated its new factory, it had a production capacity of around 300,000 pieces per year.[37] At the time, Rolex's production volume was only around 200,000 watches a year; it would not reach 300,000 until the mid-1980s. This suggests Genex sold around a third of its production to companies other than Rolex. Thus, rather than competition between suppliers, Montres Rolex SA aimed to encourage its suppliers to remain innovative in terms of quality and price – they needed to achieve a significant proportion of their turnover in a competitive market. Apart from Genex SA, Montres Rolex SA's main investment in expanding its production capacity was the opening of a small watch-movement finishing workshop in the town of Neuchâtel in

1970. Employing around thirty people when it opened, it was closed and moved back to Le Locle in 1983.[38]

The few figures available on the Rolex Group's workforce confirm its remarkable expansion between 1960 and 1990. The number of employees at Geneva-based Montres Rolex SA rose from 498 in 1964 to 593 in 1975 and 970 in 1988.[39] Between 1964 and 1988, the company's workforce grew by 95 per cent, while the Swiss watch industry lost two-thirds of all jobs in the same period.[40] The dynamics of employment at the Manufacture de Montres Rolex SA are not precisely known, but the company employed around 600 people in 1976, compared with just over 300 in the early 1960s. Its growth was also remarkable.[41]

An innovative marketing strategy

While new product development and technological innovation played only a limited role in Rolex's tremendous growth between 1960 and 1990, the company's marketing strategy enabled it to establish itself as the world's leading watch brand. Rolex certainly had an original strategy since the interwar years in terms of market positioning, with its concentration on a specific product: the high-precision, water-resistant, automatic wristwatch produced on an industrial scale. However, the Oyster model was only one type of watch at the time. Until the end of the 1950s, Rolex did not really distinguish itself from its competitors in the market, and its communication focused on the intrinsic, technical characteristics of the product: Rolex was, first and foremost, a high-quality watch like Longines, Omega or Zenith.

Narratives on product excellence did not fade after 1960. Some advertisements continued to feature Rolex as an indestructible product and as the brand that had created water-resistant watches, but they were becoming rare, even though they had largely dominated communication until then. Similarly, Rolex abandoned chronometry competitions towards the end of the 1950s. Obtaining first prizes and records was no longer considered a priority and disappeared from Rolex's communications. Thus, in the 1960s, there was a fundamental transition in the brand's discourse: Rolex was no longer simply an exceptional watch but a watch for exceptional people. It was the first watch brand to place social distinction at the heart of its marketing strategy. Rolex was the embodiment of individual success, and this was the new focus of its communication.

However, the transition was not a natural one. It was the subject of discussions and negotiations between Montres Rolex SA and its main advertising agent, JWT. In 1962, when Rolex managers were thinking of emphasising the technical innovations made to its products and the new models launched on the market, JWT proposed something completely different, with its *Great Names* campaign: "The campaign would feature leading personalities in various fields whose influence is changing the normal way of life."[42] JWT also insisted that the message about the people who ran the world was not just an advertising slogan. It had to be accompanied by actions that embodied the slogan and gave it credibility. This included ensuring that the people who count wore Rolex watches. For example, JWT advised Rolex's directors to send a brochure presenting their brand "to all the important executives employed in Switzerland by American companies [...] with a personally typed letter. [...] Rolex should send out copies, again with personal letters, to all the important executives known personally to Rolex directors".[43] This new strategy followed an initial series of advertisements launched in the 1950s on the theme *The men who guide destinies wear Rolex watches*. This discourse, which was still secondary amid a narrative strategy based on technical excellence, became dominant after 1960 (see Figure 7.4).

At the same time, on the American market, a new advertising campaign was making Rolex the "presidents' watch". The De Garmo agency, which was in charge of advertising Rolex in the United States until 1966, produced a poster showing a Rolex-equipped forearm holding a red telephone, a direct allusion to President Johnson owning a Rolex (see Figure 7.5). Company representatives in the United States insisted that Indian Prime Minister Nehru and British Prime Minister Churchill, as well as several generals, owned Rolex watches. The famous Pan Am airline also made Rolex its official watch.[44] The Oyster Day-Date thus gradually became the symbol of the presidents' watch.

Figure 7.4 Rolex advertisement, 1967

Note: It was during the 1960s that the JWT agency made Rolex a symbol of prestige and status. It was the first to develop a message about the exclusivity of its wearers, while competing brands remained focused on the classic messages of precision and aesthetics.

Source: Eastern Jeweller and Watchmaker, no. 103, 1967, p. 4. © Europa Star Archives.

The transition from functional and descriptive advertising, which explained the technical qualities of the watch, to emotional advertising messages, which transformed a product into a concept, required an adaptation of the advertising policy. The first step was to carefully select the newspapers and magazines in which the advertisements were to appear. They had to match the brand's positioning. For example, in 1962, when JWT's managers were planning market research, the directors of Montres Rolex SA explained that "the choice of media for luxury and highly priced articles cannot be guided by statistics alone [number of readers] and that the prestige of the medium chosen should also be taken into account".[45] For example, in 1965, Rolex refused to have its advertisements appear in media that did not correspond to its image, such as *Playboy*.[46] The standardisation of advertising on a global scale was also necessary to give the product concept its full force. As a first step, Rolex decided in 1962 to cease local advertising in the British market and to do away with the autonomy hitherto allowed to retailers.[47] Control of advertising content on a global scale was entrusted to JWT, which carried it out through its many subsidiaries.[48] In 1966, Rolex terminated its contract with De Garmo for the American market and handed it over to JWT. From the following year, JWT began working for Rolex in every country in the world.[49] Since then, the Montres Rolex SA and JWT teams have worked closely together to design and broadcast advertising messages.

The collaboration with JWT's American teams decisively influenced the evolution of Rolex's message. JWT was in a phase of profound change at the time.[50] It was affected by the cultural revolution sweeping the advertising profession in New York, characterised by the emergence of new values stemming from the counterculture and the use of anti-conformism, humour, and satire in advertising campaigns for major companies. From then on, it was no longer statistical analysis but the creativity of advertisers that gave agencies their legitimacy. In 1966, JWT overhauled its internal organisation, bringing its employees together in various groups that were given creative freedom. Three years later, it appointed a new creative director, Ronald Rosenfeld, one of the main initiators of the creative revolution in New York advertising. However, the

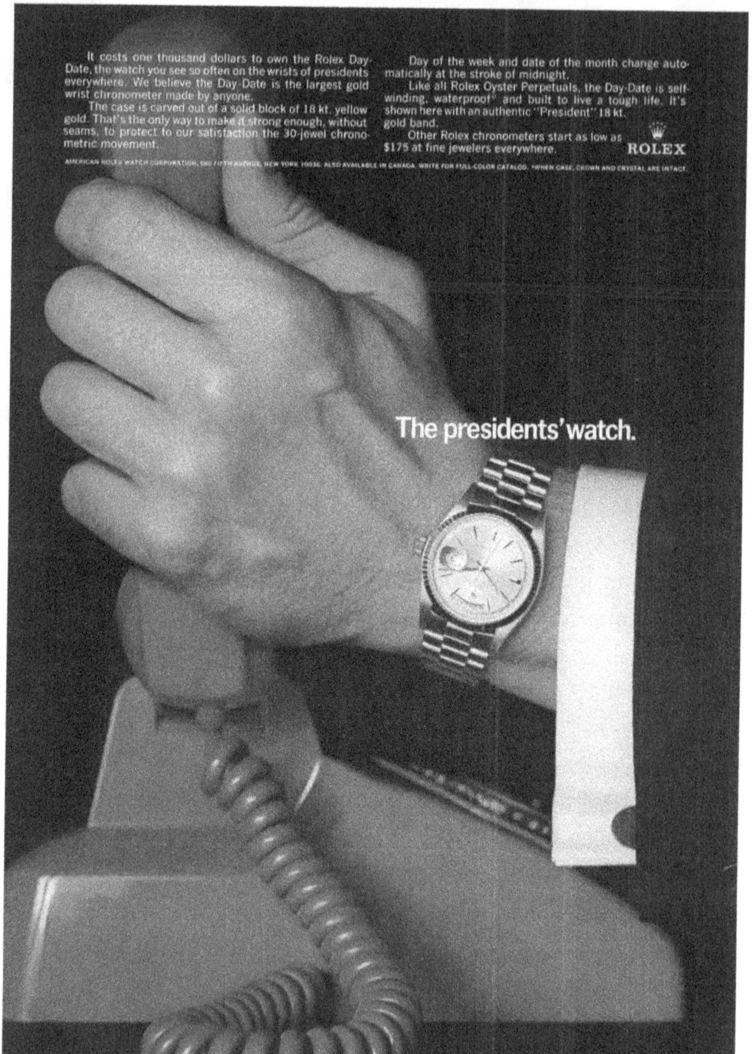

Figure 7.5 Rolex advertisement, 1966

Note: The Oyster Day-Date became the "presidents' watch" in the mid-1960s. It embodied power, ambition, and masculinity.

Figure 7.6 Working session between the management of Montres Rolex SA and the American JWT team, 1979

Note: Rolex's strategy was discussed at meetings like these, usually held in New York. Seated in the middle are André Heiniger (right) and Don Johnston, CEO and chairman of the JWT Group (left). René Dentan, director of Rolex USA, is seated to the left of Heiniger.

Source: Duke University, Rubenstein Library, J. Walter Thompson Collection, Account files collection RO1, unidentified press clipping, 1979.

incompatibility between his creative genius and the organisational rigidities of JWT led him to leave his post and set up his own company in 1970. Historian Thomas Frank explains that the impact of the counterculture did not affect all American advertising companies in the same way and that JWT remained one of the most conservative.[51]

This positioning corresponded perfectly with Rolex's expectations. The Geneva-based managers were seeking to appeal to a traditional elite, essentially male, proud of its social status and on the fringes of the sexual revolution and the hippy movement. In 1966, however, JWT managers proposed adapting Rolex's communications to the new world. It seemed beneficial to abandon the discourse on politicians and power and to refocus on personalities who embodied individual success with more glamour: sportsmen and businessmen. They explained it as follows:

> We believe that men today no longer have the same admiration for statesmen as was the case 15 years ago. [...] We have based this campaign on the idea that each man can link himself with the adventure and prestige that a Rolex

offers because in his own thoughts, he dreams of one day climbing mountains or running businesses.[52]

A new strategy was adopted in 1967.[53] A whole series of characters and individuals were gradually introduced as expressions of this exceptionality. In 1980, René Dentan, president of Rolex's American subsidiary, explained that Rolex's new partners "must be people whose prestige is parallel to ours".[54]

New strategy adopted for the 1967 campaign

In creating a contemporary campaign, the stumbling block is the hero. Attitudes have changed. The giants of the past are regarded with some cynicism and less awe. The young, aggressive, masculine, make-his-own-world man could be called a contemporary hero. But he is in so many advertisements for whisky, suits and cigarettes, he is already a cliché.

Finding the ultimate hero of all time, universally respected and admired, intelligent, ferocious, grand centrepiece of a thousand adventures turns out to be very simple.

Every man is his own hero. No matter who a man is, he dreams of great adventures, or conquering mountains or corporations or movie stars. A man does not feel these adventures are likely to happen. He seldom consciously thinks about them. But the essential point is that he feels, however remotely, that they could possibly happen. And a Rolex watch is a visible symbol of that possibility. This is why Rolex, more than any other watch is worn low on the wrist. This is why Rolex sells best where the shirt sleeves are the shortest. This is why non-swimmers buy the Submariner. Because a Rolex is designed for any situation, however rough or dangerous or heroic or exalted, it implies that the man who wears it is, potentially, a hero.

Source: HAT, JWT, HAT50/1/154/2 Rolex,
Rolex Campaign 1967, undated.

Sportsmen and women represented the main category of outstanding personalities featured by Rolex. However, unlike its competitors, Rolex no longer emphasised the sporting feats themselves. The watch was no longer a precision instrument that accompanied the sportsman in his accomplishments. Instead, the personality of the sportsman or woman, presented as the embodiment of the exceptional man or woman, was the focus of communication. One of the first to sign a contract with Rolex was the American golfer Arnold Palmer (see Figure 7.7). A charismatic personality, Palmer was considered one of the best players in the world in the early 1960s and became increasingly famous thanks to television broadcasts of golf tournaments. His agent, American businessman Mark H. McCormack, founder and owner of the International Management Group (IMG), signed a contract with Rolex's Japanese subsidiary in 1967, followed by the Geneva head office for the whole world in 1972.[55] In 1968, JWT's Tokyo subsidiary organised a first golf tournament in Japan, the Arnold Palmer Cup and Rolex Golf Tournament,[56] which contributed significantly to the reputation of Rolex in the Japanese archipelago.

This collaboration led Rolex to sponsor a series of golf tournaments in the 1970s broadcast on various television channels – the American agent even had his own sports film production company. McCormack also introduced French skier Jean-Claude Killy, who signed his first contract with Rolex in 1972 (see Figure 7.8).[57] Killy had a worldwide sports consultancy contract for Rolex and worked with JWT on advertising. During the 1970s and 1980s, McCormack organised cocktail parties and events wherever Killy and Palmer travelled in the world to meet local Rolex teams, press representatives, and select clients.

In addition, McCormack extended Rolex's sponsorship to new sports such as tennis and polo while JWT had already proposed in 1966 to take up activities in support of yachting, leading Rolex to sponsor the America's Cup in particular.[58] Tennis helped rejuvenate the brand's image, while polo reinforced Rolex's exclusivity. In 1980, Gérard Souham, a former JWT manager specialising in public relations and founder of the Société Centrale de Conseil en Communication (S3C), recommended that the Swiss manufacturer sponsor polo matches, which were enjoying a boom

Palmer and Rolex. Masters of style.

There's that magic moment in the quiet hush, the dimpled ball poised proudly on its tee. Then a sudden blur of concentrated force cracks and the streak of white arcs downcourse, lofts long and straight, bounces once, twice, and rolls to a precision stop. Then there's the famous grin, the squint, the cant of the head... no one else plays the game quite like Arnold Palmer.

It's more than the championships in the Masters, the U.S. Open, the British Open, the Ryder Cups or the Player of the Year awards. It's more than the private jets, the lucrative entrepreneurial ventures and the television commentary.

It's style. The Palmer style. The no-less-than-heroic play. No single person has done more to move golf from the elite to the masses. Arnie's Army is no misnomer. His fans are legion and he is legend; he's reinforced his reputation every step of the way.

Like the Rolex he wears... a testament to style, to endurance, to timeless value. A statement of true craftsmanship. Handmade step by step from a solid block of gold or stainless steel, there will never be another watch remotely like a Rolex. And Mr. Palmer? We're certain he's equally secure.

ROLEX

Pictured: The Rolex Day-Date Chronometer. In 18kt. gold with matching President bracelet.
Write for brochure. Rolex Watch, U.S.A., Inc., Dept. 669, Rolex Building, 665 Fifth Avenue, New York, N.Y. 10022-5383.
World headquarters in Geneva. Other offices in Canada and major countries around the world.

Figure 7.7 Rolex advertisement, 1985

Note: American golfer Arnold Palmer played an important role in Rolex's expansion into the Japanese market. He was a star among upper-middle-class men who were avid golfers. During the 1970s, he also worked with Japanese clothing manufacturer Renown to launch his fashion brand in Japan.

Quand on a vu Jean-Claude Killy descendre un spécial, on comprend pourquoi sa montre est une Rolex.

Se trouver au bas d'une piste de slalom et regarder Killy jaillir de porte en porte est un spectacle d'une beauté incroyable. Mais c'est évidemment en bord de piste, de tout près, que l'on découvre ce qui a fait de lui un skieur inégalé, un champion comme il n'en surgit qu'un tous les dix ans.

Il a la puissance nécessaire pour contrôler de foudroyantes reprises de carres.

Il a l'acuité de réflexes qui permet d'anticiper et de déjouer la plus vicieuse des chicanes.

Il a la précision de mouvements indispensable pour guider les skis au millimètre près sur la trajectoire idéale.

La montre Rolex que Jean-Claude Killy a toujours au poignet est en accord parfait avec lui-même. En accord avec cette puissance et cette précision. Son boîtier est sculpté, en 162 opérations distinctes, dans un unique bloc d'acier inoxydable spécialement traité, ou dans un lingot d'or. Il constitue un véritable blindage, sans aucune soudure, au cœur duquel se trouve un mouvement automatique à rotor : le Perpetual. Ce mouvement est si précis que l'un des Bureaux Suisses de Contrôle Officiel de la Marche des Chronomètres a effectivement décerné à la Rolex le titre de Chronomètre.

La couronne de remontoir Twinlock - invention brevetée Rolex - est, elle aussi, spéciale. Elle est vissée contre le boîtier Oyster et pour assurer une protection supplémentaire,

elle est scellée intérieurement, selon un système semblable à celui du sas de sous-marin.

Chaque Rolex exige de nos artisans une année de travail. On pourrait croire qu'ils ont repris à leur compte l'adage cité un jour à propos des exploits de Jean-Claude Killy : "L'impossible, c'est quelque chose de possible qui n'a pas été réalisé".

Ils ont réalisé la Rolex, absolument étanche - quelles que soient les circonstances - pratiquement indestructible, imperturbablement exacte. Nos artisans sont contents de "leur" Rolex. Aussi contents que Jean-Claude Killy peut l'être de cette montre qui l'a fidèlement accompagné dans toutes ses victoires, de Portillo à Grenoble et de Grenoble au Nouveau Monde.

Une Rolex mérite le prestige dont elle jouit.

👑
ROLEX
GENÈVE

Documentation sur demande à SAF des Montres Rolex, 10, avenue de la Grande-Armée, 75017 PARIS.

Figure 7.8 Rolex advertisement, 1974

Note: Cooperation between sports agents, advertisers, and watch manufacturers led to the creation of new forms of advertising that made it easier to communicate with the public.

in Europe and the United States at the time. He explained the reasons for this in the *New York Times*: "Auto races? Everybody's there. But polo, we have pre-empted the game. [...] When you see a polo player, you see snob appeal and quality. The polo audience are the natural buyers."[59]

Rolex also secured the services of new sports stars such as Formula 1 driver Jackie Stewart and tennis player John Newcombe.[60] The executive director of Montres Rolex SA, André Heiniger, asked McCormack to suggest major sports stars "who could join the worldwide Rolex family".[61] McCormack introduced him to several golf and figure-skating stars, including American golfer Nancy Lopez, about whom he insisted "she is a Rolex-type person in every respect, has a charming family, and is extremely well respected throughout the US and rest of the world".[62] Women were also becoming expressions of the individual success and exceptionalism that Rolex aimed to represent.

Finally, the collaboration with McCormack led to an extension of sponsorship into the world of classical culture. A cooperation agreement

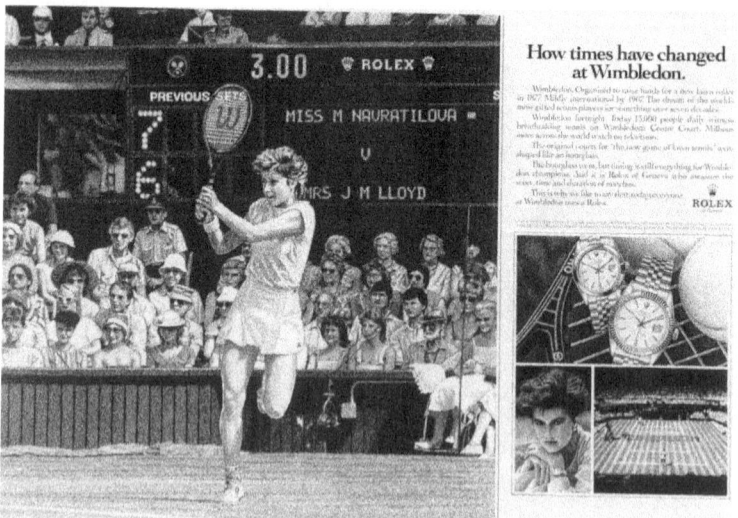

Figure 7.9 Rolex advertisement, early 1980s
Note: Since the 1980s, advertising aimed at women has been produced in a similar format to that for men. Rolex celebrates exceptional personalities across the gender divide.

was signed with Spanish opera singer Placido Domingo in the early 1980s. It was not limited to Spain or Latin America. Domingo was a global star and the collaboration with him was used to develop Rolex's presence in new markets. For example, in 1990, when Domingo was due to perform in Singapore for the first time, McCormack approached Heiniger with a proposal to finance the event, explaining the merits of such an intervention:

> Since no artist of Domingo's stature has ever performed in Singapore, this is certainly going to be the most prestigious event of its 25th anniversary year. The events will be linked to a major charity and this will ensure a high turn-out of senior government, community and business leaders. We would, of course, be able to look after the interests of Rolex as we always have.[63]

Rolex's partnerships with the world of classical music and film would develop over the coming years.

McCormack thus played a key role, alongside JWT, in the transformation of Rolex into a concept expressing the success of exceptional people. He was himself an embodiment of individual success and features in a Rolex advertisement published in 1984 (see Figure 7.10). Although they appear much less frequently than sports stars in advertisements, businessmen are another social category that expresses success. Advertisements featuring them appeared particularly in business magazines aimed at a male readership.

The launch of the Rolex Awards for Enterprise in 1976, on the fiftieth anniversary of the Oyster watch, was a major step in reinforcing the brand as the embodiment of exceptionality and individual success. It brought together men and women active in academic research and culture, as well as in the environment and new technologies. Montres Rolex SA assembled a six-member jury, which, in addition to the chairman of its Board of Directors Olivier Reverdin, professor at the University of Geneva and director of the Swiss National Science Foundation, included representatives of the international scientific community: Swiss oceanographer Jacques Piccard; Margaret Burbidge, professor at the University of San Diego and former director of the Greenwich Observatory; Derek A. Jackson, professor of nuclear physics at the CNRS in Paris; and Luis Marden, former

The man whose life is an event.

Manager. Merchandiser. Advisor to the renowned. Mark McCormack is as celebrated as the notables he represents. As a lawyer, author and competition golfer, he brings a broad spectrum of skills to his success.

Mr. McCormack studied law at Yale, taught it to the military and later joined the law firm of which he is still a partner.

As a golfer, he qualified for several U.S. and British Amateurs and one U.S. Open.

His business evolved from this rare combination of talents. Golfing led him to his first client, Arnold Palmer. His legal training established their professional relationship.

Two decades later, International Management Group, founded and directed by Mark Hume McCormack, is the largest organization of its kind in the world. And its services are as multi-faceted as its founder, ranging from sports marketing to television production, celebrity representation

to money management.

Necessarily, Mr. McCormack's lifestyle is jet-paced. He shuttles between 15 offices as far-flung as Rio and Hong Kong. And 5 homes as widespread as New York and London.

As a man of accomplishment, Mark McCormack is well-matched with his Rolex. As a man in near-perpetual motion, he is well-served by its reliability.

ROLEX

The Rolex President Day-Date Chronometer. Available in 18kt. gold, with matching bracelet.
Write for brochure. Rolex Watch, U.S.A., Inc., Dept. 608, Rolex Building, 665 Fifth Avenue, New York, N.Y. 10022. © 1984.
World headquarters in Geneva. Other offices in Canada and major countries around the world.

Figure 7.10 Rolex advertisement, 1984

Note: Successful businessmen are also embodiments of the excellence that Rolex promotes. The choice of personalities, according to nationality and field of activity, varies according to the magazine's readership and target country. However, the advertising has a similar aesthetic and structure: a photograph of the celebrity, an eye-catching headline, text that highlights the celebrity's excellence, and a photo of a Rolex watch (the model varies from magazine to magazine and from edition to edition) accompanied by its chronometric seal. JWT calls this a "case story" technique: offering a varied story (but one that always conveys the same values) within a defined framework.

A book as unique as the watch itself.

The book is Spirit of Enterprise — The 1981 Rolex Awards. And the watch, of course, is Rolex.

Simply put, we asked the worldwide scientific community for ideas that challenge the mind and quicken the heart. Projects were submitted for consideration in three broad categories: Applied Sciences and Invention, Exploration and Discovery, and The Environment.

A distinguished international committee examined thousands of entries, and, after months of deliberation, conferred five Rolex Awards for Enterprise. The prize for each Award was 50,000 Swiss francs and a gold Rolex Chronometer.

Spirit of Enterprise details the winning

SPIRIT OF
ENTERPRISE

THE 1981 ROLEX AWARDS

projects, along with hundreds of unusual, imaginative and otherwise stimulating proposals for scientific investigation.

Everything from a method that just might get useful energy from magnetism to how to save the sperm whales by cultivating a desert plant.

The Rolex Awards for Enterprise celebrate the fertility of humankind's imagination. And the book makes worthwhile, exciting reading, particularly if you're the kind of person who appreciates the spirit of Rolex itself.

Spirit of Enterprise — The 1981 Rolex Awards isn't a book for everybody. But then again, Rolex isn't a watch for everybody, either.

ROLEX

The Rolex Awards
for Enterprise

Created by Montres Rolex S.A.
to encourage
outstanding personal
enterprise

*Spirit of Enterprise — The 1981 Rolex Awards, 160 pages, suggested list price, $15.85.
Published by W. H. Freeman and Company, 660 Market Street, San Francisco, California 94104, USA. Or through your bookstore.*

24

Fortune

Figure 7.11 Rolex advertisement, 1981

Note: The Rolex Awards for Enterprise is an opportunity to communicate the brand's contribution to excellence in all areas of the arts, the environment, and knowledge. It should be emphasised that this award was not originally conceived as an early expression of a corporate social responsibility programme – although it later became one. Its primary purpose is to honour outstanding personalities who indirectly reinforce the brand's identity.

editor-in-chief of *National Geographic Magazine*.[64] Rolex announced its decision to award a sum of 50,000 francs to each of the five winners for an exceptional project. The competition was an extraordinary success, with more than 3,000 entries from all over the world.[65] The first winners were announced in 1978, and the competition has been held at regular intervals ever since. It is an opportunity to celebrate excellence in a wide range of fields.

International expansion

Rolex's continuous growth between 1960 and 1990 was clearly due to its presence in all world markets. Rolex was a global brand offering similar products to customers everywhere. However, in the absence of figures on the evolution of its market share over the three decades that have made it the leading watch brand, it is hard to know exactly which countries were behind this growth.

The JWT archives contain a few documents that give a fairly accurate idea of Rolex's presence in various world markets in the early 1960s. Table 7.2 shows changes in turnover between 1960 and 1964 based on sales figures sent to JWT by Montres Rolex SA. It includes the total for the Rolex and Tudor brands. Four main conclusions can be drawn from this table. First, the growth in sales, which rose from 38.4 million francs to 57.9 million, was mainly due to an increase in volume (+26 per cent), with the average value of the watch increasing by only 19 per cent. In 1964, the average value of a watch was 279 francs (or just over 1,000 francs in 2023). This does not mean, however, that these figures include a high proportion of Tudor watches. It refers to the value of watches sold to distributors, who add their own margin before retailers do the same. According to another document, the price of a steel Rolex Oyster in British jewellers was £40 in early 1965, or about 500 francs. This is roughly double the average value of Rolex and Tudor watches sold by Montres Rolex SA that year, which corresponds approximately to the distributor's and retailer's margins.

*Table 7.2   Turnover (thousands of francs) and sales volumes (number of watches)
of Rolex and Tudor, 1960–1964*

		1960	1961	1962	1963	1964
Switzerland	Value	5,297	5,225	5,188	5,968	6,127
	Volume	15,473	15,049	14,087	14,605	15,298
	Average value	342	347	368	409	401
Europe	Value	5,898	6,924	6,619	7,620	8,685
	Volume	34,133	25,683	27,523	31,110	38,921
	Average value	173	270	240	245	223
Africa	Value	500	748	704	968	964
	Volume	1,860	2,611	2,010	2,847	3,023
	Average value	269	286	350	340	319
Middle East	Value	4,089	4,349	4,830	4,575	5,213
	Volume	12,269	18,229	17,224	16,785	19,252
	Average value	333	239	280	273	271
India and Asia	Value	13,339	16,469	18,440	18,825	22,813
	Volume	55,448	62,354	62,060	62,547	70,351
	Average value	241	264	297	301	324
North America	Value	2,853	3,347	3,925	3,648	4,457
	Volume	17,902	22,960	25,958	24,853	26,629
	Average value	159	146	151	147	167
Central America	Value	1,041	1,264	2,165	1,983	1,925
	Volume	3,271	3,843	6,580	5,663	5,286
	Average value	318	329	329	350	364
South America	Value	1,657	1,298	1,662	1,683	2,541
	Volume	5,037	4,129	5,380	4,792	7,960
	Average value	329	314	309	351	319
Australia, N.-Z.	Value	525	737	775	3,186	2,100
	Volume	5,985	9,015	9,274	12,260	10,316
	Average value	88	82	84	260	204
Armies	Value	3,185	1,202	1,512	1,592	3,079
	Volume	12,285	4,872	5,588	5,795	10,642
	Average value	259	247	271	275	289
TOTAL	Value	38,384	41,563	45,820	50,048	57,904
	Volume	163,663	168,745	175,684	181,257	207,678
	Average value	235	246	261	276	279

Source: HAT, JWT, HAT50/1/154/2/1-5, Rolex Tudor exports, n.d.

Second, the main growth market during the first part of the 1960s was Asia. This region's share even rose from 31 per cent to 39.4 per cent, while the average value of watches there was slightly higher than for the world as a whole. A market study carried out in 1963 by JWT explains that "the Far East contains our largest markets and may be classed in the following order: Hong Kong, Singapore, Japan, Australia".[66] For the most part, these were British colonies or areas of British influence, but American businessmen were probably an important clientele (see p. 140). Rolex (Hong Kong) Ltd was one of the first foreign subsidiaries founded by the Group, in 1967.[67] The situation was similar in Africa, where the main markets in 1963 were Rhodesia and South Africa.[68]

Third, European markets were in relative decline, although for different reasons. Italy was the largest European market in 1963. Rolex did not yet have a subsidiary or agent for the whole country. Its presence was based on a multitude of contracts by city and by region with local retailers. However, sales were experiencing difficulties in several other European countries. This was particularly the case in France:

> This is a market which has been neglected by Rolex for many years due to the extremely high customs duties and the restrictions on licences. These restrictions have been modified and we are now conducting a small national campaign, but any intensive effort will have to wait for two or three years, in which time we hope to have set up a properly working dealer network.[69]

As for Sweden, its development was still very slow: "For a long time this has been a difficult territory for Rolex as the distributors are not really used to selling top-grade merchandise."[70] Finally, the Swiss domestic market remained the one in which Rolex watches were the most expensive. It was controlled by Bucherer and the Geneva retailer Béguin, who sold mainly to tourists.[71]

Fourth, the United States and Latin America showed only limited growth. The American market was even the one in which Rolex watches were the cheapest in 1964, but the strength of the dollar meant that American nationals often bought their watches outside the country. It was especially after 1970 that this market entered a phase of strong expansion.

Rolex's expansion in the American market and worldwide between 1965 and 1990 is difficult to analyse due to a lack of figures. However, an impressionistic analysis, based on correspondence with sports agent McCormack, JWT advertising campaigns, and the international press, highlights the decisive role played by two countries: the United States and Japan.

The American market exerted a decisive influence on Rolex's development from the second half of the 1960s. Against the backdrop of the Cold War, the tremendous economic boom, the myth of the American dream, and the cult of the self-made man provided a cultural context highly conducive to the reception of the new message developed by JWT.[72] Rolex embodied the exceptionality of successful men. This strong and coherent marketing positioning responded to a desire for social expression on the part of the white middle and upper classes. According to André Heiniger, Rolex's sales on the American market increased fivefold in the 1970s. In 1969, sales in the United States amounted to around $7.5 million.[73] This rose to around $11 million in 1973.[74] This fast-growing market accounted for around 20 per cent of total sales in 1980, compared with just 7.7 per cent in 1964.[75] At that time, the United States accounted for just 12 per cent of all Swiss watch exports.[76] While Rolex was virtually absent from this market before 1945, it had become one of the main bases of its growth. In 1977, the Geneva-based company bought a building on the famous Fifth Avenue in New York for $15 million. The firm's directors explained that "this decision was a sign of their confidence in the expansion of the American market".[77] Sales in the United States continued to grow throughout the 1980s. According to *L'Impartial*, in 1987 the American luxury watch market (watches costing more than $3,500) was worth between $800 million and $1 billion. It was occupied by ten major Swiss brands, of which Rolex accounted for half.[78] A few years later, a journalist from *Le Nouveau Quotidien* caricatured the profile of the typical Rolex customer in the United States as "a man in his fifties who likes to feel and show off 250 grams of gold on his wrist".[79]

Japan was the second market in which Rolex expanded rapidly. The brand was represented in the post-war period by the Swiss trading company Liebermann, Waelchli & Co, which represented various luxury brands in Japan, including Cartier and Chanel. The boom in parallel exports of Rolex watches in the early 1970s reflected the brand's success in Japan. Other European luxury brands, such as Louis Vuitton, were experiencing the same problem at the time.[80] As the parallel market in luxury goods was damaging in terms of price, profit, and brand image, manufacturers tried to combat the practice. In the case of Rolex, Liebermann Waelchli & Co. decided to refuse access to its after-sales service network to customers who had bought Rolex watches outside the official network. In 1973, however, the Japanese competition authorities ruled against the company, claiming that official retailers were monopolising the market.[81] The desire to strengthen control over distribution and marketing in the Japanese market led to the foundation of Rolex Japan Ltd in 1980.[82] Sales accelerated during the 1980s. Rolex represented access to wealth and luxury for the upper middle classes, who benefited from the rise in the yen and the financial bubble of 1985–1991. The watch brand represented luxury in the same way as Christian Dior or BMW.[83] This context was also favourable to a revival of parallel imports, which were now carried out by companies with sufficient capital to extend their sales network and set up their own technical service to maintain the products they sold.[84] Rolex Japan was now trying to restrict the supply of parts to its authorised retailers, leading parallel importers to seek parts supplies from Rolex agents in Europe and the United States.[85]

Other important markets included Switzerland and the then-British colony of Hong Kong. In 1972, Rolex entered a business relationship with Emperor Watch and Jewellery Ltd, one of Hong Kong's leading watch retailers.[86] Five years later, Hong Kong absorbed around 15 per cent of the watches manufactured by Rolex.[87] As for the Swiss market, it was based on collaboration with the Lucerne jeweller Bucherer. Its turnover, which also included jewellery and watch brands other than Rolex, was 109.6 million francs in 1978 and 329.1 million in 1985.[88] From 1984, Montres Rolex SA also operated a shop in Geneva called Chrono Time,[89] which would have been the only boutique to belong directly to the Geneva company.

Rolex's international expansion after the 1970s was driven by a new strategy that turned the brand into a concept expressing individual excellence and social success. It was the first watch brand to adopt an accessible luxury positioning. Statistics on sales of Rolex watches in Great Britain by price category show a clear upward trend between 1959 and 1964 (see Table 7.3). Although the heart of the price range remained in the £25–50 category, in which steel Rolex Oyster watches were particularly found, there was a sharp increase in the higher price categories. Watches costing more than £100 rose from 7 per cent to 18.5 per cent of sales, and those costing between £50 and £100 rose from 15 per cent to 20 per cent, leading to the veritable collapse of the entry-level segment (including Tudor watches), which fell from 35 per cent to 11 per cent of sales. In April 1965, the price of the steel Rolex Oyster even increased to £44, while its direct competitor, the steel Omega Seamaster, was still selling for £36.[90] Rolex's new positioning enabled it to remain competitive while increasing its prices. The transition from measuring instrument to concept generated juicy profit margins.

However, it was above all in the mid-1970s that a general upward trend in prices became visible. The prices of watches mentioned in sales catalogues for the years 1957–2023, compiled and posted online by the watchmaking blog Minus4plus6, provide a perfect illustration of this increase (see Figure 7.12). Deflated and represented in 1957 dollars, the prices of two of the most popular Rolex watches, the Datejust in steel and the Submariner Date in steel, show a steady increase in price.[91] They rose from around $250 and $270 in the second half of the 1970s to $538 and $572 respectively in 1989. Their price, measured

Table 7.3   Retail prices of Rolex watches on the UK market, market share in % by price category, 1959–1964

	Up to £25	£25–50	£50–100	Over £100
1959	35	43	15	7
1960	27	50	15	8
1961	26	45	17	12
1962	15	51	21	13
1963	13	48	23	16
1964	11	49	20	20

Source: HAT, JWT, HAT50/1/154/2/2/1-5, Rolex UK sales, 25 May 1965.

Figure 7.12 Rolex watch prices in constant dollars, 1957–2023

Note: The steel Datejust includes references 116200/126300/126200/126300 (Oyster Bracelet) and the steel Submariner Date includes references 1680/16610 /116610N/126610LN. Values are in 1957 dollars.

Source: www.minus4plus6.com/PriceEvolution.php# (consulted 8 August 2023). Inflation was calculated using figures from www.dollartimes.com/inflation/ (consulted 8 August 2023).

in constant dollars (without inflation), doubled during the 1980s. Furthermore, if we compare these values with changes in the average working wage over the same period, we can see that it was becoming increasingly difficult for the working classes to acquire such watches. In 1989, it took 179 hours' work to buy a Rolex Submariner and 168 for a Rolex Datejust, compared with around seventy hours' work in the second half of the 1970s (see Figure 7.13). The discourse on the exceptionality of men was accompanied by a social distancing of customers through price.

Rolex becomes world number one

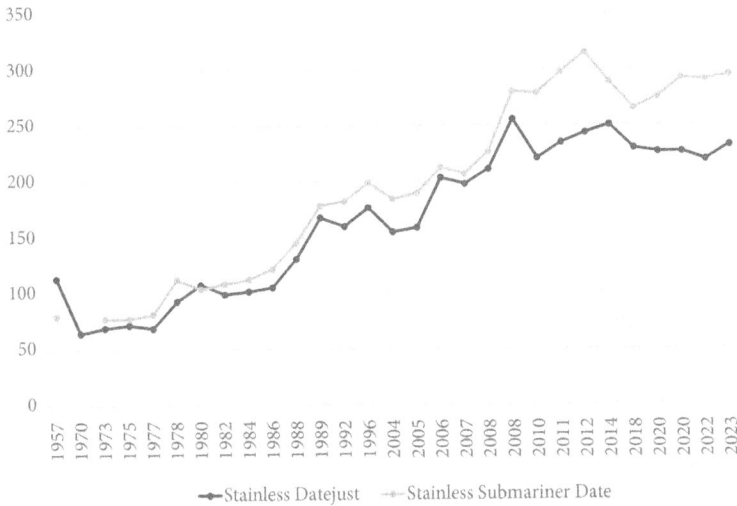

Figure 7.13 Number of working hours required for an American worker to buy a Rolex watch, 1957–2023

Source: See Figure 7.12 and Annual Wages, Unskilled Labor and Manufacturing Workers, hourly compensation in current USD, www.measuringworth.com/datasets/uswage/ (accessed 8 August 2023).

A company unaffected by the crisis

While the Swiss watch industry faced one of the biggest crises in its history between 1975 and 1985, one that threatened its very existence, Rolex got through the decade without any major problems. For example, in 1977 the Swiss ambassador to Canada deplored the decline of Swiss positions in the domestic watch market due to Japanese competition but added that "expensive Swiss watches still sell very well. The Rolex representative, for example, even increased his sales slightly last year."[92]

Better still, the watchmaking crisis strengthened Rolex's position and ensured its undisputed status as the world's leading watch brand. The statistics on chronometry certificates perfectly illustrate Rolex's resistance to the crisis, particularly in the face of its competitor Omega (see Figure 7.3). After reaching a peak of 230,341 certificates in 1974,

Rolex experienced two years of sharp decline. In 1976, it recorded just 135,501 certificates, its lowest level since 1967. In two years, the number of certificates fell by 42 per cent. The company was hit hard by the crisis, but this fall can probably also be explained by the liquidation of stocks and the desire to limit their replenishment. March 1975 was also the only time the Swiss press reported a slowdown in the Rolex group, announcing a reduction in working hours and short-term working at the Bienne and Geneva factories.[93] However, the number of certificates began to rise again in 1977, just as the Swiss watch industry was sinking into crisis. The record level set in 1974 was surpassed in 1980, ushering in a period of tremendous growth, so much so that the level of 580,000 chronometers was surpassed in 1990. This momentum was even more remarkable given that all of Rolex's direct competitors were experiencing major difficulties. The economic crisis was both short-lived and violent. It resembled a cyclical shock, whereas the oil crisis sent other Swiss watchmaking companies into a structural crisis that lasted until the mid-1980s.[94] How can such resilience be explained?

Gold prices and the watchmaking crisis according to the FTMH union (1980)

Gold to blame?

Omega watches are not selling well – or as well as they used to – because a large proportion of them are made of gold. And gold is now so expensive that watches are reaching unaffordable prices. This explanation is provided by the management of the SSIH. It is not convincing.

Omega's main competitor in this product range is Rolex, which doubled its production and sales during the 1970s. This company buys 10 to 12 tonnes of gold a year (nearly 300 million francs), making it the country's leading industrial user of precious metal.

And Rolex is doing very well.

Source: *La Lutte syndicale*, 5 November 1980.

First, it should be remembered that this major crisis did not originate with the advent of the quartz watch. This technical innovation strengthened the competitiveness of the Japanese competitor, but it was not the cause of the crisis.[95] The causes were structural (an industry based on the existence of a very large number of small and medium-sized companies) and strategic (the desire of Swiss watchmaking companies to be present in all market segments, from the entry-level Roskopf watch to the top-of-the-range watch). Swiss watchmakers wanted to offer a wide choice of products to consumers around the world, as they had done successfully since the mid-nineteenth century, but they did not have the industrial capacity to mass-produce this wide variety of products. Japanese competitors, Seiko in particular, adopted a diametrically opposed strategic objective since the beginning of the twentieth century: to mass-produce a limited number of high-quality watch models. This enabled them to invade the world market in the 1960s with cheap, precise mechanical watches.[96] The quartz revolution only strengthened Seiko's competitive advantage but did not establish it. In this context, Rolex was the only Swiss watch company to follow a similar strategy to Seiko. Its models were limited in number, industrially produced, and of very high quality. What's more, unlike Seiko, which focused its communication strategy solely on the excellence and affordability of its products, Rolex had a unique positioning (products of excellence for personalities of excellence) that made it a luxury brand.

The quartz revolution had a considerable impact on the competitiveness of watch brands. This new technology made precision inexpensive and accessible to all. Except for Rolex, the strategy of the major Swiss watch manufacturers, which was based on the development of high-precision instruments, became obsolete. A watch's reputation no longer rested on its ability to tell the exact time. This is all the more true given that, following the collapse of the Bretton Woods monetary system, the Swiss franc became extremely strong against the dollar, particularly in comparison with the yen. This reduced the attractiveness of Swiss watches on the American market. Rolex, however, was completely unaffected by this phenomenon, even experiencing strong growth in the

American market, where the price of its watches rose sharply. The reason for this success was that Rolex was not just a watch: it was a marker of social status. In August 1974, when the Swiss franc was soaring and the oil crisis had begun, JWT managers wrote in a report that Rolex sales were continuing to rise in the United States, even though the price had been increased twice since the beginning of 1973. Rolex's positioning in the luxury market enabled it to escape the crisis: "This has not seemed thus far to affect consumer acceptance of Rolex in that narrow income stratum which can afford it."[97] Although the situation deteriorated rapidly in 1975, Rolex's strategy enabled it to emerge from the crisis very quickly.

This positioning does not mean Rolex had no interest in new electronic technologies. On the contrary, it was one of the main Swiss companies to develop R&D activities in the field of quartz watches. On the one hand, it was a major partner of the Centre Electronique Horloger (CEH), a research company with capital of 480,000 francs, founded in 1962 by various partners led by Ebauches SA and the Fédération Horlogère to develop quartz technology for watchmaking.[98] Several watchmaking companies also took a minority stake of 5,000 francs, mainly IWC, Mido, Omega, Tissot, and Montres Rolex SA.[99] The CEH was the first company in the world to develop a prototype quartz watch, which took part in the chronometric competition held by the Neuchâtel Observatory in 1967.[100] While continuing its in-house work, Rolex remained involved with the CEH until the creation of the Centre Suisse d'Electronique et de Microtechnique SA (CSEM) in 1983, which took over the CEH laboratory. Montres Rolex SA remained a shareholder in the CSEM after it was founded.[101] It also sent its directors to sit on the bodies of the CEH. Marc Nardin, briefly technical director of Montres Rolex SA, was a member of the Board of Directors of the CEH when it was founded. In 1969, he gave a lecture entitled "The CEH Quartz Wristwatch" at an event organised by the Geneva National Institute.[102] His successor, René Le Coultre, an engineer with a degree from the Swiss Federal Institute of Technology in Zurich and former technical adviser to the Fédération Horlogère, had led the team that developed the first quartz watch prototype at the CEH. He became president of the CEH in 1981, a position he held until 1992.[103]

On the other hand, Rolex also developed intense in-house R&D activity in the field of electronic watches. The statistics on patent applications highlight the importance of this, since more than one in three patents obtained between 1960 and 1990 related to quartz watches (see above, p. 158). In 1971, André Heiniger hired Le Coultre to develop a Rolex quartz watch.[104] The Geneva company opened its own electronics laboratory that year. A series of Oyster quartz watches was launched on the market in 1977. Rolex did not grant any special status to these watches, which were also submitted to the COSC.

The statistics on chronometry certificates illustrate Rolex's quartz watch strategy (see Figure 7.14). In 1977, the Group obtained an initial series of eighty-three certificates. Industrial production was launched in the years that followed, with a total of 83,995 chronometry certificates obtained by Rolex for quartz movements during the 1980s. This number may seem high, but it represents only 2.4 per cent of the total of 3.5 million Rolex chronometers during this decade. This perfectly illustrates the brand's continued concentration on mechanical products. Moreover, Rolex only held a 23.5 per cent share of the total number of chronometry certificates awarded by the COSC for quartz movements during the 1980s, compared with 90.3 per cent for all chronometers. Other companies, therefore, were much more actively involved in electronic chronometry. This is particularly true of Omega, which had virtually abandoned mechanical chronometers and had obtained more than 170,000 certificates for quartz movements. Girard Perregaux SA received more than 60,000. Thus, for Rolex, the development of quartz watches should be understood first and foremost as a technology watch activity. In the late 1970s and early 1980s, it was important to master this technology, whose potentially disruptive effects could not yet be assessed. However, this new technology did not in any way call into question the brand's strategy. In fact, after 1986, there was a steady decline in the number of Rolex quartz chronometers. None was registered in 1990.[105]

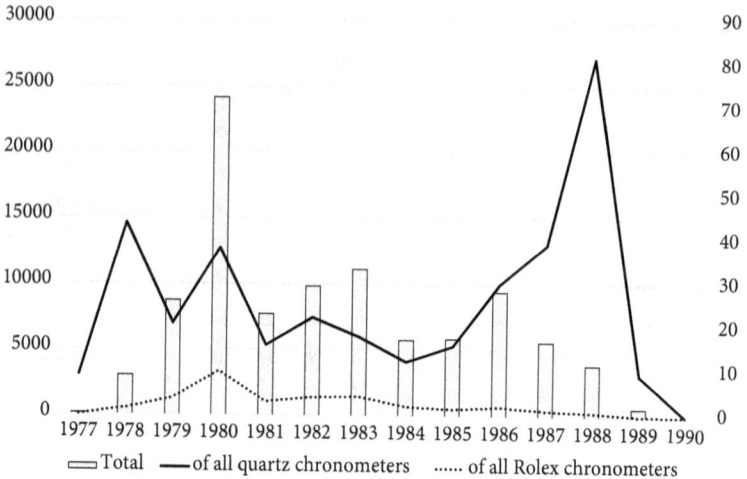

Figure 7.14 Rolex quartz chronometers, 1977–1990
Source: COSC reports, 1977–1990.

Rolex's position in the Swiss watch industry strengthened considerably during the crisis. In the canton of Geneva, according to federal business censuses, the largest watchmaking employer, Montres Rolex SA, saw its workforce grow from 593 in 1975 to 813 in 1985, representing 14.1 per cent and 18.9 per cent respectively of total watchmaking employment in the canton.[106] In addition, Rolex's competitiveness during this period contributed to an in-depth transformation of the Swiss watchmaking industry and made Geneva the place par excellence for the sale and distribution of luxury watches.[107] The canton of Geneva's share of the total value of Swiss watch exports rose from 12.7 per cent in 1972 to 37 per cent in 1985. It remained at around a third until the beginning of the twenty-first century.[108] This transformation largely reflects the success of Rolex and the importance of this brand in the Swiss watch industry.

Counterfeiting: the price of success

Rolex's worldwide reputation and power of attraction quickly made it one of the most copied watches. Counterfeiting, imitation, and misuse of the brand have been evident at least since the post-war years. Reports from Swiss consulates and embassies around the world informed Rolex of these abuses. In 1952, for example, the Singapore consulate reported that "for some days now, small Chinese and Hindu street traders have been selling lighters bearing the Omega and Rolex marks on this market for S$2.50. The sellers admit that these lighters are made in Japan, although there is no mention of where they were manufactured."[109]

However, counterfeiting became a worrying activity, especially since the mid-1960s, because of the industrial dimensions it acquired. The Swiss watchmaking industry was partly responsible for the growth of this phenomenon. Between 1961 and 1965, the major manufacturers obtained the end of state control over the industry. It was then possible to manufacture parts, such as cases and dials, and assemble movements outside Switzerland. In addition, in the mid-1960s, the Swiss Federation of the Watch Industry encouraged the transfer of the production of case components to Hong Kong.[110] The internationalisation of watch production systems led to a rapid increase in counterfeiting. Workshops based mainly in Asia, but also in Italy and Switzerland, began copying on a large scale. The counterfeiting market rapidly became international, as the reports drawn up by Swiss diplomats posted abroad attest. This affected not only Rolex but all luxury brands such as Cartier, Omega, Piaget, and Longines – but Rolex's particular positioning, with its brand image expressing individual success, made it a prime target of counterfeiters.

Letter from the Swiss ambassador to Senegal to Montres Rolex SA, Geneva, 8 August 1967

To the Executive Director,

For some time now, Rolex watches have been sold on the streets of Dakar, under the cloak, at the fanciest prices. The sellers, generally young unemployed people, are looking to sell their wares, preferably to tourists.

I have not been able to determine how these watches were imported into Senegal. I assume that they were smuggled in from

---

the Far East, by sailors or via the port of Bathurst in Gambia. There is a large smuggling trade between Gambia and Senegal.

The Rolex watch being sold, a specimen of which is enclosed, is certainly a fake. I thought I was doing the right thing by buying one after haggling over the price. I paid 2,000 CFA francs, or 35 Swiss francs, which is undoubtedly still very expensive for the quality of this watch. But asking prices vary between 15 and 20,000 CFA francs. The seller claims that it's a Swiss watch, more precisely a Rolex made in Switzerland, as the dial seems to attest.

In view of this situation, I think that you should take action to find out where this manufacture originated. For my part, I am prepared to draw the attention of the Senegalese authorities to the existence of this clandestine traffic. However, I wouldn't want to do this without your formal agreement.

A copy of this communication is being sent, for information, to the Trade Division of the Federal Department of Economic Affairs and to the Watchmaking Federation in Bienne.

Yours sincerely

The Swiss ambassador.

Source: Swiss Diplomatic Documents, dodis.ch/60599.

Since the 1970s, Montres Rolex SA has developed intense legal activity to combat smuggling and imitations without mercy. In particular, it collaborates closely with the Federation of Watch Industry, which has had an analysis service to examine cases of counterfeiting since 1969, and with the Office of the Public Prosecutor of the Confederation.[111] Interpol and the Swiss diplomatic network make it possible to intervene anywhere in the world and arrest Italian or Swiss traffickers.[112] The fight against the boom in counterfeit watches, which has not yet been the subject of any major academic study, is not limited to Rolex. It is also a subject not directly related to the issues addressed in this book, which is why the analysis of this dimension of Rolex's success is not developed further here.

Conclusive remarks

In 1965, Montres Rolex SA inaugurated its new headquarters in the Acacias district of Geneva. The buildings, made of concrete, glass and aluminium, expressed the power of the brand (see Figure 7.15). A few months earlier, André Heiniger had been appointed executive director of the company. He was to implement an original strategy, unique in the watch industry, that would make Rolex the world's leading watch brand. This strategy could be described as conservative in industrial terms and innovative in marketing terms.

On the one hand, Heiniger maintained the product portfolio and production system put in place over the previous two decades without making any major changes. In terms of design management, Rolex represented technical excellence in Swiss watchmaking, embodied by

Figure 7.15 New head office of Montres Rolex SA, 1965

Note: The architecture of the new headquarters of Montres Rolex SA, inaugurated in 1965, expresses the technical characteristics that the Rolex Oyster is intended to embody: an indestructible, hermetically sealed monolith.

a handful of iconic models mass-produced in the Group's factories. Its products were of the highest quality and had a very high profile in the market. Admittedly, the style of these products was slightly adapted over time, but there was no fundamental innovation in this area, unlike the competition, which multiplied models and collections. The data on trademark registrations well illustrate Rolex's product development policy. Between 1960 and 1990, the Group registered a total of fifty-eight trademarks, all of which concerned existing collections, apart from Cellini and Cosmograph, which were launched in the early 1960s. In addition, Montres Tudor SA registered only nine trademarks for its various collections, and the Marconi Watch was no longer active in the watchmaking sector.[113] According to the *New York Times*, Tudor watches, sold for less than $500, accounted for less than 10 per cent of sales in 1980.[114] Rolex, therefore, concentrated on a limited number of models, which were high-precision watches, generally with chronometry certificates. This choice enabled the industrial production of quality watches. Such an industrial strategy is rare in the Swiss watchmaking industry. Rolex's main competitors, notably Longines, Omega, and Zenith, multiplied their models to respond to the diversity of demand, which made it difficult, if not impossible, to establish true mass production. The only company to adopt a similar industrial strategy to Rolex was Japanese watchmaker Seiko.[115]

Heiniger was also extremely innovative in his marketing strategy for Rolex. Working with advertising agents and public relations specialists and consultants, mainly American, including JWT, he succeeded in transforming the very nature of his brand. Between the second half of the 1960s and the early 1970s, Rolex underwent a profound transformation of its image: it no longer expressed the high precision of its watches but the exceptionality of those who wore them. It conveyed a strong emotional value. Rolex was now an accessible luxury item.[116] In October 1980, the *New York Times* published a long article entitled "The Rolex: How the Swiss Sell Status", in which it was asserted that "individual achievement and appreciation of the timepiece are linked".[117]

The years 1960–1990, therefore, represent a pivotal period in the history of Rolex. Its managers succeeded in establishing a competitive advantage based on both a perfectly mastered production system and an original marketing position. Moreover, the Geneva-based group maintained this dual policy throughout the decades. The emergence of the Japanese competitor – targeting the mass market – and the advent of the quartz watch had little influence on Rolex's strategy, which enabled it to get through the great crisis of 1975–1985 unscathed. Better still, it was during this crisis that the Geneva-based brand definitively won out over its direct competitor, Omega.

Finally, Rolex's tremendous success has made it a benchmark in terms of marketing positioning for other Swiss watch companies. By demonstrating that a watch is much more than a precision instrument, Rolex has highlighted the importance of integrating a narrative dimension into product development – what I call intangible design. During the 1980s, this new way of designing watches led to great success for several companies, both in the entry-level segment (Swatch) and the exclusive luxury segment (Blancpain). Since 1990, the gradual transformation of Swiss watchmaking into a luxury industry has been based on a product development strategy whose origins can be traced back to that implemented by Rolex in the 1960s.[118]

Notes

1 *Tribune Le Matin*, 27 September 1977. This represents approximately $72 million in 2022; indexed to the consumer price index; www.measuri ngworth.com/index.php (accessed 15 October 2023).

2 Donzé, "L'industrie de la montre roskopf en Suisse".

3 Donzé, *Longines*, Chapter 4.

4 Donzé, "Dynamics of Innovation in the Electronic Watch Industry".

5 *Recensement 2017*, La Chaux-de-Fonds: Convention patronale, 2018, p. 9. The level of employment once again exceeded 60,000 in 2022, for the first time since 1975, but it is still a long way from the peak of the 1960s; https://cpih. ch/statistiques/ (accessed 15 October 2023). The repositioning of the watch industry towards luxury is generating huge profits, but the effects remain limited on employment in Switzerland.

6 *FOSC*, 10 October 1960.

7 In his book, based in part on interviews with Betty Wilsdorf-Mettler, widow of Hans, and Hans-Helmut Kübel, Gisbert L. Brunner highlights the tensions between the Wilsdorf heirs and André Heiniger. Brunner, *The Watch Book*, p. 12.

8 SFA, E4264#2006-96, *Rapport d'enquête du Service cantonal des naturalisations*, Geneva, 8 June 1962.

9 *FOSC*, 20 February 1964.

10 Duke University, Rubenstein Library, J. Walter Thompson Papers, Review Board Records, Account Summary, 31 January 1973.

11 Ibid., July 1968.

12 Ibid., 20 July 1973.

13 *FOSC*, 14 May 1970 and 3 June 1970. This company had been bought by the American watch manufacturer Bulova in 1966 and experienced major managerial and financial difficulties in the 1970s and 1980s. See Donzé, *L'invention du luxe*, pp. 144–145.

14 *FOSC*, 7 August 1972 and 29 July 1975.

15 *FOSC*, 29 July 1975.

16 *FOSC*, 7 August 1972 and 18 August 1987.

17 Ginalski et al., *Les élites économiques suisses au XXᵉ siècle*.

18 *Nouvelle Revue de Lausanne*, 2 February 1965.

19 Izuishi, *Rorekkusu no himitsu*, pp. 199–209.

20 The "Benvenuto Cellini" trademark was registered in 1956 and "Cellini" in 1968. WIPO, www3.wipo.int/madrid/monitor/fr/# (accessed 29 October 2021).

21 Izuishi, *Rorekkusu no himitsu*, p. 227.

22 Donzé, *L'invention du luxe*, pp. 133–136.

23 May, "Rolex: The Timeless Timepiece".

24 *New York Times*, 19 October 1980.

25 Kapferer and Bastien, *The Luxury Strategy*.

26 For example, patent no. 377726 obtained in 1962; Espacenet, https://worldwide.espacenet.com (accessed 16 February 2022).

27 Espacenet, https://worldwide.espacenet.com (accessed 16 February 2022).

28 Donzé, "Global Competition and Technological Innovation".

29 Donzé, *Histoire sociale et économique de la chronométrie*, p. 155.

30 *L'Impartial*, 2 October 1970.

31 *L'Impartial*, 15 September 1972.

32 *L'Impartial*, 26 October 1973.

33 *FOSC*, 1959, p. 1747, 1982, p. 3278, and 1985, p. 1470; Marti, *Le renouveau horloger*, p. 78.

34 *FOSC*, 1979, p. 1187.

35 *FOSC*, 1974, p. 312, and 1982, p. 1535.

36 Marti, *Le renouveau horloger*, p. 78.

37 *Journal de Genève*, 27 March 1971.

38 SFA, E7211A#20037#376.

39 SFA, E7175B#1976197#883, letter from the Federal Office for Industry, Trade and Labour to the Federal Aliens Police, 3 February 1965, *La lutte syndicale*, 12 October 1988, and Federal Census of Enterprises, 1975.

40 Convention patronale, *Recensement 2007*, La Chaux-de-Fonds: CPIH, 2008.

41 *La lutte syndicale*, 14 September 1977.

42 HAT, JWT, HAT50/1/154/1 Rolex, reports of meeting, 23 January 1962.

43 HAT, JWT, HAT50/1/154/1 Rolex, report of a meeting held in Geneva on 9 March 1962.

44 *New York Times*, 22 September 1966.

45 HAT, JWT, HAT50/1/154/1 Rolex, report of a meeting held in Geneva on 20 July 1962. Rolex offered the following publications for Great Britain: *The Observer, Sunday Times, Sunday Telegraph, The Economist, Punch, Vogue, The Queen, Birmingham Post, Leeds Yorkshire Post, The Scotsman, Glasgow Herald.*

46 HAT, JWT, HAT50/1/154/1 Rolex, reports of meeting, 20 October 1965. A year later, however, Rolex advertised in this magazine to target young men with high incomes and because the Eterna watch brand was considering doing so. Ibid., 22 February 1966.

47 HAT, JWT, HAT50/1/154/1 Rolex, reports of meeting, 19 September 1962.

48 HAT, JWT, HAT50/1/154/1, a brief summary of Rolex and Tudor advertising country by country, 1 March 1963.

49 Duke University, J. Walter Thompson Company Newsletter Collection, vol. 21, no. 42, 30 December 1966.

50 Frank, *The Conquest of Cool*.

51 Ibid., pp. 102–103; *New York Times*, 13 September 1997.

52 HAT, JWT, HAT50/1/154/1 Rolex, reports of meeting, 8 November 1966.

53 HAT, JWT, HAT50/1/154/2 Rolex, *Rolex Campaign 1967*, undated.

54 *The New York Times*, 15 December 1980.

55 University of Massachusetts Library (UML), Mark H. McCormack Papers (MHM), letter to Garmo, McCaffery Incorporated, 17 December 1967, and to André Heiniger, 22 July 1972.

56 Duke University, J. Walter Thompson Company Newsletter Collection, vol. 23, no. 38, 15 November 1968.

57 UML, MHM, Letter from Mark H. McCormack to André Heiniger, 22 July 1972. In 1985, René Dentan, director of Rolex's American subsidiary, stated in the American press that Rolex did not give money to celebrities with whom it collaborated but only a watch and the fame that came with appearing in

the brand's advertisements (Duke University, Rubenstein Library, J. Walter Thompson Collection, Account files, RO1, *Modern Jeweler*, February 1983, p. 53). McCormack's archives show, however, that the celebrities for whom he was the agent, notably Palmer and Killy, received substantial financial contributions, and that some of them regularly asked for increases.

58 HAT, JWT, HAT50/1/154/1 Rolex, reports of meeting, 8 November 1966.

59 *New York Times*, 9 September 1980.

60 UML, MHM, letter from Mark H. McCormack to R.A.A. Holt, 13 July 1981.

61 UML, MHM, letter from Mark H. McCormack to Andre J. Heiniger, 8 September 1987.

62 Ibid.

63 UML, MHM, letter from Mark H. McCormack to Andre J. Heiniger, 30 March 1990.

64 *Journal de Genève*, 24 September 1976.

65 *Journal de Genève*, 3 March 1978.

66 HAT, JWT, HAT50/1/154/1, a brief summary of Rolex and Tudor advertising country by country, 1 March 1963.

67 *Rolex Magazine*, no. 2, 2014, p. 132.

68 HAT, JWT, HAT50/1/154/1, a brief summary of Rolex and Tudor advertising country by country, 1 March 1963.

69 Ibid.

70 Ibid.

71 Ibid.

72 Samuel, *The American Dream*.

73 Duke University, Rubenstein Library, J. Walter Thompson Papers, Review Board Records, Account Summary, 29 January 1970.

74 Ibid., 20 July 1973.

75 *New York Times*, 19 October 1980; HAT, JWT, HAT50/1/154/2/1–5, Rolex Tudor exports, n.d.

76 Swiss foreign trade statistics, 1980.

77 *Tribune Le Matin*, 27 September 1977.

78 *L'Impartial*, 29 April 1987.

79 *Le Nouveau Quotidien*, 24 April 1993.

80 Donzé, *Selling Europe to the World*, p. 12. Parallel imports exploded in the 1970s as a result of sharp fluctuations in the foreign exchange market following the end of the Bretton Woods system.

81 *Nouvelle Revue de Lausanne*, 23 May 1973.

82 *Zainichi gaishikei kigyo fairu.*

83 *Nihon keizai shimbun*, 30 September 1985 and 14 November 1985.

84 *Nihon keizai shimbun*, 6 and 11 November 1986.
85 *Nihon keizai shimbun*, 22 December 1986.
86 www.emperorwatchjewellery.com/en/brand-heritage.php (accessed 5 January 2022).
87 *24 Heures*, 3 February 1977.
88 *Journal de Genève*, 14 February 1987.
89 *FOSC*, 30 July 1984.
90 HAT, JWT, HAT50/1/154/2/2/1-5, Rolex UK sales, 25 May 1965.
91 I chose steel models to avoid the impact of sharp fluctuations in the price of gold and silver over the long term.
92 Swiss diplomatic documents (DODIS), letter from the Swiss ambassador to Canada to the Trade Division, 13 May 1977, https://dodis.ch/50990 (accessed 15 July 2023).
93 *Tribune Le Matin*, 21 March 1975. It should be noted, however, that Rolex's subcontractors, particularly the case and bracelet manufacturers, were harder hit by the crisis. Several of Rolex's suppliers in Geneva in particular experienced industrial action and conflicts with the unions during the crisis. Steinauer, *L'horloge flétrie*.
94 Donzé, "Global Competition and Technological Innovation"; Bohlhater, *Die Uhrenkrisen der 1930er- und 1970/80er-Jahre in der Schweiz*.
95 Donzé, "Global Competition and Technological Innovation".
96 Donzé, *Industrial Development*, pp. 160–170.
97 Duke University, Rubenstein Library, J. Walter Thompson Papers, Review Board Records, no. 26, 20 July 1973.
98 Perret et al., *Microtechniques et mutations horlogères*, Chapter 4.
99 Ibid., p. 142.
100 However, it was the Japanese company Seiko that was the first in the world to market a quartz watch, in December 1969. Donzé, *Industrial Development*, p. 137.
101 Perret et al., *Microtechniques et mutations horlogères*, p. 240.
102 *Journal de Genève*, 22 March 1969.
103 Trueb, *Zeitzeugen der Quarzrevolution*, pp. 47–51.
104 Trueb, Ramm, and Wenzig, *Die Elektrifizierung der Armbanduhr*, pp. 182–185.
105 A few thousand certificates were obtained again in the second half of the 1990s.
106 Federal Census of Enterprises, 1975 and 1985, quoted in Donzé, *L'invention du luxe*, pp. 124–125.
107 Donzé, *L'invention du luxe*.

108 Ibid., p. 126.
109 MIH, CSH, letter from CSH to Rolex Watch, 4 November 1952.
110 Donzé, *The Business of Time*, pp. 104–109.
111 *FAN – L'Express*, 21 May 1989.
112 AF, E4327#199094#64.
113 WIPO database.
114 *New York Times*, 19 October 1980.
115 Donzé, "The Hybrid Production System".
116 Researchers in luxury management distinguish between exclusive luxury, aimed at a small elite and based on extremely expensive products generally made by hand, and accessible luxury, aimed at the upper-middle classes, which includes industrial goods with a high emotional value. See Allérès, "Spécifictés et stratégies marketing des différents univers du luxe".
117 *New York Times*, 19 October 1980.
118 Donzé, "La transformation de l'horlogerie suisse en industrie du luxe".

8

Rolex and the changing luxury goods industry (since 1990)

Since 1990, the Swiss watchmaking industry has been repositioning itself towards luxury, characterised by a sharp increase in the value of exports coupled with a steady decline in volumes. The average export value of a Swiss watch rose from 143 francs in 1990 to 1,501 francs in 2022, an increase mainly due to mechanical watches, which represented only 41 per cent of the total value of exports in 1990 but 87 per cent in 2019.[1] Luxury watches are certainly nothing new. They have existed since the eighteenth century, and Rolex is precisely the expression of the importance of this market for certain companies. However, until the 1990s, luxury was only a specific segment of the watch market – most companies were targeting a mass market. The structural transformation of the Swiss watch industry over the past three decades has seen the entire industry reposition itself towards luxury. Luxury watchmaking is no longer the exception; it has become the norm.

The rise in the average price of watches is one of the most visible expressions of this phenomenon. Between 1989 and 2012, the price of a Rolex at US retailers, measured in constant dollars, almost doubled, before entering a phase of stagnation (see Figure 7.12, p. 182). Compared with the purchasing power of the American worker, the trend is similar. Today, it takes almost 300 hours of work to hope to acquire a steel Submariner, nearly four times as much as in the early 1970s (see Figure 7.13, p. 183). The situation is identical for all luxury brands. An Audemars Piguet watch, for example, now costs an average of 45,000 francs, whereas its iconic Royal Oak model was launched in 1972 for around five times less, which at the time seemed exorbitant.[2]

For Rolex, the main consequence of this industrial transformation was the emergence of new competitors who attempted to challenge its position of absolute domination of the luxury watch market – essentially the Omega and Cartier brands. Both underwent a major revival in the 1990s, as part of their respective groups, the Swatch Group and Compagnie Financière Richemont. Omega benefited from a new marketing strategy implemented after the arrival in 1992 of Jean-Claude Biver as the head of the marketing and communication department.[3] As for Cartier, it underwent an initial phase of strong development as part of its cooperation with Ebel and its director Pierre-Alain Blum, with whom it founded a factory in La Chaux-de-Fonds in 1992 before opening its own manufacturing company in 2000.[4] These two brands adopted a strategy similar to that of Rolex – namely, the mass production of quality watches aimed at the accessible luxury segment. However, despite their undeniable growth since the 1990s, they have not succeeded in overturning Rolex's status as the world's leading watch brand. Rolex's sales also showed strong growth between 1990 and 2022, and Rolex remains far ahead of its two main competitors (see Table 8.1). The gap is even widening. In 2022, Rolex generated 3.4 times more sales than Cartier and 3.8 times more than Omega.

The statistics on chronometry certificates issued by the COSC perfectly illustrate the transformation of the competitive environment and Rolex's continued leadership (see Figure 7.3, p. 160). Rolex saw the number of its certifications continue to rise, from 583,108 in 1990 to 795,716 in 2015. However, although it remains, by far, the largest registrant, its share of the total has fallen sharply, dropping from a virtual monopoly in 1990 (94.2 per cent) to just under half of all registrations in 2015 (46 per cent). The main competitor is Omega, with a 29.6 per cent share of certifications in 2015. On the same date, Cartier, which has not incorporated technical excellence into its heritage strategy, had no chronometry certificates.

Other watch brands have also seen strong sales growth over the past two decades. By 2022, four other companies had sales of over one billion francs. However, their products are positioned in different segments

Table 8.1   *Estimated sales of Rolex, Omega, and Cartier, in millions of francs,*
1990–2022

	1990	2000	2010	2022
Rolex	1,400	2,200	4,400	9,300
Omega	600	1,100	1,750	2,470
Cartier	510	850	1,800	2,750

Sources: L'Hebdo, 16 June 1988 (Rolex 1990 measured in an extension based on COSC statistics of 1987 estimate provided here); Compagnie Financière Richemont, Annual Report, 1991 and 2001 (Cartier 1990 and 2000; Cartier brand accounts for around 75 per cent of Luxco SA division sales and watchmaking 43 per cent, according to the 1990 annual report and L'Impartial, 27 April 1988; similar proportion for 2000); Swatch Group, Annual Report, 1990 and 2000 (Omega 1990 and 2000; estimated at 35 per cent of watch sales); L'Hebdo, 26 November 1999 (Rolex 2000); Vontobel (2010), Morgan Stanley (2023).

from Rolex: exclusive luxury for the independent manufacturers Patek Philippe, Audemars Piguet, and Richard Mille, and premium for Longines, a Swatch Group subsidiary.[5] They are, therefore, not direct competitors to Rolex.

As a result, Rolex has been able to maintain and strengthen its status as the world's leading watch brand despite the dramatic change in competitive conditions. This chapter discusses four main elements that contributed to strengthening Rolex's leadership: the creation of a centralised group, the continuation of the same marketing strategy, a stronger presence in the global luxury market, and the role of the Tudor brand.

The creation of a centralised group

The repositioning of many watch brands towards luxury led to strong competition for the supply of mechanical movement components on the one hand and exterior parts (cases, bracelets, and dials) on the other. While Swatch Group holds a near-monopoly position for some of the former, the move to Asia to relocate production of the latter has led to a scarcity of Swiss manufacturing.[6] In order to develop and market high-quality mechanical watches, watch brands need to guarantee their ability to acquire the necessary components. Since 2000, there has been a major drive in the Swiss watch industry to buy out suppliers and invest in production resources.[7] At Rolex, this policy of control takes two forms, leading to the vertical integration of production within a centralised manufacturer: the in-house development of watch components and movements and the purchase of suppliers of watch parts.

At the turn of the twenty-first century, Geneva-based Montres Rolex SA began acquiring its main suppliers, successively purchasing Virex (1998) and Joli Poli (1999) cases; Gay Frères (1998) bracelets; Beyeler (2000) dials; and Boninchi (2001) winding crowns. A few years later, it reorganised its production sites in Geneva, opening a factory in Plan-les-Ouates (2005), transforming its Acacias Centre (2006), and opening a new site in Chêne-Bourg (2007).[8] As a result of this reorganisation, the number of sites in the canton of Geneva fell from seventeen in 2004 to just three in 2008.[9] Vertical expansion was accompanied by rationalisation of investments and concentration. This has helped make Rolex Geneva's largest watchmaking employer, with several thousand employees.[10] Immigrant workers and cross-border commuters helped Rolex grow. In 1995, Gil Baillod, editor-in-chief of *L'Impartial* and a moral authority on the Swiss watchmaking industry, wrote in the columns of his daily newspaper: "Carmen, Angela, Maria, Francesca and all their Spanish, Italian and cross-border sisters are responsible for the legendary good workmanship of the largest watch manufacturer in Switzerland and indeed in the world!"[11] Meanwhile, the Manufacture des Montres Rolex SA in Bienne acquired the micromechanics company Micrometal AG, based in the same town (2001).[12]

In parallel with the redeployment of activities in Geneva, Montres Rolex SA merged with its movement producer, Manufacture des Montres Rolex SA, in Bienne. In 2001, Harry Borer stepped down as chairman of the latter after more than thirty years in the business. The next generation of Aegler–Borer family descendants preferred to sell the business to the Geneva company rather than continue managing it.[13] Montres Rolex SA acquired the company in 2004. Bertrand Gros and Patrick Heiniger, respectively chairman and executive director of Montres Rolex SA, joined the Bienne-based company's Board of Directors that year to oversee its takeover, which was officially completed in 2005 (see Table A.1, p. 235). However, the production centre and jobs were maintained in Bienne – new factories were even built in the city between 2009 and 2012.

The 2000s saw a profound transformation in the way Rolex was organised. It became a truly integrated manufacturer with power concentrated in the Geneva head office. In 2002, Montres Rolex SA was renamed Rolex SA, illustrating the Genevan company's desire for centralised power. This change was the work of Patrick Heiniger, son of André, who was appointed executive director of Montres Rolex SA in 1992 and a member of its Board of Directors in 1997. Born in Argentina in 1950, Patrick Heiniger studied law in Geneva and New York before becoming a partner in the law firm, Heiniger, Gros & Waltenspühl, founded in Geneva in the early 1980s.[14] Specialising in real estate and finance, he first joined the Board of Directors of Montres Rolex SA in 1984,[15] his father having decided to train a young man in his thirties to become his successor. Patrick Heiniger subsequently rose through the ranks, becoming sales director in 1986 before relinquishing his directorship the following year.[16] He then joined the boards of Marconi Watch SA (a financial company affiliated with Montres Rolex SA) and Rolex Holding SA.[17]

Bertrand Gros, a business lawyer and Patrick Heiniger's partner, played a key role alongside Heiniger at the helm of Rolex. A director of numerous financial and real estate companies, Gros joined the Board of Directors of Montres Rolex SA in 1990 and became chairman in 1997, succeeding André Heiniger. He held this position for twenty-five years until 2022. In addition to his activities at the head of Rolex, Gros was also involved with the Federation of the Swiss Watch Industry, where he was an expert on the legal commission and the anti-counterfeiting group.[18]

The management of Montres Rolex SA remained stable throughout the 1990s and 2000s. The Heiniger–Gros pair ran Rolex without major interference from the Board of Directors. During these two decades, it was mainly Genevan notables, apart from Olympic champion Jean-Claude Killy, who were appointed to the board. The links with the Swiss business elite remained superficial. The professional profiles of the board members also suggest limited knowledge of managing a luxury watch brand. As had been the case since the late 1950s, their presence was intended to ensure harmonious relations with the owner of Montres Rolex SA, the Hans Wilsdorf Foundation. Recruitment to the Board of Directors thus continued its elitist tradition.

It should also be noted that the company was then run by business lawyers, which suggests that managing the war chest accumulated since the 1960s was as important as that of the watch brand itself. Rolex's independence, as well as its ability to verticalise and reorganise its production in the 1990s and 2000s through self-financing, is a remarkable achievement in itself. A comparison with the Swatch Group (SG) easily highlights Rolex's financial strength. Between 1990 and 2020, SG distributed a total of 5.8 billion francs to its shareholders – mainly the Hayek family.[19] Moreover, these juicy cash distributions were not at the expense of investment in SG's production facilities, which remain among the most modern in the world. SG's financial independence was also strengthened during this period, with the equity ratio rising from 54.6 per cent in 1990 to 85 per cent in 2020. By comparison, Rolex has no shareholders other than the Wilsdorf Foundation. Nor does it have to spend hundreds of millions of francs to buy back its own shares on the stock market in order to improve their price and distribute them to its managers, unlike SG and, above all, Richemont.[20] Belonging to a foundation, therefore, has a decisive positive impact on Rolex's independence. Rolex sets aside the funds necessary for its operations and remits the balance to the Hans Wilsdorf Foundation, which ensures the growth of its watchmaking brand. The wealth accumulated by Rolex and the Hans Wilsdorf Foundation, estimated for the latter at around ten billion francs in 2008,[21] does not come solely from the sale of watches. Profits are reinvested in various financial and property transactions. In 1994, a dispute between the Union Bank of Switzerland (UBS) and its main shareholder, BK Vision, publicly revealed some of Rolex Holding SA's stock market investments. The latter held not only 17.4 per cent of the capital of BK Vision (founded in 1991 by BZ Gruppe, the company of asset manager Martin Ebner, to manage a fund of around two billion francs in UBS and Zurich Insurance) but also 17.4 per cent of the capital of a second BZ Gruppe investment fund, Pharma Vision (four billion francs in assets in Swiss and foreign pharmaceutical companies).[22] Rolex and the Wilsdorf Foundation also have major financial investments in the United States.[23]

Finance was, therefore, essential to Rolex's independent development, which is no doubt why the firm's management was entrusted to two business lawyers in the 1990s. Patrick Heiniger resigned at the end of 2008 under unclear circumstances, probably linked to losses on the financial markets during the Global Financial Crisis of 2007–2008. Executive management was taken over in 2009 by chief financial officer (CFO) Bruno Meier, a former manager of Deutsche Bank's Geneva subsidiary who moved to Rolex in 2005.[24]

However, this appointment was only temporary due to a financial emergency. Increased competition in the global luxury market, particularly in China, meant that Rolex needed strategists rather than financiers at the helm. After just two years as chief executive officer (CEO), Meier left the company in 2011, replaced by Gian Riccardo Marini, director of the Italian subsidiary, who knew the brand inside out.[25] But his presence was short-lived also, as in 2015, aged sixty-seven, he retired, although he remained on good terms with Rolex SA and sat on its Board of Directors until 2019.

Jean-Frédéric Dufour was appointed CEO of Rolex SA in 2015. Born into an old family of Geneva industrialists and a graduate of the University of Geneva, he had considerable experience in the watch industry, beginning his career with Chopard in 1994 before moving on to the Swatch Group and Ulysse Nardin and then being appointed CEO of Zenith in 2009.[26] Experience in luxury management was now an essential resource when it came to running Rolex. Moreover, Dufour's arrival as CEO was accompanied by a fundamental change in the way Board members were recruited. Representatives of Geneva's upper class were no longer the target but managers with experience in the luxury goods industry. The six new directors appointed since 2015 include the owner of Bon Génie department stores (Nicolas Brunschwig), an independent

Figure 8.1 Rolex SA's head office

Note: Business growth and company takeovers made Rolex the largest employer in the canton of Geneva at the end of the 2010s. The number of employees rose from 2,585 in 1999 to 4,513 in 2019 (Tribune de Genève, 2 October 2019).

Source: Rolex SA.

jeweller (Manuel Bouvier), a former CEO of LVMH's watch and jewellery division (Philippe Pascal), and the commercial director of Zurich Opera (Christian Berner) (see Table A.3, p. 240). For the first time since Wilsdorf's death, Board members were helping define Rolex's strategy.

Finally, to conclude this analysis of Rolex's governance, it is worth noting the extraordinary growth in the number of managers since the 1980s. In August 2023, according to the Geneva Trade Register, Rolex SA had a CEO (Jean-Frédéric Dufour), nine directors, ten deputy directors, forty assistant directors, and no fewer than 128 authorised representatives.[27] The creation of a centralised group gave rise to a gigantic organisation (around 6,000 employees in 2018)[28] run by a bloated bureaucracy.

The continuation of the marketing strategy

Rolex's marketing strategy after 1990 did not change fundamentally. The model put in place during the previous period – exceptional watches for exceptional people – continues to this day. Such positioning, in the context of an industry undergoing profound change, may be perceived as conservative. But this is precisely what makes Rolex strong and gives legitimacy to its discourse on excellence. The main new model launched during this period was the Sky-Dweller annual calendar and dual-time watch, introduced in 2012.[29] However, although it is a real novelty in technical terms, this watch takes up the aesthetic codes of the Day-Date and is in line with the brand's continuity (see Figure 8.2). As a result, Rolex remains attached to the models developed up to the 1960s (Oyster Perpetual, Day-Date, Submariner, Daytona, etc.). Of course, they come in various colours and materials, their aesthetics matching the atmosphere of the era. The new multicoloured Rolex Oyster model launched in 2023 has even been hailed by critics for its audacity because it breaks with the aesthetic tradition of sober elegance while keeping the collection's style intact (see Figure 8.3).

At the same time, this attachment to historic models is accompanied by a continued focus on individual success and the excellence of personal destinies. Rolex continues to sponsor exceptional individuals in

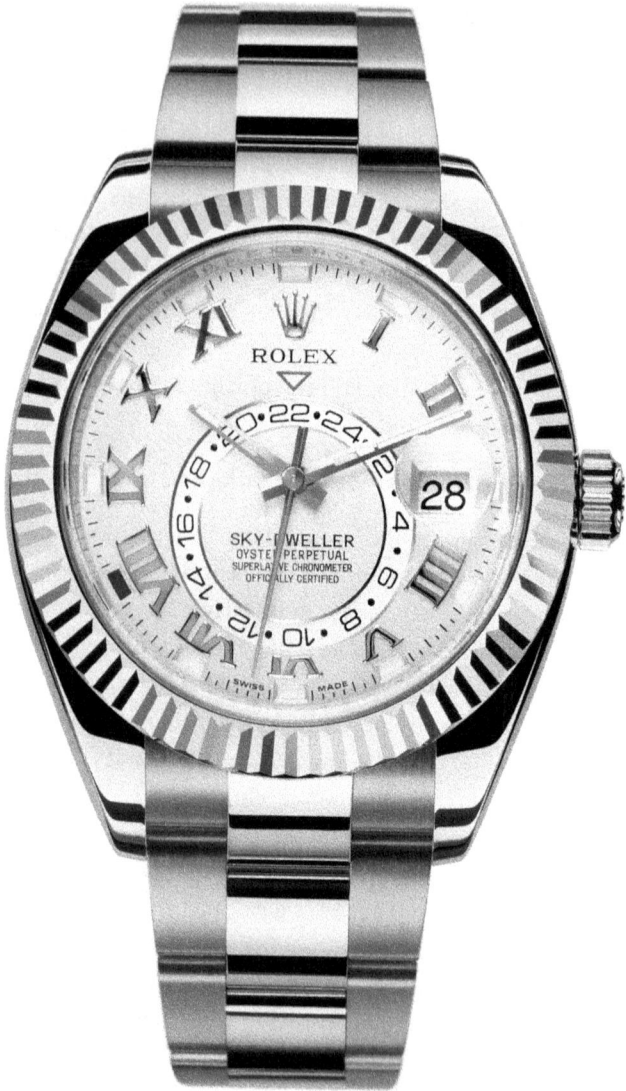

Figure 8.2 Rolex Sky-Dweller, 2012

Note: The Rolex Sky-Dweller is an illustration of product development carried out within the aesthetic framework of the Oyster. This makes it possible to innovate while keeping the brand's style intact, a continuity that meets the discourse on excellence.

Source: Rolex SA.

A last word to start

OF SWEETS AND SKELETONS

BY PIERRE MAILLARD

What's going on? Rolex is having fun decorating the dial of its Oyster Perpetual with colourful bubbles, as if for a child's birthday party. And then there's the Day-Date with *Love, Peace, Faith, Eternity, Hope* and *Happy* in the day window, along with 31 emojis in the date window. Oris has launched a green watch that has Kermit the frog emerging on the first of every month. Hermès is exploring all the colours of the rainbow. Patek Philippe has created an ode to the colour purple. Claude Meylan presents a sculpted, painted cow in a meadow, with a ladybird... We could fill an entire page with examples. In these unusually grey times, veering to black for many, there's an urgent need for an injection of colour. We've seen it before. In fact, this situation has played out thousands of times throughout history. In times of trouble, we like nothing more than a good party! During plague years, artists would paint scenes of dancing skeletons, decked out in riotous colours and extravagant costumes. In more recent memory, some people wore masks printed with a smile.

In a way, this urge to add some colour and joy when everything is dark is a form of magical thinking. It's both an exorcism and a release valve.

What could be more normal? Watchmaking is no exception. It doesn't exist outside the world – it's a reflection of the world. There's no such thing as a genuine tool watch any more – they're trinkets. You wear them to match your mood. They're an ornament like any other – although more valuable than many.

In 2019, Richard Mille became the butt of many jokes after releasing the provocative "Bonbon" collection, featuring marshmallows, liquorice and various other candies. In fact, he was ahead of his time. If he were to release it today, it's a safe bet that no one would bat an eye. It would be considered a haute horlogerie antidote to the general climate of unease.

It's as if the watch industry had said, "Let's think about something other than the bleak times we're living through" and wasted no time capitalising on the widespread and entirely human desire to make light of any situation. Except that, for the time being, the remedy it offers is accessible to only a very small slice of the population. Some might think it in poor taste. Like dancing on your yacht, while the boats all around you are sinking. Take the Billionaire Timeless Treasure, yours for just 20 million euros. It's a "skeleton tourbillon" set with yellow diamonds. You could almost call it a dancing skeleton... Now, what does that remind you of? ◆

146

Figure 8.3 Editorial by watch journalist Pierre Maillard, 2023

Note: The specialist watch press celebrates the ability of Swiss watchmakers, from Rolex to Richard Mille, to meet the aesthetic expectations of new generations of luxury consumers in the early 2020s.

Source: Europa Star, no. 373, 2023, p. 146. © Europa Star Archives.

Figure 8.4 Rolex advertisement, 2008

Note: The use of personalities from sports and the arts has been an essential feature of Rolex communications since the 1970s. It is not the direct contribution of Rolex watches to their exploits that is highlighted but the match between exceptional personalities and exceptional products.

Source: Europa Star, no. 289, 2008, p. 2. © Europa Star Archives.

traditional and elitist sports (golf, tennis, sailing), the arts (architecture, cinema), and the exploration of wide-open spaces. Arnold Palmer may have given way to tennis star Roger Federer (see Figure 8.4), but Rolex still focuses on a similar profile: the man or woman with exceptional qualities rather than the achievement itself. In November 2021, the manufacturer's website stated that "sponsorship is intimately linked to the perpetual pursuit of excellence found in all of the brand's activities".[30] It is also with this in mind that Rolex is perpetuating its Awards for Enterprise.

Rolex SA also pursues a zealous defence of its iconic models. In collaboration with the Federation of the Swiss Watch Industry (FH), it continues its fight against counterfeits. In addition, imitating Rolex watches has come under increasing scrutiny. The success of models such as the Submariner has led many watch brands to launch watches inspired by this design. However, as the dispute between Rolex and Titoni AG of Grenchen in the second half of the 1990s shows, the legal battle against imitations is difficult and limited. In 1994, Titoni was expelled from the FH for copying Rolex. This exceptional sanction was voted on by secret ballot. François Habersaat, president of the FH, claimed that Titoni had "systematically and slavishly imitated an entire Rolex collection".[31] Its Cosmo line was largely inspired by certain Oyster models.[32] Titoni defended itself by explaining that imitating certain Rolex models is commonplace and that it was being made a scapegoat for the success of its models in Asia, particularly China.[33] A complex legal battle ensued. In 1995, the Solothurn Cantonal Court ruled against Rolex, stating that the Oyster models had entered the public domain. In 1996, the Court of Appeal of the Canton of Berne overturned Titoni's exclusion from the FH. This decision was confirmed the following year by the Federal Court.[34] This case illustrates the attraction that iconic models exert on the entire industry and the difficulty of putting an end to it through the legal system. Titoni, among others, continues to launch models largely inspired by the most famous Rolexes (see Figure 8.5).

However, despite an apparent conservatism regarding product development, the verticalisation of production within manufacturing has a considerable impact on R&D activities. Between 1990 and 2019, the

Figure 8.5 Titoni advertisement, 2022

Note: Imitations of the design of iconic Rolex models, such as the Submariner, have become extremely common since the 1980s. The phenomenon is not only affecting Asian counterfeiters but also Swiss watchmaking companies.

Source: Europa Star, 2022, no. 370, p. 79. © Europa Star Archives.

number of patents filed accelerated (see Figure 2.2, p. 37). The 276 patents obtained during these three decades even represent almost half of all patents obtained by Rolex since the end of the nineteenth century (45.8 per cent). This growth in R&D is largely the result of the in-house development of external parts. Bracelets, cases, and dials were the subject of a total of ninety patents, or around a third of the total during this period (32.6 per cent). The other main areas of research concerned mechanical movement (27.5 per cent), watch production and assembly methods and processes (17.4 per cent), and materials (9.4 per cent). The design of new watches concerned only nine patents (3.3 per cent) and the development of complication mechanisms only 26 (9.4 per cent). These figures reveal that product diversification was not a fundamental challenge for Rolex in the years 1990–2019. Continuing to improve the precision and durability of watches, as well as perfecting the production system, were at the heart of R&D. The development of anti-magnetic balance springs, which enabled Rolex to break away from the monopoly exercised by Nivarox, a subsidiary of SMH (Swatch Group since 1998), in the early 1990s, also falls within this context.[35] The importance of external parts illustrates not only the verticalisation of these activities but also the need to innovate in these areas in order to offer new variations on the collections.

The main new type of product developed by Rolex during this period was the chronograph watch, for which a total of seven patents were obtained. However, this was not a new model in the brand's collections as such. Rolex chronographs had been on sale since the 1930s and the famous Cosmograph Daytona was launched in 1963. These models were equipped with Valjoux calibres, a company acquired in 1944 by Ebauches SA, which later became ETA SA, a subsidiary of the Swatch Group. Rolex's desire to distance itself from its technological dependence on ETA, particularly for image reasons, led it to turn to Zenith and use a modified version of its El Primero chronograph movement. This was then used for the Oyster Perpetual Cosmograph Daytona model. Rolex thus mastered the technical know-how of the chronograph through research. Its first chronograph movement developed in-house was designed in 2000.[36]

The conservative product development strategy has enabled Rolex watches to become truly iconic products sought after by collectors since the early 1990s. We have seen above that the real price of Rolex watches, excluding inflation, roughly doubled between 1989 and 2012. The increase is much greater for second-hand products, which are becoming the object of a veritable competition between collectors the world over. The Rolex Daytona is one of these iconic products. In the mid-1980s, it fetched around $1,000 at auction, rising to $20,000 in the mid-1990s and several hundred thousand dollars by 2020.[37] In October 2017, a Daytona that belonged to the American actor Paul Newman sold for $17.8 million.[38] These figures fascinate many observers, some of whom have even published books to encourage collectors.[39] The phenomenal literature on Rolex watches, most of it written after 1990, was born of this phenomenon.

This frenzied race to buy historical models is primarily the result of a new strategy on the part of auction houses. The Galerie Genevoise d'Horlogerie Ancienne (later renamed Antiquorum), founded in 1974 by Osvaldo Patrizzi and Gabriel Tortella, played a key role in this process. First, it was the first to launch themed sales of watch brands, with *The Art of Patek Philippe* (1989) and then *The Art of Breguet* (1991). Accompanied by illustrated catalogues that tell the story of the watchmakers and the brands, these sales were a great success, encouraging other auction houses to follow suit, most notably Christie's and Sotheby's. Second, Antiquorum innovated by offering themed sales of wristwatches. It is no longer the watchmakers of past centuries that are celebrated, but contemporary brands. Specialist sales of Rolex watches were held in Milan (1992), Geneva (2006), and New York (2008). Christie's did the same in London (1997) and Geneva (2017), Sotheby's in Hong Kong (2002), Artcurial in Paris (2004), and Philips in Geneva (2015).[40]

The exponential growth in prices and records after 2000 is not, however, the only consequence of the auction houses' new strategies. It should be remembered that the world's growing income inequality and the formidable enrichment of the wealthy classes play a key role in encouraging the continuing rise in demand. According to the World Inequality

Database, after several decades of stability, the share of pre-tax national income earned by the richest 10 per cent began to grow rapidly in the 1980s. Between 1980 and 2020, it rose from 31 per cent to 34 per cent in France, from 36 per cent to 44 per cent in Japan, from 23 per cent to 32 per cent in Sweden, from 28 per cent to 38 per cent in the UK and from 33 per cent to 46 per cent in the US.[41] The continuing growth in the incomes of the dominant classes is a key factor in explaining the boom in the consumption of luxury goods and the dizzying rise in their prices. This less-than-glamorous dimension of the luxury goods industry is not generally cited as a factor in its growth by economic journalists and analysts – who depend on the advertising revenues of these brands. Yet it is an essential dimension of contemporary luxury.[42] The celebration of individual success and social distinction makes Rolex a brand that embodies the winners of this transformation of modern society.

A stronger presence in the global luxury market

By the end of the 1980s, Rolex already had a strong presence in the world's major luxury markets, from the United States to Japan, including Latin America, Western Europe, and the Middle East. The end of the Cold War and the gradual opening of China to foreign companies led to a profound upheaval in the luxury goods market. On the one hand, it entered a phase of strong growth. According to the consulting firm Bain & Co, global demand for luxury consumer goods, including watches, rose from €73 billion in 1994 to a peak of €281 billion in 2019, on the eve of the COVID-19 crisis.[43] We also witness the globalisation of luxury brands – that is, the standardisation of their identity and positioning across the world, a process carried out under the direct control of headquarters.[44] The global luxury market is thus characterised by a high degree of homogeneity throughout the world. For many Swiss watch brands, which had built their expansion on exporting movements and adapting their products to local markets, the 1990s saw a profound process of reorganisation.[45] One of the most visible elements of the growing control of luxury companies over their brands is the verticalisation of distribution and retailing. For the Richemont group, for example, the proportion of sales generated by its own network of boutiques rose from 31.1 per cent in 1996 to 63.5 per cent in 2020.[46] Internalising retail not only increases profits but also gives the brand control over its identity.

In this context, Rolex benefits from its early adoption of a global brand strategy. While most of its competitors, notably Cartier and Omega, focused on reorganising their marketing and distribution strategies to present themselves as global luxury brands, Rolex did not need to go through this stage. It has a long history of iconic products and a standard message to consumers around the world that has not changed since the mid-1960s. As a result, it did not develop any fundamentally new models and did not change its communications. Rolex remains an exceptional watch for exceptional people. It can therefore focus on the conditions for its entry into new luxury markets, such as China, and strengthen its distribution strategy.

Although not officially represented in the country during the Maoist period, Rolex watches were not completely absent. In the 1950s, like other luxury watch brands, they were smuggled in, mainly by Communist bureaucrats passing through Hong Kong.[47] In 1967, a sales subsidiary was opened in the British colony under the name Rolex (Hong Kong) Ltd (see p. 178). Despite the absence of a direct presence in the country, Rolex managed to establish its reputation in China. In 1994, according to a study carried out by the consulting firm Beijing Market Research, Rolex was a brand known to 76 per cent of Chinese consumers. Admittedly, this was a long way behind Coca-Cola, which was then the best-known foreign brand because it was mass-produced and distributed in the country (98 per cent). But Rolex was one of the main luxury brands known to the public, along with Mercedes (93 per cent) and Pierre Cardin (80 per cent).[48] However, it was mainly after 2000 that Rolex entered the Chinese market. In 2002, it reportedly obtained permission to set up an after-sales service centre, which opened two years later under the name Rolex (Beijing) Ltd, with similar centres subsequently opened in Shanghai and Guangzhou.[49] These various organisations represent the points through which Rolex oversees its presence in China. As elsewhere in the world, however, Rolex does not invest directly in distribution and retailing in the Chinese market, unlike the major watch and luxury groups.[50] Partnerships are formed with the main local companies that control vast networks of boutiques, such as Xinyu Hengdeli, the company in which Swatch Group invested in 2005,[51] Chow Tai Fook, now the world's largest jewellery company in terms of turnover, and Dickson Watch & Jewellery in Hong Kong.

These partnerships were accompanied by a new marketing strategy aimed at focusing on the Rolex brand, whereas Tudor had initially been used to penetrate the Chinese market. These changes helped to make Rolex the leading watch brand in China after the COVID-19 pandemic, overtaking the Swatch Group brands that had dominated this market since 2000. According to the consulting firm Euromonitor, in 2013 Rolex was still only ranked third in the Chinese luxury watch market (with a market share of 16.1 per cent), behind Longines (20.7 per cent) and Omega (20.8 per cent). Omega then entered a phase of steady decline (11.4 per cent in 2022). Longines initially managed to strengthen its position (over 22 per cent in 2018 and 2019) before collapsing (16.8 per cent in 2022). Faced with these two competitors, and the emergence of Cartier (8.8 per cent in 2013 and 16.5 per cent in 2022), Rolex was able to strengthen its presence and establish itself in first place, ahead of Longines, from 2021. Its market share was estimated at 22.6 per cent in 2022.[52]

The experience gained in the Chinese market was undoubtedly essential to ensure Rolex's growth in the global luxury market. Indeed, in 2011, when the Board of Directors of Rolex SA decided to create the position of director of foreign subsidiaries, it was the head of the brand in China, Daniel Neidhart, who was appointed.[53] The growing competition between the major watchmaking groups to verticalise retailers and control boutique networks for their own benefit required particular attention from headquarters. The strategic choice not to invest directly but to collaborate over the long term with independent retailers with excellent reputations has been maintained. Rolex is thus continuing its partnerships with companies such as Tourneau in the United States (acquired by

Bucherer in 2018),[54] Mercury in Russia, The Hour Glass in Singapore, and Ahmed Seddiqi & Sons in the United Arab Emirates. However, a major strategic change was made in 2023 with the acquisition of Bucherer, a family business that had no buyer.[55] It is still too early to say whether this acquisition marks the turning point in a new strategy aimed at verticalising retail activities.

Finally, we should mention the recent decision to embark on the certification of pre-owned watches. To guarantee the authenticity of Rolex watches offered for sale on the resale market, which has been experiencing tremendous growth since 2020, Rolex SA has decided to launch its own Certified Pre-Owned (CPO) programme.[56] Here also, it is still too early to gauge the effects of this decision on the development of the second-hand Rolex market.

The role of the Tudor brand

Tudor continues to be used as a second brand by Rolex, particularly to penetrate new markets such as China. During the 1990s, the Tudor brand featured prominently in magazines aimed at Chinese consumers (see Figure 8.6). In the 2000s, Tudor watches were widely associated with Rolex and sold in the same boutiques opened in major Chinese cities.[57] This is still the case today, for example, with Chow Tai Fook and its thousands of boutiques across the country. According to the Swiss business press, China accounted for 90 per cent of this brand's sales in 2016.[58] Rolex's second brand no longer occupied a secondary place in the Group's formidable growth between 1960 and 1990. However, its positioning in a lower-price segment made it an attractive brand in the emerging markets that were opening to watchmaking and luxury goods during the 1990s. It was this brand that the directors of Montres Rolex SA used in their strategy to enter the Chinese market.

However, Rolex management adopted a new strategy for Tudor in the second half of the 2000s, with the ambition of making it an autonomous and complementary brand with its own identity. In the context of strong competition in the accessible luxury segment (Rolex, Omega, Cartier), the aim was to have a powerful brand in a lower segment (core price

Figure 8.6 Tudor advertising for the Chinese market, 1998

Note: *In the 1990s, Rolex set out to conquer the newly opened Chinese market with its Tudor brand. It was associated with Rolex in many jewellery stores across the country, attracting the attention of a new clientele unaccustomed to luxury brands.*

Source: Europa Star, *Chinese edition, no. 43, 1998, p. 2. © Europa Star Archives.*

between 2,000 and 4,000 francs),[59] to prevent competitors from dominating this segment and expanding into the higher segment where they could establish themselves as new competitors to Rolex. The main brands targeted were TAG Heuer and Longines.

In 2009, Rolex gave its second brand the resources it needed to fulfil its ambitions. While the brand had always been managed by Rolex directors, independent management was put in place under the direct supervision of Bertrand Gros, who became chairman of the Board of Directors of Montres Tudor SA that year.[60] Management was then entrusted to a distribution specialist, Philippe Peverelli, who had notably overseen the creation of a global network of boutiques for Chopard.[61] When he left in 2016, his right-hand man, Eric Pirson, took over. A former employee of Rolex, which he joined during his apprenticeship, Pirson was previously production director at Tudor. He is responsible for the brand's autonomous production.[62]

Two challenges were essential if Tudor was to become a competitive brand in the high-end segment. First, it had to differentiate itself from Rolex and build its own identity; second, it had to free itself from its dependence on China and build a truly global presence. It launched new models with specific designs and initially focused on sports watches. A collaboration was set up with the car manufacturer Porsche (2009) and the Italian motorbike manufacturer Ducati (2011). The collaboration with the motoring world thus made it possible to create a world of its own for Tudor, centred on classic watchmaking communication themes such as mechanical performance and precision (see Figure 8.7). The message is therefore quite distinct from that of Rolex. After 2010, Tudor also launched modernised versions of models developed in the second half of the twentieth century in order to communicate its historical roots and market its first ladies' watches.[63] Finally, although it used customised ETA movements, it developed its own in-house automatic calibre in 2015.[64] It also obtained its first chronometry certificates from the COSC in 2014.[65] Then, in 2021, some of Tudor's models received the title of Master Chronometer for the first time, awarded by the Swiss Federal Institute of Metrology (METAS) for watches that have undergone more stringent tests than those of the COSC. Not only was it the only brand in its segment

Figure 8.7 Tudor advertisement, 2011
Note: Collaborating with luxury automobile brands allows Tudor to communicate on common themes such as performance, precision, and the beauty of mechanical objects.
Source: Europa Star, no. 305, 2011, p. 76 © Europa Star Archives.

to achieve such a feat, but it also thumbs its nose at Omega, which in 2015 launched a collaboration with METAS to distinguish itself from the competition's COSC chronometers in a much higher price segment.[66]

Eventually, Tudor gradually gained industrial independence from Rolex and implemented its own verticalisation. The process began in 2012, with the creation in Delémont, in the canton of Jura, of Kenissi SA, a company investing in industrial projects. With a capital of 100,000 francs, it was headed by Philippe Dalloz, a manufacturer of sapphire crystals for watches and a former supplier to Rolex.[67] Renamed Kenissi Holdings SA in 2015, it saw its capital increase to 125,000 francs and the appointment of a second director in the person of Frédéric Grangié, CEO of Chanel's watchmaking subsidiary. The Board of Directors was again reorganised in 2018: Dalloz remained chairman and was joined by Pascal Bratschi (Manufacture des Montres Rolex SA) and Eric Pirson (CEO of Tudor). Jean-Paul Girardin, vice-president of Breitling, who is said to have delivered chronograph calibres to Tudor, was appointed managing director.[68] The head office of Kenissi Holdings was transferred to Le Locle in 2022. At the same time, in 2016, a new company was founded under the name Kenissi SA, still in Delémont, with a capital of CHF 100,000 and Philippe Dalloz as its chairman. Its head office was transferred to Geneva in 2018, to the premises of the financial company Kendra Securities House SA. The following year, it changed its name to Kenissi Manufacture SA, with the same Board of Directors as Kenissi Holdings. Its registered office was also transferred to Le Locle.[69] The reasons for the creation of a dual legal structure are not clear but may have been related to tax optimisation. The Kenissi Group's relationship with Rolex and Chanel remains opaque, but the composition of the companies' governing bodies suggests that these companies had a stake in their capital. Kenissi is said to specialise in the production and sale of sapphire crystals, but it quickly moved into the production of watch calibres.[70] In 2018, the transfer of Kenissi Manufacture to Le Locle coincided with the announcement of a major industrial project: the creation of the Tudor and Kenissi manufacturers, united in a single building.[71] The new building opened in 2023. Tudor–Kenissi also supplies calibres to Chanel, which acquired a 20 per cent stake in Kenissi SA in 2018, as well as independent brands such as Breitling, Bell & Ross, and Fortis.[72]

Tudor's second major strategic objective was freeing itself from its dependence on China and building a truly global presence. In particular, it made its debut in the United States (2013), Great Britain (2014), and Japan (2018).[73] To achieve this, it has been investing massively in advertising and communications since 2010.[74] In addition to collaborations with Porsche and Ducati, Tudor created its own network of ambassadors to communicate with a global audience, signing contracts with David Beckham and the All Blacks (2017).[75]

Tudor's transformation into a competitive brand in the global market for watches between 2,000 and 5,000 francs has been a success. According to the Vontobel Bank, in 2014 Tudor was still only a secondary player in its price segment (1,500–8,000 francs). Its market share was estimated at just 6 per cent, far behind Longines (25 per cent) and TAG Heuer (14 per cent), but close to Rado (7 per cent) and slightly ahead of numerous secondary brands such as Frédérique Constant, Mido, and Titoni (all at 4 per cent).[76] However, by the end of the 2010s, Tudor was enjoying exceptional growth. For the year 2020, Morgan Stanley analysts ranked it fourteenth among all Swiss watch brands, all segments combined, with sales estimated at 390 million francs. It was still a long way behind Longines (1.1 billion) but closer to TAG Heuer (589 million).[77] Tudor also ended its dependence on China. In 2016, China accounted for just under half of sales.[78] In January 2022, the Tudor Boutique network offering the brand's exclusive products comprised a total of forty-nine points of sale, spread across the globe, from Europe to Japan, via the United States and the Middle East. China certainly represented a significant presence (twelve boutiques in mainland China, nine in Hong Kong, and one in Macao), but this amounted to less than half of the shops.[79]

Conclusion

The transformation of watchmaking into a luxury industry after 1990 posed no threat whatsoever to Rolex, which even saw its position of dominance strengthen during the first two decades of the twenty-first century. This success is based on maintaining an unchanged strategic positioning. The brand's iconic models may have been slightly modernised, but their aesthetic continuity remains unchanged. Similarly, Rolex's values remain unchanged. They continue to embody the narrative established in the 1960s: exceptional watches for exceptional people.

This conservative marketing strategy was supported by Patrick Heiniger's in-depth transformation of the industrial organisation. The various acquisitions and reorganisations gave rise to a truly centralised industrial group that strengthened Rolex's independence. In addition, the company's governance, characterised by its membership of a foundation, ensured the accumulation of several billion francs in profits, which made these reorganisations possible. From this point of view, the boom in the luxury goods industry, marked by a sharp rise in prices, strengthened Rolex's financial autonomy, as the growing profits were not distributed to shareholders, unlike other watch brands. The centralisation of executive management and Rolex's financial strength made it easier to make decisions on development choices, such as the autonomy of Tudor, expansion in China, and the takeover of Bucherer. It is hard to imagine what could put an end to Rolex's bold domination of the world watch market.

Notes

1 Federation of the Swiss Watch Industry.
2 The Royal Oak was put on the market in 1972 at a price of 3,300 francs, a value equivalent to around 9,000 francs in 2023. *Europa Star*, 2022, no. 129, p. 27; Morgan Stanley, *Swiss Watches*, 2023.
3 Donzé, *A Business History of the Swatch Group*, p. 75.
4 Donzé, *L'invention du luxe*, p. 160.
5 Morgan Stanley, *Swiss Watches*, 2023.
6 Donzé, *History of the Swiss Watch Industry*, pp. 139–143.
7 Ibid., pp. 134–135.
8 Marti, *Le renouveau horloger*, p. 184.
9 *Le Temps*, 27 December 2008.
10 *L'Hebdo*, 3 March 2003; *Bilan*, 13 February 2013.

11 *L'Impartial*, 2 June 1995.

12 *FOSC*, 28 December 2001.

13 *Le Temps*, 27 March 2004.

14 *Financial Times*, 9 March 2013. The firm was apparently not officially registered but was first mentioned in the *FOSC* on 18 November 1982.

15 *FOSC*, 5 September 1984.

16 *FOSC*, 18 August 1987; *Financial Times*, 9 March 2013.

17 *FOSC*, 18 August 1987, and 21 September 1987.

18 *Le Temps*, 13 June 2014.

19 Swatch Group, Annual Reports, 1990–2020. The Hayek family's share of these dividends amounts to 30–40 per cent.

20 Since 1999 at least, Richemont has spent tens of millions of francs each year to buy back its own shares, generally distributed internally in the form of stock options. Compagnie Financière Richemont, Annual Reports, 1999–2020.

21 *Le Temps*, 27 December 2008.

22 *L'Hebdo*, 13 October 1994, and 17 November 1994.

23 *Bilan*, vol. 5, 1995.

24 *Le Temps*, 22 December 2008 and *FOSC*, 14 September 2009.

25 *Le Temps*, 4 May 2011.

26 Biographical information provided to the author by Rolex SA, 25 August 2023.

27 Geneva Trade Register.

28 *Le Temps*, 10 September 2018.

29 Brunner, *The Watch Book*, pp. 196–199.

30 www.rolex.com/fr/world-of-rolex/rolex-and-partners.html (accessed 19 November 2021).

31 *Le Nouveau Quotidien*, 25 November 1994.

32 *Le Nouveau Quotidien*, 8 September 1995.

33 *Le Nouveau Quotidien*, 25 November 1994.

34 *Le Nouveau Quotidien*, 20 March 1997.

35 Marti, *Le renouveau horloger*, pp. 108–109.

36 Brozek, *The Rolex Report*, p. 67.

37 Patrizzi and Cappelletti, *Investir dans les montres Rolex*, p. 8.

38 *New York Times*, 10 August 2022.

39 See, for example, Patrizzi and Cappelletti, *Investir dans les montres Rolex*.

40 Catalogue of the MIH library, https://bib.rero.ch/ (accessed 2 May 2022).

41 World Inequality Database, https://wid.world/data/ (accessed 4 July 2024).

42 Donzé, *Selling Europe to the World*, pp. 22–23; Piketty, *Le capital au XXIe siècle*.

43 Bain & Co, *Luxury Goods Market Study*, 2015; Bain & Co, *The Future of Luxury: Bouncing Back from COVID-19*, 2021.

44 Donzé, *Selling Europe to the World*.

45 For the example of Longines, see Donzé, "The Transformation of Global Luxury Brands".

46 Compagnie Financière Richemont, Annual Reports, 1996–2020.

47 According to a confidential report by the Beijing Embassy's chargé d'affaires, Revilliod, sent to the Trade Division in 1957, "the Rolex, Omega, Longines and Cyma watches on sale here would not be bought directly by interested Chinese circles but would be supplied by overseas Chinese". SFA, 220.174, 1971/46, letter from the Beijing embassy to the Division of Commerce, 7 September 1957.

48 Hooper, "Globalisation and Resistance in post-Mao China", pp. 443–444.

49 *Rolex Magazine*, no. 2, 2014, p. 133.

50 Theurillat and Donzé, "Retail Networks and Real Estate".

51 Donzé, *A Business History of the Swatch Group*, pp. 111–112.

52 Euromonitor International, Passport database, https://login.euromonitor.com (accessed 8 November 2023).

53 *Le Temps*, 4 May 2011.

54 *Forbes*, 1 February 2018.

55 *Le Temps*, 24 August 2023.

56 *Le Temps*, 1 December 2022.

57 *Europa Star*, vol. 279, 2006, pp. 77–79.

58 *Le Temps*, 14 December 2016.

59 *Europa Star*, vol. 295, 2009, p. 18.

60 *FOSC*, 30 September 2009.

61 Under his management, the number of Chopard boutiques is said to have risen from eight (1998) to 126 (2006). *Le Temps*, 7 April 2016.

62 *Le Temps*, 7 April and 14 December 2016; Geneva Trade Register.

63 *Europa Star*, vol. 309, 2011, p. 11.

64 *Le Temps*, 30 May 2017; Arm, "Tudor, des coulisses à l'avant-scène", pp. 64–67; Gachet, "Tudor–Kenissi", p. 7.

65 COSC, Annual Report, 2014.

66 Donzé, *Histoire sociale et économique de la chronométrie*, p. 182.

67 Trade Register, www.zefix.ch (accessed 3 July 2023); *Les Echos*, 23 September 1996.

68 Gachet, "Tudor–Kenissi".

69 Trade Register, www.zefix.ch (accessed 3 July 2023).

70 *Le Temps*, 19 November 2018.

71 *Le Temps*, 18 November 2018.

72 Gachet, "Tudor–Kenissi".

73 *Le Temps*, 30 May 2017; www.gressive.jp/brand/tudor/news/164693 (accessed 14 January 2022).

74 *Europa Star*, vol. 301, 2010, p. 26.

75 *Le Temps*, 30 May 2017.

76 Vontobel, *Watch Industry*, 2015, p. 22.

77 Morgan Stanley, *King Rolex*, 2021.

78 *Le Temps*, 7 April 2016.

79 www.tudorwatch.com/en/tudor-boutiques-selection (accessed 14 January 2022).

Conclusion

The deconstruction of the manufacturer of excellence proposed in this book has enabled me to shed light on the conditions under which Rolex succeeded in establishing itself as the world's leading watch brand in the 1970s. The historical analysis admittedly contains some gaps due to the lack of access to the archives of the companies in the Rolex group. Certain hypotheses, therefore, remain uncertain. However, the wide range of sources consulted, and the use of an analytical model inspired by work in design management, make it possible to gain a good understanding of the process by which Rolex became what it is today.

Its historical development can be divided into four successive phases. First, from the founding of the company in 1905 and the launch of the Rolex brand in 1908 to the early 1920s, Hans Wilsdorf's business focused on the design, manufacture, and sale of high-precision wristwatches. He was inspired by the strategy followed by the major manufacturers of the day, his aim being to be recognised as one of them. For the most part, Wilsdorf subcontracted product development: the Aegler factory in Bienne manufactured the movements, while numerous small workshops supplied the parts for the casing. Communication focused on technical quality and performance. Rolex embodied Swiss industrial excellence.

Second, the design of the Oyster, launched on the market in 1926, represented a breakthrough in the sense that Wilsdorf internalised product development, both technically and aesthetically. It forged closer links with the Aegler factory, acquired numerous patents relating to the water resistance of watches, invested in the case manufacturer Genex and registered many watch models. It was in this context that the self-winding wristwatch Oyster Perpetual (1931) was also developed. The internalisation of tangible design (the style and aesthetics of watches) was not, however, accompanied by a change in the brand's identity. Rolex remained the expression of high-precision watchmaking. Moreover, one must guard against a teleological reading of history. Until the Second World War, the Oyster remained one model among many. Rolex continued to develop and sell a wide variety of watches. The top-of-the-range Prince model, launched in 1928, illustrates Wilsdorf's trial and error: he was looking for the right watch and the right concept that would sell in his markets. But he did not know which one would yet.

Third, based on these organisational capabilities, a dozen iconic products were created in the fifteen years following the end of the Second World War. The different functions of the watches gave rise to collections with strong aesthetic and identity characteristics. The wide variety of products from the interwar period was abandoned – the Prince model was discarded in the 1940s. In addition, the new iconic models embodied a global brand: they were the same in every market in the world. There was no longer any need to adapt to local conditions. The Rolex Day-Date, Submariner, and Cosmograph met with great success, enabling the Geneva-based brand to rival Omega. However, Rolex remained attached to a traditional concept of design, concentrating on tangible aspects: technical excellence expressed in a dozen or so models with a strong visual identity.

Fourth, the second half of the 1960s was a time of fundamental change. Collaboration with American advertising agents and businessmen, principally J. Walter Thompson, led to a profound transformation in Rolex's strategy. The discourse on excellence was soon no longer limited to watches. It was extended to the people who wore them. Rolex became a brand that expressed individual achievement, professional success, and the exceptional nature of great men. These essentially masculine values corresponded to the expectations of the white, upper-middle-class man of the years of economic growth – and of all those who were seduced by this discourse. The genius of André Heiniger, who has run Montres Rolex SA since 1964, was to combine this revolutionary marketing strategy in the watchmaking industry with an extremely conservative product policy. In fact, the last major model launched by Rolex in the post-war years dates back to 1963 (Cosmograph Daytona). It is remarkable that when Heiniger took over the helm of the company, he virtually ceased product innovation – of course, new variations of the collections were proposed and the Cellini collection was launched, but the company no longer created fundamentally new products. Instead, Heiniger concentrated on exploiting the few existing collections and transforming them into iconic products that expressed Rolex's excellence. It was under his reign that the legend of this brand was born, built on the triple exceptionality of the Oyster watch, its designer Hans Wilsdorf, and its customers around the world. This narrative allowed Rolex to establish itself in the long term and in the continuity of technical excellence – there was no need to innovate in terms of product development since the iconic models developed from 1945 to 1963 embodied the industrial excellence of watchmaking. The quality and robustness of Rolex watches were taken for granted. It was then possible to focus communication on the exceptional nature of those who wore them. Rolex was no longer a watch. It had become a narrative on social status.

This determination to base the Rolex brand on the concept of exceptionality and to maintain this positioning intact over the long term was the work of André Heiniger. In 1985, the American directors of JWT explained in a memo that Heiniger "did not wish to change his 30-year-old advertising strategy and felt that the advertising clearly reflected the marketing strategy and the very nature of the Rolex product".[1]

The new business model developed in the second half of the 1960s, which corresponds to the shift towards an intangible design strategy (the product as the expression of a concept), has not been challenged to this day. Of course, Rolex has adapted its communication and its products to the spirit of the times (with greater attention to ladies' watches, for example), but always within the existing conceptual and aesthetic framework. The transformation of the production system, with the centralisation of power in Geneva and the verticalisation of the manufacturing of external parts, was also an important step that strengthened Rolex's competitiveness. However, the brand's strategic positioning has never changed. Today, this continuity gives Rolex a legitimacy that no other brand possesses.

The historical analysis in this book highlights the two main competitive advantages that have enabled Rolex to become one of the world's leading luxury brands and the undisputed leader in watchmaking. The first advantage stems from the separation between production and sales. Wilsdorf was a salesman. From the launch of the Rolex brand in 1908, his company focused on sales. He knew the markets, the customers, and their desires, and sought to offer them a watch that met their expectations. To achieve this, he quickly took control of the decoration of his watches, because tangible design was a major element of a sales strategy, as well as brand management. However, the industrial production of movements was not one of his concerns. His partner in Bienne, the Manufacture des Montres Rolex SA, run by the Aegler–Borer family, was responsible for production activities. With ambition and success. Rolex movements quickly won prizes in observatory competitions and accumulated thousands of chronometry certificates. This separation of production and marketing is unique in the Swiss watch industry, and worldwide, for a company the size of Rolex. Until the 1980s, the directors of other major watch manufacturers, such as Longines, Omega, IWC and Zenith, had to supervise both the production activities of their companies and the sale of their watches around the world. Since the 1950s, however, the desire to break out of the straitjacket of the Swiss federal state control (so-called *Statut horloger*), the issue of relocating production to Asia, the introduction of Swiss Made legislation, and industrial restructuring in the wake of the crisis have captured the attention of watch company directors. Hans Wilsdorf and, above all, André Heiniger did not have to ask themselves these questions because Emil and Harry Borer did. They were able to concentrate on developing their brand and creating a unique concept, thanks to their cooperation with JWT, almost three decades before the other brands.

Conclusion

Rolex's second competitive advantage lies in its identification of a new market: accessible luxury, a segment that incorporates the codes of classic luxury (social distinction through the consumption of specific products that embody intangible values) while limiting the distance through price. Rolex watches may be expensive, but they are not inaccessible to the middle classes. They represent a dream product that the average consumer can hope to acquire one day. Until then, luxury watchmaking, embodied by the manufacturers Patek, Philippe & Cie and Vacheron & Constantin, followed the classic business model also found in haute couture and jewellery: one-off pieces or (very) small batches of products, made in part by hand, aimed at a wealthy clientele – the *happy few*. Rolex brought luxury within reach of the middle classes in the second half of the 1950s. It was not only the first watch company to understand the potential offered by such a positioning but also one of the first in the entire luxury industry. Indeed, it was not until the 1970s that the first fashion designers, such as Yves Saint Laurent, and jewellers, such as Cartier, included accessible products in their ranges. The LVMH (Moët Hennessy Louis Vuitton) group was also created in 1987 based on the strategy of accessible luxury aimed at the global market.[2] Rolex's pioneering position is not limited to watchmaking. It is one of the main creators of the contemporary luxury industry.

Notes

1 Duke University, Rubenstein Library, J. Walter Thompson Collection, Wally O'Brien Papers, 22, undated note [1985].
2 Donzé, *Selling Europe to the World*.

Appendix

Table A.1   *Members of the Board of Directors of Manufacture des Montres Rolex SA, Bienne, 1921–2005*

Years	Name	Profession and mandates
1921–1960	Hans Wilsdorf	Chairman (1921–1940). Founder and executive director of Montres Rolex SA, Geneva.
1921–1944	Hermann Aegler	Chairman (1940–1944). Executive director of Manufacture des Montres Rolex SA
1921–1926	Émile Béha	Director of Montres Rolex SA, Geneva.
1927–1936	Fred G. Gruen	Owner of Gruen Watch, Cincinnati (USA) and Bienne. Brother of Georg.
1927–1936	Georg J. Gruen	Owner of Gruen Watch, Cincinnati (USA) and Bienne. Brother of Fred.
1936–1967	Emil Borer	Chairman (1944–1967). Nephew of Hermann Aegler and director of Manufacture des Montres Rolex SA.
1944–1961	Hans Aegler	Son of Hermann Aegler and senior manager of Manufacture des Montres Rolex SA.
1948–1951	Albert Kohler	Chairman of Fiduciaire Kohler SA, Bienne, director of Fabrique de La Glycine, Bourquin Frères SA, and Société des Produits Houghton SA, Bienne, and Léon Charpilloz SA, Moutier.
1948–1961	Emilie Aegler	Wife of Hermann Aegler.
1961–1972	Alfred Aegler	Manufacturing director of Manufacture des Montres Rolex SA.

Appendix

Years	Name	Profession and mandates
1961–2000	Hermann Müller-Aegler	Director of Manufacture des Montres Rolex SA.
1961–2000	Hans Cottier-Aegler	Doctor, professor at the University of Bern.
1967–2005	Harry Borer	Chairman (1967–2001). Son of Emil and executive director of Manufacture des Montres Rolex SA. Director of numerous financial companies.
1974–1993	Hans Sautter-Borer	Administrative director of Manufacture des Montres Rolex SA.
1979–1993	Ernst Jaberg	Doctor of law, lawyer, judge, and member of the Bern cantonal government. Director of the Aarberg sugar refinery and the Jungfrau railways; chairman of Berner Kantonalbank.
1987–2000	André Heiniger	Executive director of Montres Rolex SA, Geneva.
1987–2005	Willy Meier	Doctor of law and notary, president of Bienne Fair, director of numerous companies, Bienne.
1990–2005	Rosemarie Borer-Christen	Wife of Harry Borer.
1993–2005	Franziska Borer Winzenried	Daughter of Harry Borer, lawyer, director of Manufacture des Montres Rolex SA.
1993–2005	Daniel Borer	Chairman (2001–2002). Son of Harry Borer, director of Skywork and owner of luxury hotels.
2001–2005	Tony Reis	Chairman (2002–2005). Manager of IBM, CEO of Swisscom, director of Clariant and various industrial companies.
2004–2005	Bertrand Gros	Chairman of Montres Rolex SA, Geneva
2004–2005	Patrick Heiniger	Chairman (2005). Executive director of Montres Rolex SA, Geneva.

Note: The composition of the company's Board of Directors prior to 1921 is unknown. The company was acquired in 2005 by Rolex SA, Geneva.

Source: FOSC, 1921–2005.

Table A.2 Members of the Board of Directors of Montres Rolex SA, Geneva,
1920–2023

Years	Name	Profession and mandates
1920–1945	Hermann Aegler	Chairman (1920–1935 and 1941–1945). Executive director of Manufacture des Montres Rolex SA.
1920–1960	Hans Wilsdorf	Chairman (1935–1941). Founder and executive director of Montres Rolex SA.
1920–1926	Émile Béha	Director of Montres Rolex SA and member of the Board of Directors of Manufacture des Montres Rolex SA.
1938–1939	Antoinette Gagnebin	Employee of Montres Rolex SA.
1938–1939	Marguerite Gagnebin	Employee of Montres Rolex SA.
1939–1972	Fernand Lilla	Lawyer, secretary to the Board of Directors.
1941–1945	Lucie Cécile Huguenin	Employee of Montres Rolex SA.
1945–1968	Emil Borer	Chairman (1945–1961). Executive director and chairman of Manufacture des Montres Rolex SA.
1960–1975	Victor Maerky	President of the Grand Council, director of Roto-Sadag SA.
1960–1978	Jean Malche	Director and then chairman of the Board of Directors of Tribune de Genève.
1961–1974	Maurice Merkt	Chairman (1962–1974). Lawyer in Geneva, director of Fiduciaire Suisse SA, close to the Bettencourt family (L'Oréal), chairman of the Wilsdorf Foundation.
1970–1973	Raymond Déonna	Chairman of the Board of Directors of Journal de Genève, Liberal national councillor.
1970–1975	Jean Merminod	Former ambassador.
1972–1990	Claude Barbey	Executive director of Cosa Liebermann, member of the Swissair Board of Directors.
1972–2000	Martin Peter	Former rector of the University of Geneva.
1972–1997	André Heiniger	Chairman (1992–1997). Executive director of Montres Rolex SA.
1973–1993	Olivier Reverdin	Chairman (1974–1992). Professor at the University of Geneva, Liberal member of the National Council and the Council of States.

Appendix

Years	Name	Profession and mandates
1974–1980	Paul Waldvogel	Executive director of Ateliers des Charmilles SA, chairman of the Geneva Chamber of Commerce and Industry, member of the Vorort Committee.
1979–1993	Gustave Schilplin	Director of Sodeco-Saia SA.
1984–1987	Patrick Heiniger	Business lawyer, son of André Heiniger, executive director of Montres Rolex SA (since 1992).
1988–1999	Harry Borer	Chairman of Manufacture des Montres Rolex SA, son of Emil Borer.
1988–1992	Alexandre Hay	Lawyer, chairman of the Board of the Swiss National Bank, chairman of the International Committee of the Red Cross.
1988–2008	Guy Waldvogel	Executive director of Givaudan and director of a number of financial companies.
1990–2022	Bertrand Gros	Chairman (1997–2022). Business lawyer, director of a number of financial companies.
1993–2015	Pierre-Yves Firmenich	Executive director of Firmenich SA.
1995–2010	Gérard Bernheim	Businessman active in finance.
1995–2001	Jean-Louis Delachaux	Head of Credit Suisse Geneva.
1995–2000	Peter Martin	Unidentified.
1997–2009	Patrick Heiniger	Business lawyer, son of André Heiniger, executive director of Montres Rolex SA.
1999–2001	Franziska Borer Winzenried	Daughter of Harry Borer, lawyer, director of the Manufacture des Montres Rolex SA.
2000–2015	Jean-Claude Killy	Former skier and Olympic champion, member of the Coca-Cola Board of Directors.
2006–2023	Henri Turrettini	Private banker in Geneva.
2009–2019	Daniel Treves	Private banker in Geneva.

(continued)

Table A.2 (Cont.)

Years	Name	Profession and mandates
2010–	Franck Riboud	CEO of Danone, member of the boards of Accor SA, Lacoste SA and Renault SA. Graduate of EPFL.
2011–2019	Gian Riccardo Marini	Former director of Rolex Italy.
2015–	Nicolas Brunschwig	Chairman (2022–). Director and owner of Bon Génie department stores, member of the UBP Board of Directors.
2018–	Manuel Bouvier	Independent jeweller, former Cartier employee, and chairman of the IC Fabergé Foundation.
2020–	Anne Bobillier	Company director, vice-Chairwoman of Romande Energie.
2021–	Philippe Pascal	Former CEO of the watch and jewellery division of LVMH.
2022–	Christian Berner	Commercial director, Zurich Opera House.
2022–	Michel Juvet	Private banker in Geneva.

Source: FOSC, 1920-2023 and Geneva Trade Register, www.ge.ch/recherche-entr eprises-dans-registre-du-commerce-geneve (accessed 8 August 2023); Journal de Genève archives and Swiss elite database Obelis.

Appendix

Table A.3 *Members of the Board of the Hans Wilsdorf Foundation, Geneva, 1945–2023*

Years	Name	Profession and mandates
1945–1965	Maurice Merkt	Chairman (1945–1965). Lawyer in Geneva, director of Fiduciaire Suisse SA, close to the Bettencourt family (L'Oréal).
1945–1976	Gustave Martin	Chairman (1975–1976). Notary in Geneva.
1945–1957	Alfred Chapuis	Professor at the Neuchâtel School of Commerce; watchmaking historian.
1945–1957	Francis Guyot	Head of Credit Suisse Geneva.
1945–1954	Eugène Jaquet	Director of the Geneva School of Watchmaking; watchmaking historian.
1945–1957	Lucie Huguenin	Employee, Montres Rolex SA, Geneva.
1945–1957	Juliette Ihne	Employee, Montres Rolex SA, Geneva.
1957–1991	Émile Dupont	Chairman (1976–1991). Conservative state councillor, Geneva.
1957–1975	Max Gamper	Chairman (1965–1975). Director of Crédit Suisse Genève.
1957–1979	Jean Malche	Director and then chairman of the Board of Directors of *Tribune de Genève*.
1957–1974	Robert Rauber	Unidentified person of German nationality; probable relative of Hans Wilsdorf.
1957–1960	Jean-Laurent Comtesse	Director of Banque Romande, lecturer at the University of Neuchâtel, and founder of financial companies in Liechtenstein.
1960–1970	Dieter-Heinrich Kübel-Wilsdorf	Director of numerous companies in French-speaking Switzerland, nephew of Hans Wilsdorf.
1965–1986	Georges Bickel	Former professor of medicine at the University of Geneva.
1965–1970	Jean Babel	Trustee director and Christian Democrat councillor of state.
1974–1996	Hans-Helmut Kübel-Wilsdorf	Director of Montres Rolex SA, grand-nephew of Hans Wilsdorf.
1975–2005	Jean-Louis Delachaux	Head of Credit Suisse Geneva.
1975–1976	Maurice Kervan	Notary in Geneva.
1976–2000	Wolfgang Stromer Von Reichenbach	Professor at the Freien Universität Berlin and the Friedrich-Alexander-Universität Erlangen-Nürnberg.
1976–2013	Pierre Mottu	Chairman (1991–2013). Notary in Geneva.

(continued)

Table A.3   *(Cont.)*

Years	Name	Profession and mandates
1979–1995	Alexandre Hay	Lawyer, chairman of the Board of the Swiss National Bank, chairman of the International Committee of the Red Cross.
1981–2005	Michel Vallotton	Professor at the University of Geneva.
1995–2003	Martine Brunschwig Graf	Radical-Democratic state councillor and member of the National Council.
1995–2016	Pierre-Yves Firmenich	Executive director of Firmenich SA.
1996–2008	Heinrich Ulrich Martin Kübel	Heir to Hans Wisldorf
2000–	Kurt Weissen	Historian, private banker, and director of Swiss companies.
2004–	Costin van Berchem	Chairman (2013–). Notary in Geneva.
2005–2023	Christian de Saussure	Psychiatrist in Geneva.
2006–	Henri Turrettini	Private banker in Geneva.
2009–2012	Bruno Mettler	Director of Rolex SA.
2012–2016	Anita Christine Kübel	Heiress of Hans Wilsdorf.
2012–2020	Serge Bednarczyk	Head of social institutions and chairman of the Geneva Liberal Party. Secretary of the Wilsdorf Foundation.
2014–2022	Nicolas Brunschwig	Director and owner of Bon Génie department stores, member of the Board of Directors of UBP, chairman of the Board of Directors of Rolex SA.
2016–	Nathalie Canonica	President of the Butini Foundation.
2017–	Guillaume Fatio	Lawyer in Geneva.
2018–	Anita Kübel	Heiress of Hans Wilsdorf.
2022–	Christian Berner	Commercial director, Zurich Opera House.
2023–	Bénédicte Montant	Architect in Geneva.

Source: See Table A.2

Figures

Figures

Figures

Tables

References

Archives

Association Patronale de l'Horlogerie et de la Microtechnique (APHM), Bienne

Archives of the Association cantonale bernoise des fabricants d'horlogerie (ACBFH)

State Archives, Canton Berne (AEB)

FTMH Papers
   V Unia 405–409 Protokollbuch Comité général, 1916–1961.
   V Unia 578–585 Uhrenarbeiter/Horloger, Protokollbuch Vorstand, 1900–1956.
   V Unia 1186–1187 Uhrenarbeiter/Horloger, Protokollheftm, 1892–1893 and 1899–1900.

State Archives, Geneva (AEG)

General Secretariat of the Department of the Public Economy (DPE)
   1986 va 9.18.58.
   1986 va 9.62.7
Cantonal Population Office
   CH AEG 2003va042, dossier no 157288
FTHM Papers
   CH AEG Private papers 631.4.28
   CH AEG Private papers 397.8.1

References

Swiss Federal Archives (SFA), Berne

E2001: Political Federal Department
E2200: Diplomatic Representations
E2500: Political Federal Department, personal files
E3375: Swiss Science Council
E4327: Office of the Public Prosecutor
E6300: Federal Tax Administration
E6351: Central Customs Department
E7004: General Secretariat of the Federal Department of Public Economy: Watchmaking
E7110: Political Federal Department, Division of Commerce
E7115: Political Federal Department, Central Division
E7184: Federal Office for Industry, Trade and Labour
E7211: Federal Office for Industry, Trade and Labour

Duke University, Rubenstein Rare Book & Manuscript Library, Durham, North Carolina (USA)

J. Walter Thompson Company (JWT) Collections
J. Walter Thompson Company Newsletter Collection, online access: https://repository.duke.edu/dc/jwtnewsletters

History of Advertising Trust (HAT), The Michael Cudlipp Research & Study Centre, Norfolk (UK)

The J. Walter Thompson (JWT), London, Advertising Agency, Client Account Files

Musée international d'horlogerie (MIH), La Chaux-de-Fonds

Archives de l'horlogerie, 1881–1920.
Papers of the Chambre suisse d'horlogerie, correspondence, 1895–1982.
Robert Berthoud, Watchmaking patents records, 1954.

University of Massachusetts Library (UML), Amherst, Massachusetts (USA)

Mark H. McCormack Papers (MHM)

References

Websites

Dictionary of Jura, www.diju.ch

European Patent Office, database, https://worldwide.espacenet.com/

Forbes, www.forbes.com/

German Historical Institute, Immigrant Entrepreneurship, www.immigrantentre
preneurship.org/

House of Commons, Parliamentary Papers, London, https://parlipapers.proqu
est.com/parlipapers

Intellectual Property Office, London, https://trademarks.ipo.gov.uk

Oxford Dictionary of National Biography, Oxford University Press, 2011, www.
oxforddnb.com/

Scopus, www.scopus.com

Swiss Central Business Name Index, www.zefix.ch

Swiss Diplomatic Documents (DODIS), https://dodis.ch

Swiss Historical Dictionary (DHS), https://hls-dhs-dss.ch/

Swiss National Library, catalogue, www.helveticat.ch

United States Patent and Trademark Office, Trademark Electronic Search System
(TESS), https://tmsearch.uspto.gov

World Inequality Database, https://wid.world/data/

Newspapers and printed sources

24 Heures, 1972–.

Adam: Revue des modes masculines en France et à l'étranger, 1925–1973.

The Anatomy of Time, Geneva: Rolex, s.d. [1950].

Archives commerciales de la France, 1874–1955.

Bain & Co., *Luxury Goods Market Study*, 2015.

Bain & Co., *The Future of Luxury: Bouncing Back from Covid-19*, 2021.

Belles Lettres de Lausanne: Livre d'or du 175 anniversaire, 1906–1981,
Lausanne: Belles Lettres, 1981.

Bienneer Tagblatt, 1904–1995.

Bilan, 1989–.

Centenaire de la fabrique, 1878–1978, Bienne: Manufacture des Montres Rolex
SA, 1978.

The China Press, 1946–.

Compagnie Financière Richemont, Annual Report, 1996–2020.

Contrôle officiel suisse des chronomètres (COSC), Annual Report, 1974–.

Convention patronale, *Recensement 2007*, La Chaux-de-Fonds: CPIH, 2008.

References

Deutsche Uhrmacher-Zeitung, 1877–1942.

Le Droit du Peuple, Organe officiel du Parti socialiste suisse, des Partis ouvrier-socialiste vaudois et ouvrier-socialiste lausannois, 1917–1940.

The Eastern and Jeweller and Watchmaker, 1950–1995.

Europa Star, 1959–.

FAN–L'Express, 1738–2018.

La Fédération horlogère suisse, 1886–1947.

Feuille officielle suisse du commerce (FOSC), Berne, 1883–.

Financial Times, 1888–.

Gazette de Lausanne, 1816–1991.

L'Hebdo, 198 1–2017.

L'Illustré, 192 1–.

L'Impartial, 188 1–2018.

Indicateur Davoine [various titles], La Chaux-de-Fonds, 1864–1950.

The Japan Times, 1897–.

Journal de Genève, 1826–1898.

Journal du Jura, 1876–1995.

Journal suisse d'horlogerie, 1876–.

Le Jura, 1852–1970.

La Lutte syndicale, 1908–1998.

Montres Rolex, *Vade mecum Rolex*, 4 volumes, Geneva: Montres Rolex SA, 1945.

Morgan Stanley, *King Rolex*, 2021.

Morgan Stanley, *Swiss Watches*, 2023.

Morgan Stanley, *Swiss Watches: The Power of Icons*, 2023.

New York Times, 1851–.

Nikkei keizai shimbun, 1876–.

Le Nouveau Quotidien, 1991–1998.

Nouvelle Revue de Lausanne, 1868–2012.

Recensement 2017, La Chaux-de-Fonds: Convention patronale, 2018.

La Revista Relojera el Orfebre, 1942–1979.

Rolex Jubilé 1905–1920–1945, Geneva: Montres Rolex SA, 1945.

Rolex Magazine, 2013–.

La Sentinelle, 1890–1971.

Statistique annuelle du commerce extérieur de la Suisse [various titles], Berne: Central Customs Department, 1886–.

Swatch Group, Annual Report, 1983–2022.

Le Temps, 1998–.

The Times, 1785–.

References

La Tribune de Genève, 1879–.
Vontobel, *Watch Industry*, 2015.
Watch Around, 2007–.
Zainichi gaishikei kigyo fairu, Tokyo: Nihon Keizai Shimbun, 2001.

Books and articles

Acklin, Claudia and Alexander Fust, "Towards a Dynamic Mode of Design Management and Beyond", *Proceedings of the 19th DMI: Academic Design Management Conference*, 2014, pp. 1908–1920.

Allérès, Danielle, "Spécifictés et stratégies marketing des différents univers du luxe" [Specificities and Marketing Strategies of the Different Luxury Sectors], *Revue française du marketing*, vol. 132, 1991, pp. 71–96.

Angell, Svein Ivar and Mads Mordhorst, "National Reputation Management and the Competition State: The Cases of Denmark and Norway", *Journal of Cultural Economy*, vol. 8, no. 2, 2015, pp. 184–201.

Arm, Jean-Philippe, "Tudor, des coulisses à l'avant-scène" [Tudor, from Behind the Scenes to the Forefront], *Watch Around*, vol. 19, 2015, pp. 64–67,

Béguelin, Sylvie, "Naissance et développement de la montre-bracelet: histoire d'une conquête" [Birth and Development of the Wristwatch: The History of a Conquest], *Actes du 5ᵉ Congrès européen de chronométrie*, 1994, pp. 65–68.

Billings, Mark and Lynne Oats, "Innovation and Pragmatism in Tax Design: Excess Profits Duty in the UK during the First World War", *Accounting History Review*, vol. 24, no. 2–3, 2014, pp. 83–101.

Blaszczyk, Regina Lee. *Imagining Consumers: Design and Innovation from Wedgwood to Corning*. Baltimore, MD: Johns Hopkins University Press, 2000.

Blaszczyk, Regina Lee. *The Color Revolution*. Cambridge, MD: MIT Press, 2012.

Boettcher, David, "The Rolex Screw Down Crown (and its Antecedents)", *NAWCC Watch & Clock Bulletin*, December 2010, pp. 677–688.

Bohlhater, Bruno, *Die Uhrenkrisen der 1930er- und 1970/80er-Jahre in der Schweiz: Entstehung und Bewältigung Von der ASUAG und der SSIH zur Swatch Group AG* [The Watch Crises of the 1930s and 1970/80s in Switzerland: Origins and Management from ASUAG and SSIH to Swatch Group]. University of Fribourg, unpublished PhD dissertation, 2015.

Boillat, Johann, *Les véritables maîtres du Temps: le cartel horloger suisse (1919–1941)* [The True Masters of Time: The Swiss Watchmaking Cartel, 1919–1941]. Neuchâtel: Alphil, 2014.

References

Booker, Peter J., *A History of Engineering Drawing*. London: Chatto & Windus, 1963.

Bottge, Delphine, *Les fondations actionnaires en Suisse: Ces fondations qui détiennent des entreprises* [Shareholder Foundations in Switzerland: Foundations that Own Companies]. Geneva: Slatkine, 2022.

Brown, John K., *The Baldwin Locomotive Works, 1831–1915: A Study in American Industrial Practice*. Baltimore, MD: Johns Hopkins University Press, 1995.

Brozek, John E., *The Rolex Report: An Unauthorized Reference Book for the Rolex Enthusiast*, 4th edition. Saint Petersburg: InfoQuest, 2002.

Brunner, Gisbert L., *The Watch Book: Rolex*, 2nd edition, Augsburg: teNeues, 2022.

Bubloz, Gustave, *La Chaux-de-Fonds, métropole de l'industrie horlogère suisse*. La Chaux-de-Fonds: Société des fabricants d'horlogerie de La Chaux-de-Fonds, s.d. [1912].

Bucherer, Carl F., "Célébration de 125 ans d'histoire suisse du temps" [Celebrating 125 Years of Swiss Time History], *Insight*, no. 7, 2013.

Chachereau, Nicolas, *Les débuts du système suisse des brevets d'invention (1873–1914)* [The Beginnings of the Swiss Patent System, 1873–1914]. Neuchâtel: Alphil, 2022.

Chandler, Alfred D., *Strategy and Structure: Chapters in the History of the American Industrial Enterprise*. Cambridge, MA: MIT Press, 1962.

Chandler, Alfred D., *Scale and Scope: The Dynamics of Industrial Capitalism*. Cambridge: Belknap Press, 1990.

Chapuis, Alfred and Eugène Jaquet, *La montre automatique ancienne: un siècle et demi d'histoire, 1770–1931* [The Antique Automatic Watch: A Century and a Half of History, 1770–1931]. Neuchâtel: Griffon, 1952.

Chessel, Marie-Emmanuelle, *La publicité: Naissance d'une profession, 1900–1940* [Advertising: Birth of a Profession, 1900–1940], Paris: CNRS Éditions, 1998.

Chung, Doug J., *Rolex SA*. Boston, MA: Harvard Business School, case no. 521034, 2021.

Cooper, Rachel, Sabine Junginger, and Thomas Lockwood, "Design Thinking and Design Management: A Research and Practice Perspective", *Design Management Review*, vol. 20, no. 2, 2009, pp. 46–55.

Cross, Nigel, *Design Thinking: Understanding How Designers Think and Work*, Oxford and New York: Berg, 2011.

Cunningham, Brendan, *Selling the Crown: The Secret History of Marketing Rolex*, self-published, 2022.

da Silva Lopes, Teresa and Paul Duguid, *Trademarks, Brands, and Competitiveness*. London and New York: Routledge, 2010.

Dahlén, Marianne, "Copy or Copyright Fashion? Swedish Design Protection Law in Historical and Comparative Perspective", *Business History*, vol. 54, no.1, 2012, pp. 88–107.

References

Davis, Rhiannon, "Negotiating Local and Global Knowledge and History: J. Walter Thompson Around the Globe 1928–1960", *Journal of Australian Studies*, vol. 36, no. 1, 2012, pp. 81–97.

Dietrich, Robert, *A Brief History of the Gruen Watch Company*. Indianapolis: KenRo Printing Company, 1991.

Donzé, Pierre-Yves, *Histoire d'un syndicat patronal horloger: l'Association cantonale bernoise des fabricants d'horlogerie (1916–2001)* [History of a Watchmaking Employers' Union: The Bernese Cantonal Association of Watch Manufacturers, 1916–2001]. Neuchâtel: Alphil, 2006.

Donzé, Pierre-Yves, *Les patrons horlogers de La Chaux-de-Fonds (1840–1920): Dynamique sociale d'une élite industrielle* [The Watchmaking Business Leaders of La Chaux-de-Fonds (1840–1920): Social Dynamics of an Industrial Elite]. Neuchâtel: Alphil, 2007.

Donzé, Pierre-Yves, *History of the Swiss Watch Industry from Jacques David to Nicolas Hayek*. Bern: Peter Lang, 2011.

Donzé, Pierre-Yves, "The Hybrid Production System and the Birth of the Japanese Specialized Industry: Watch production at Hattori & Co. (1900–1960)", *Enterprise & Society*, vol. 12 no. 2, 2011, pp. 356–397.

Donzé, Pierre-Yves, *Longines: From Family Business to Global Brand*. Saint-Imier: Editions des Longines, 2012.

Donzé, Pierre-Yves, "Global Competition and Technological Innovation: A New Interpretation of the Watch Crisis, 1970s–1980s", in Thomas David, Jon Mathieu, Janick Marina Schaufelbuehl, and Tobias Straumann (eds), *Crises: Causes, interprétations et consequences* [Crises: Causes, Interpretations and Consequences]. Zurich: Chronos, 2012, pp. 275–289.

Donzé, Pierre-Yves, "L'industrie de la montre roskopf en Suisse" [The Roskopf Watch Industry in Switzerland], in Jean-Michel Piguet (ed.), *La drôle de montres de Monsieur Roskopf*. La Chaux-de-Fonds: Musée international d'horlogerie, 2013, pp. 77–95.

Donzé, Pierre-Yves, *A Business History of the Swatch Group: The Rebirth of Swiss Watchmaking and the Globalization of the Luxury Industry*. Basingstoke: Palgrave Macmillan, 2014.

Donzé, Pierre-Yves, *Industrial Development, Technology Transfer, and Global Competition: The Japanese Watch Industry from 1850 to the Present Day*. New York: Routledge, 2017.

Donzé, Pierre-Yves, *L'invention du luxe: histoire de l'horlogerie à Genève de 1815 à nos jours* [The Invention of Luxury: History of Watchmaking in Geneva from 1815 to the Present Day]. Neuchâtel: Alphil, 2017.

References

Donzé, Pierre-Yves, "Dynamics of Innovation in the Electronic Watch Industry: A Comparative Business History of Longines (Switzerland) and Seiko (Japan), 1960–1980", *Essays in Economic & Business History*, vol. 37, 2019, pp. 120–145.

Donzé, Pierre-Yves, "National Labels and the Competitiveness of European Industries: The Example of the 'Swiss Made' Law Since 1950", *European Review of History: Revue européenne d'histoire*, vol. 26, no. 5, 2019, pp. 855–870.

Donzé, Pierre-Yves, "Industrial Leadership and the Long-Lasting Competitiveness of the Swiss Watch Industry", in Martin Guttmann (ed.), *Historians on Leadership and Strategy: Case Studies From Antiquity to Modernity*. Cham: Springer, 2020, pp. 171–191.

Donzé, Pierre-Yves, "The Transformation of Global Luxury Brands: The Case of the Swiss Watch Company Longines, 1880–2010", *Business History*, vol. 62, no. 1, 2020, pp. 26–41.

Donzé, Pierre-Yves, "La transformation de l'horlogerie suisse en industrie du luxe" [The Transformation of Swiss Watchmaking into a Luxury Industry], in Blancheton Bertrand (ed.), *Vers le haute de gamme made in France*. Paris: Histoire économique et financière de la France, 2021, pp. 181–198.

Donzé, Pierre-Yves, *The Business of Time: Global History of the Watch Industry*. Manchester: Manchester University Press, 2022.

Donzé, Pierre-Yves, *Histoire sociale et économique de la chronométrie* [Social and Economic History of Chronometry]. Neuchâtel: Alphil, 2023.

Donzé, Pierre-Yves, *Selling Europe to the World: The Rise of the Luxury Fashion Industry, 1980–2020*. London: Bloomsbury, 2023.

Donzé, Pierre-Yves and Shigehiro Nishimura, "Patent Management and the Globalization of Firms: The Case of Siemens (1890–1945)", *Journal of Management History*, vol. 28, no. 2, 2022, pp. 199–214.

Fallet, Estelle, *Tissot, 150 ans d'histoire: 1853–2003* [Tissot, 150 Years of History, 1853–2003]. Le Locle: Tissot SA, 2003.

Foulkes, Nicholas, *Patek Philippe: The Authorized Biography*. London: Random House, 2016.

Frank, Thomas, *The Conquest of Cool: Business Culture, Counterculture, and the Rise of Hip Consumerism*. Chicago: University of Chicago Press, 1997.

Gachet, Stéphane, "Tudor–Kenissi: Mouvement de fond" [Tudor-Kenassi: Undercurrent Movement], *Watch Around*, no. 67, 2023.

Giertz-Mårtenson, Ingrid, "H&M: Documenting the Story of One of the World's Largest Fashion Retailers", *Business History*, vol. 54, no. 1, 2012, pp. 108–115.

Ginalski, Stéphanie, André Mach, Thomas David, and Félix Bühlmann, *Les élites économiques suisses au xxᵉ siècle* [Swiss Economic Elites in the 20th Century]. Neuchâtel: Alphil, 2016.

References

Hansen, Per H., "Business History: A Cultural and Narrative Approach", *Business History Review*, vol. 86, no. 4, 2012, pp. 693–717.

Hansen, Per H., *Danish Modern Furniture 1930–2016: The Rise, Decline and Re-emergence of a Cultural Market Category*. Odense: University Press of Southern Denmark, 2018.

Heskett, John, *Industrial Design*. Oxford: Oxford University Press, 1981.

Hirano, Mitsuo, *Seikosha shiwa*. Tokyo: Hattori Seiko, 1968.

Hooper, Beverley, "Globalisation and Resistance in Post-Mao China: The Case of Foreign Consumer Products", *Asian Studies Review*, vol. 24, no. 4, 2000, pp. 430–470.

Huguenin, Régis and Gianenrico Bernasconi, *L'heure pour tous, une montre pour chacun: un siècle de publicité horlogère* [Time for Everyone, a Watch for Everyone: A Century of Watch Advertising]. Neuchâtel: Alphil, 2019.

Hultquist, Clark Eric, "Americans in Paris: The J. Walter Thompson Company in France, 1927–1968", *Enterprise & Society*, vol. 4, no. 3, 2003, pp. 471–501.

Izuishi, Shozo, *Rorekkusu no himitsu* [The Secrets of Rolex]. Tokyo: Kodansha, 2002.

Jansen, Sue Curry, "Designer Nations: Neo-liberal Nation Branding – Brand Estonia", *Social Identities*, vol. 14, no. 1, 2008, pp. 121–142.

Jequier, François, *De la forge à la manufacture horlogère (xviiiᵉ-xxᵉ siècles): Cinq générations d'entrepreneurs de la vallée de Joux au cœur d'une mutation industrielle* [From the Forge to Watchmaking (18th–20th Centuries): Five Generations of Vallée de Joux Entrepreneurs at the Heart of Industrial Change]. Lausanne: Bibliothèque vaudoise, 1983.

Jevnaker, Birgit Helene, "Building Up Organizational Capabilities in Design", in Margaret Bruce and Birgit Helene Jevnaker, *Management of Design Alliances. Sustaining Competitive Advantage*. New York: John Wiley & Sons, 1998, pp. 13–38.

Jewkes, John, David Sawers, and Richard Stillerman, "Self-Winding Wrist-Watch", in John Jewkes, David Sawers, and Richard Stillerman, *The Sources of Invention*. Basingstoke: Palgrave Macmillan, 1969, pp. 293–295.

Jones, Geoffrey, *Deeply Responsible Business: A Global History of Value-Driven Leadership*. Cambridge, MA: Harvard University Press, 2023.

Jones, Geoffrey and Alexander Atzberger, *Hans Wilsdorf and Rolex*. Boston, MA: Harvard Business School, case no. 9-805-138, 2006.

Kapferer, Jean-Noël and Vincent Bastien, *The Luxury Strategy: Break the Rules of Marketing to Build Luxury Brands*, 2nd edition. New York: Kogan, 2009.

Kleisl, Jean-Daniel, *Le patronat de la boîte de montre dans la vallée de Delémont: l'exemple de E. Piquerez SA et de G. Ruedin SA à Bassecourt*

References

(1926–1982) [Watch Casemaking Business Owners in the Delémont Valley: The Example of E. Piquerez SA and G. Ruedin SA in Bassecourt, 1926–1982]. Delémont: Alphil, 1999.

Koller, Christophe, *"De la lime à la machine": L'industrialisation et l'Etat au pays de l'horlogerie* ["From the File to the Machine": Industrialisation and the State in the Land of Watchmaking]. Courrendlin: Editions CJE, 2003.

Kretzschmar, Anders, *The Economic Effects of Design.* Copenhagen: Danish National Agency for Enterprise and Housing, 2003.

Kristoffersson, Sara. *Design by IKEA: A Cultural History.* London: Bloomsbury Publishing, 2014.

Laboratoire de recherches horlogères, "L'influence du champ magnétique", *Bulletin annuel de la Société suisse de chronométrie*, 1933, pp. 52–74.

Lachat, Stéphanie, *Le Temps Longines: Histoires de Montres* [Longines Time: Histories of Watches]. Saint-Imier: Edition des Longines, 2017.

Mariana, Mazzucato, *The Entrepreneurial State: Debunking Public vs. Private Sector Myths.* London: Anthem Press, 2013.

Maielli, Giuliano, "Path-dependent Product Development and Fiat's Takeover of Lancia in 1969: Meta-routines for Design Selection between Synergies and Brand Autonomy", *Business History*, vol. 59, no. 1, 2017, pp. 101–120.

Marti, Laurence, *Le renouveau horloger. Contribution à une histoire récente de l'horlogerie suisse (1980–2015)* [The Watchmaking Revival: A Contribution to a Recent History of the Swiss Watchmaking Industry, 1980–2015]. Neuchâtel: Alphil, 2016.

May, David, "Rolex: The Timeless Timepiece", *Campaign*, 13 November 1987.

Meikle, Jeffrey, *Twentieth Century Limited: Industrial Design In America 1925–1939.* Philadelphia: Temple University Press, 1979.

Melchior, Marie Riegels, "From Design Nations to Fashion Nations? Unpacking Contemporary Scandinavian Fashion Dreams", *Fashion Theory*, vol. 15, no. 2, 2011, pp. 177–200.

Merlo, Elisabetta and Mario Perugini, "Making Italian Fashion Global: Brand Building and Management at Gruppo Finanziario Tessile (1950s–1990s)", *Business History*, vol. 62, no. 1, 2020, pp. 42–69.

The Millennium Watch Book: Montres de plongée [The Millenium Watch Book: Diving Watches]. Geneva: GMT Publishing, 2022.

Moore, Charles W., *Timing a Century: History of the Waltham Watch Company.* Cambridge, MA: Harvard University Press, 1945.

Mordhorst, Mads, "The Creation of a Regional Brand: Scandinavian Design", in Haldor Byrkjeflot, Lars Mjøset, Mads Mordhorst, and Klaus Petersen (eds), *The Making and Circulation of Nordic Models, Ideas and Images*. London: Routledge, 2021, pp. 251–270.

Niemitz, Hans-Ulrich. *Dampfturbinenkonstruktion bei der Brown Boveri AG & Cie nach dem Zweiten Weltkrieg* [Steam Turbine Design at Brown Boveri AG and Cie after the Second World War]. New York: Peter Lang, 1993.

Nourrisson, Didier, *L'Amérique en bouteille: Comment Coca-Cola a colonisé le monde* [America in a Bottle: How Coca-Cola Colonised the World]. Paris: Vendémiaire, 2023.

Paratte, Véronique, *Marketing et publicité dans l'horlogerie: le cas Longines de 1900 à 1962* [Marketing and Advertising in the Watchmaking Industry: The Case of Longines from 1900 to 1962]. University of Neuchâtel, unpublished Master's dissertation, 2003.

Pasquier, Hélène, *La "Recherche et Développement" en horlogerie: Acteurs, stratégies et choix technologiques dans l'Arc jurassien suisse (1900–1970)* [Research and Development in Watchmaking: Actors, Strategies and Technological Choices in the Swiss Jura Mountains, 1900–1970]. Neuchâtel: Alphil, 2008.

Patrizzi, Osvaldo, *Orologi da polso Rolex: Wristwatches Rolex*. Geneva: G. Mondani, 1992.

Patrizzi, Osvaldo and Mara Cappelletti, *Investir dans les montres Rolex* [Investing in Rolex Watches]. Lutry: Watchprint, 2021.

Perret, Thomas, André Beyner, Pierre Debély, Laurent Tissot, and François Jeanneret, *Microtechniques et mutations horlogères: clairvoyance et ténacité dans l'Arc jurassien* [Microtechnology and Change in the Watchmaking Industry: Foresight and Tenacity in the Jura Arc]. Hauterive: Editions Gilles Attinger, 2000.

Piketty, Thomas, *Le capital au XXIᵉ siècle* [Capital in the Twenty-first Century]. Paris: Seuil, 2013.

Pouillard, Véronique, *La publicité en Belgique, 1850–1975: Des courtiers aux agences internationales* [Advertising in Belgium, 1850–1975: From Brokers to International Agencies]. Brussels: Académie royale de Belgique, 2005.

Pouillard, Véronique, "American Advertising Agencies in Europe: J. Walter Thompson's Belgian Business in the Inter-war Years", *Business History*, vol. 47, no. 1, 2005, pp. 44–58.

Pouillard, Veronique and Tereza Kuldova, "Interrogating Intellectual Property Rights in Post-war Fashion and Design", *Journal of Design History*, vol. 30, no. 4, 2017, pp. 343–355.

Richon, Marco, *Omega Saga*. Bienne: Fondation Adrien Brandt en faveur du patrimoine Omega, 1998.

References

Rieben, Henri, Madeleine Urech, and Charles Iffland, *L'horlogerie et l'Europe* [Watchmaking in Europe]. Lausanne: University of Lausanne, 1959.

Samuel, Lawrence R., *The American Dream: A Cultural History*. Syracuse, NY: Syracuse University Press, 2012.

Scheurer, Frédéric, *Les crises de l'industrie horlogère dans le canton de Neuchâtel* [The Crises of the Watchmaking Industry in the Canton of Neuchâtel]. La Neuveville: Ed. Beerstecher, 1914.

Seyffer, David, *Die Unternehmensgeschichte von IWC Schaffhausen: Ein Schweizer Uhrenhersteller zwischen Innovation und Tradition* [The Company History of IWC Schaffhausen: A Swiss Watch Manufacturer between Innovation and Tradition]. Oberhausen: Athena, 2015.

Siegenthaler, Hansjörg and Heiner Ritzmann-Blickenstorfer, *Statistique historique de la Suisse* [Historical Statistics of Switzerland]. Zurich: Chronos, 1996.

Skou, Niels Peter and Anders V. Munch, "New Nordic and Scandinavian Retro: Reassessment of Values and Aesthetics in Contemporary Nordic Design", *Journal of Aesthetics & Culture*, vol. 8, no. 1, 2016.

Steinauer, Jean, *L'horloge flétrie* [The Withered Clock]. Lausanne: Diffusion Éd. d'en bas, 1984.

Theurillat, Thierry and Pierre-Yves Donzé, "Retail Networks and Real Estate: The Case of Swiss Luxury Watches in China and Southeast Asia", *The International Review of Retail, Distribution and Consumer Research*, vol. 27, no. 2, 2017, pp. 126–145.

Tonnerre, Quentin, "Une question de prestige dans le domaine international de l'industrie horlogère: Diplomatie suisse et chronométrage sportif (1964–1970)" [A Question of Prestige in the International Watch Industry: Swiss Diplomacy and Sports Timekeeping, 1964–1970], *Relations internationales*, 2019, no. 1, pp. 129–144.

Trueb, Lucien F., *Zeitzeugen der Quarzrevolution* [Witnesses of the Quartz Revolution]. La Chaux-de-Fonds: MIH, 2006.

Trueb, Lucien F., Günther Ramm, and Peter Wenzig, *Die Elektrifizierung der Armbanduhr* [The Electrification of the Wristwatch]. Ulm: Ebner Verlag, 2011.

Veyrassat, Béatrice, "Sortir des montagnes horlogères: les faiseurs de globalisation (1750–années 1830/1840)" [Moving Out of the Watchmaking Mountains: The Makers of Globalisation, 1750–1830s/1840s], in Marie-Claude Schöpfer, Markus Stoffel, and Françoise Vannotti (eds), *Unternehmen, Handelshäuser und Wirtschaftsmigration im neuzeutlichen Alpenraum*. Brigue: Rotten Verlag, 2014, pp. 257–279.

Vivas, Sébastian, *L'ancre et la plume: le Journal suisse d'horlogerie, 1876–2001, acteur et miroir de la culture horlogère* [The Anchor and the Pen: The Swiss

References

Horology Journal, 1876–2001, Mirror and Actor of Watchmaking Culture].
La Chaux-de-Fonds: Éditions l'homme et le temps, 2007.

West, Douglas C., "From T-Square to T-Plan: The London Office of the J. Walter Thompson Advertising Agency 1919–70", *Business History*, vol. 29, no. 2, 1987, pp. 199–217.

Zajtmann, David, "Une révolution dans la mode: le prêt-à-porter des couturiers parisiens (1965–2000)" [A Revolution in Fashion: Ready-to-wear by Parisian Couturiers (1965–2000)], *Entreprises et histoire*, vol. 3, 2022, pp. 52–63.

Index

Index

Index

EU authorised representative for GPSR:
Easy Access System Europe, Mustamäe tee 50,
10621 Tallinn, Estonia
gpsr.requests@easproject.com

www.ingramcontent.com/pod-product-compliance
Lightning Source LLC
Chambersburg PA
CBHW071017280326
41935CB00011B/1381